WORLD BANK WORKING PAPER NO. 184

Comparing European and U.S. Securities Regulations

MiFID versus Corresponding U.S. Regulations

Tanja Boskovic
Caroline Cerruti
Michel Noel

I0126280

THE WORLD BANK
Washington, D.C.

ISBN: 978-0-8213-8253-0
eISBN: 978-0-8213-8254-7
ISSN: 1726-5878   DOI: 10.1596/978-0-8213-8253-0

Library of Congress Cataloging-in-Publication Data has been requested.

Contents

Acknowledgments

This Report has been prepared by Tanja Boskovic, Caroline Cerruti, and Michel Noel (all World Bank).

The authors thank Sophie Sirtaine (Sector Manager, ECSPF, World Bank) for her guidance and support. They thank the peer reviewers: Burçak Inel Martenczuk (Deputy Secretary General, Federation of European Securities Exchanges), Oliver Fratzscher (Senior Financial Economist, GCMSM, World Bank), and Tadashi Endo (Senior Financial Sector Specialist, GCMSM, World Bank) for agreeing to provide comments on the report. The authors are grateful to John Pollner (Lead Financial Officer, ECSPF, World Bank), Luca Fossati (Policy Adviser, Securities Markets Policy and Company Law, Federation of European Securities Exchanges), Rosa Armesto (Economics and Statistics Adviser, Federation of European Securities Exchanges), Thomas Gira (Executive Vice-President, FINRA), and Jon Kroeper (Senior Vice-President, FINRA) for their valuable inputs. All errors and omissions are authors' alone.

The authors' views expressed in this publication do not necessarily reflect the views of the World Bank or any of its affiliates.

Acronyms and Abbreviations

AML	Anti-Money Laundering
ATS	Alternative Trading System
BIS	Bank for International Settlements
CAR	Capital Adequacy Requirement
CDS	Credit Default Swaps
CESR	Committee of European Securities Regulators
CFTC	Commodity Futures Trading Commission
DJIA	Dow Jones Industrial Average
ECN	Electronic Communication Network
EU	European Union
EC	European Commission
FESE	Federation of European Securities Exchanges
FHC	Financial Holding Companies
FINRA	Financial Industry Regulatory Authority
FRB	Federal Reserve Board
FSAP	Financial Services Action Plan
IOSCO	International Organization of Securities Commission
ISD	Investment Services Directive
MiFID	Market in Financial Instruments Directive 2004/39/EC
MTF	Multilateral Trading Facility
NASD	National Association of Securities Dealers
NASDAQ	National Association of Securities Dealers Automated Quotations
NMS	National Market System
NYSE	New York Stock Exchange
OTC	Over-the-Counter
Reg ATS	Regulation Alternative Trading Systems
Reg NMS	Regulation National Market System
RM	Regulated Market
SEC	Securities and Exchange Commission
SI	Systematic Internalizer
SRO	Self-Regulatory Organization
TRACE	Trade Reporting and Compliance Engine
UCITS	Undertaking for Collective Investments in Transferable Securities

Executive Summary

The purpose of this paper is to compare the EU and U.S. securities regulations. In November 2007, the Market in Financial Instruments Directive 2004/39/EC (MiFID) came into force in the EU, and brought about deep changes in the market infrastructure. The same year Regulation NMS in the United States was fully enacted and reformed equities markets. This study compares MiFID with the corresponding U.S. regulations, and primarily focuses on the regulatory and supervisory framework, trading venues, and the provision of investment services. Implementation of the rules, enforcement, and right to redress are beyond the scope of this paper. Likewise, the paper does not intend to judge the effectiveness of the two regulatory systems.

The international financial crisis evidenced some gaps in securities regulations. Main issues have focused on the imperfect oversight of large interconnected institutions, the low transparency of OTC markets, especially derivatives, and the insufficient liquidity and capital across financial institutions. Regulators on both sides have announced plans to address them:

- **A better supervision of large and interconnected institutions**: Under the U.S. regulatory reform plans, the Federal Reserve would have the power to conduct consolidated supervision and regulation of all large interconnected financial firms. These firms will be subject to the non-financial activities restrictions of the Bank Holding Company Act, regardless of whether they own insured depositary institutions. In the EU, a Systemic Risk Council would be established to identify systemic risks to the financial system, and the European System of Financial Supervisors would enhance the supervision of cross-border institutions. One substantial difference remains the plan to separate financial and commercial activities in the United States, while this is not currently considered in Europe.
- **Increase market transparency:** In the United States, the Treasury unveiled a comprehensive reform of OTC derivatives in May 2009: all "standardized" OTC derivatives would be cleared, dealers and firms who create large exposures to counterparties would be subject to tough regulation (with conservative capital requirements, business conduct standards, margin requirements), and un-cleared trades would be reported to a regulated trade repository. The EU Commission is examining several courses of action for OTC derivatives: standardization, central data repository, central counterparty clearing and moving trading to more public venues. In both regions, there is a risk of adding carve-outs to the regulation of derivatives as industrial firms claim that the clearing would incur significant costs. As regards OTC equity markets, the SEC and CESR are currently investigating whether dark pools should be subject to stricter regulation.
- **Enhance capital and liquidity requirements:** The U.S. draft systemic risk legislation proposes to raise capital and risk management requirements for all

Financial Holding Companies. In the EU a comprehensive reform of the Capital Requirement Directives is currently under review. Both approaches consider stricter capital requirements to address the exposure to securitized products.

The paper argues that rules in the current securities regulations may differ on both sides of the Atlantic, but objectives and some of the outcomes are comparable. Differences are related to:

- **The scope of trading venues:** MiFID is not currently applied to dark pools, while in the United States, dark pools are considered as ATS and register as broker-dealers. They have to make their quotes available to the public above a certain trading volume threshold.
- **EU regulators have more discretion in authorizing investment firms** and intervening in their management since they can judge whether the managers of investment firms or Regulated Markets are sufficiently experienced and reputable, while the U.S. regulator can only control their reputation and competences. The EU regulations go one step further in allowing supervisors to control the integrity of ultimate controllers of Regulated Markets regardless of their ownership, while the U.S. rules generally base the notion of control on ownership.
- **Organizational requirements** are broader in scope for exchanges in the United States and focus on disciplinary powers, which is explained by the self-regulatory role of exchanges in the United States versus a more limited role in the EU.
- **Capital requirements** are risk-based in the EU and based on the concept of maintaining a highly liquid core of capital in the United States.
- **The mitigation of conflicts of interest** is a broad and general obligation for investment firms in Europe while it is focused on more specific situations in the United States.
- **Investor protection rules** in Europe are two-tiered between retail and professional investors (client categorization is binding), while the U.S. regulatory scheme protects all investors, with some carve-outs for institutional investors.
- **Best execution** in the United States covers a number of factors, with price being typically the most important; in Europe price is one factor among others to assess whether the client has obtained the best possible result for the execution of its trade.
- **Data consolidation on equity trades:** in the United States, quotes and transaction data reported by national exchanges and associations are consolidated into a single system and disseminated to market participants, whereas in Europe, quotes and trades are fragmented between multiple trading venues and no consolidation is required.

However, the objectives of the securities regulations are similar, and some outcomes are comparable:

- Both regulatory systems aim to maintain fair and orderly markets, protect investors, and provide price transparency.
- **Equity securities are subject to more scrutiny** and transparency requirements than bonds or derivatives. In the two regions, pre and post-trade transparency requirements apply to equities while there is no or limited transparency regime for derivatives and bonds.
- **Investor protection regimes are broad** and offer better protection to individual investors, whether the rules to achieve such protection are strictly tiered or not.
- **Competition has increased in Europe**, but trading has become more fragmented and liquidity has moved from exchanges, raising the concern of "fragmented liquidity" that led *inter alia* to the adoption of Reg NMS in the United States. In both regions consolidation between exchanges stepped up and it seems that an increasing share of equity trading moved to dark pools.
- **There are concerns on both sides regarding the fragmentation of oversight**. The U.S. SEC does not oversee futures and government bonds; it shares supervisory responsibility with the banking supervisors which oversee commercial banks dealing with securities. In Europe, MiFID is implemented by 27 national supervisors which may lead to different interpretations.

A discussion on the outcomes cannot really be achieved without looking at the implementation of the securities regulations. Thus, the study suggests some directions for future research:

- Assess enforcement on both sides, at the SEC and SRO level in the United States, and at the level of the 27 supervisors in the EU;
- Deepen the knowledge of dark pools on both sides and examine how to improve disclosure and price discovery;
- In Europe in particular, examine ways to achieve quotes and trades consolidation.

Introduction

This paper aims to compare the European Union (EU) and U.S. securities regulations. In November 2007, the Market in Financial Instruments Directive 2004/39/EC (MiFID) came into force in the EU and unleashed competition in European securities markets. The same year came into force in the United States the Regulation NMS (Reg NMS) which was designed to foster competition among individual equities markets and orders. This study compares MiFID with the corresponding U.S. regulations, and primarily focuses on the regulatory and supervisory framework, trading venues, and the provision of investment services. The implementation of the rules, enforcement, and right to redress are beyond the scope of this study. Likewise, the paper does not intend to judge the effectiveness of the two regulatory systems.

In recent months, the international financial crisis has revealed gaps in securities regulations. Main issues have focused on the imperfect oversight of large interconnected institutions, the low transparency of OTC markets, especially derivatives, and the insufficient liquidity and capital across financial institutions. As regulators have announced plans to address those issues, a comparison of the securities regulations in Europe and the United States helps to understand where we are coming from.

The paper focuses on the 2004/39/EC MiFID Directive and its two implementing legislations in Europe; in the United States, it mostly encompasses the 1934 Securities Exchange Act, the FINRA rules and the Reg NMS. The U.S. framework is characterized by a powerful supervisor and important powers assigned to self-regulatory organizations. In the EU, legislation is more recent and unified and characterized by the absence of a supra-national supervisor; self-regulatory organizations have more limited powers. The study looks at the regulatory frameworks in the EU and United States, the scope and objectives of securities regulations, the rules implementing the different objectives, and draws some crisis-related lessons.

CHAPTER 1

Regulatory Framework and Oversight

At a glance, one difference between the EU and U.S. securities regulations is the existence of a unified regulation in the EU under MiFID while in the United States, several regulations and oversight bodies co-exist: the federal level, the state level, and the industry (so-called "Self-Regulatory Organizations"—SROs—in the 1934 Securities Exchange Act). The EU securities framework is relatively close to the United States: MiFID being a Directive, it had to be transposed and its implementation may vary from country to country despite harmonization efforts by the Committee of European Securities Regulators (CESR). Each member state has its own securities supervisor. And exchanges in Europe enact their own rules for their members as do SROs in the United States.

Historically, securities regulation has moved from the state level (member state in the EU) to the federal level (EU institutions level) in both places. A significant difference is however the existence of a powerful federal securities supervisor in the United States versus none in the EU as of now. Under the EU Commission communication on reforming financial regulation broadly endorsed by the EU Council of Ministers on June 19, 2009,[1] CESR would be given legal personality and would have powers on its own, but these would be in specific areas (for example, settling disputes between national supervisors). The power of the SEC is also limited as it does not oversee commodity derivatives and government bonds, and it shares supervisory responsibility with banking supervisors over commercial banks dealing with securities.

EU Securities Framework

The MiFID Directive 2004/39/EC provides a unified framework for securities: it encompasses investment firms, Multilateral Trading Facilities (MTF), Regulated Markets (ie exchanges) and financial instruments (transferable securities,[2] money-market instruments, units in collective investment undertakings and derivatives, excluding bonds and securitized debt).

The Directive, referred to as "Level 1" due to its mode of adoption jointly by the EU Parliament and the Council, sets the principles. It needs to be transposed. It is complemented by "Level 2" texts which consist of implementing measures. They have been adopted by the member states without involving the EU Parliament: Directive 2006/73/EC which needs to be transposed, and Commission Regulation 1287/2006 applicable in the member states without transposition.[3]

Though a unified framework, MiFID had to be implemented by 27 national legislators and its oversight is conducted by national supervisors. So the EU regulatory framework for securities offers in reality as much diversity as the U.S. framework, albeit without a supra-national supervisor as to date. It has to be noted that MiFID is complemented by the Prospectus and Transparency Directives for the disclosure requirements of public companies.[4]

By comparison to the United States, the rule-making powers given to regulated exchanges by MiFID are more limited, and they are focused on the provision of fair and orderly trading, the admission of financial instruments to trading, and the access to the regulated exchanges (articles 39, 40 and 42 of the MiFID Directive). EU regulated exchanges do not have any powers to regulate the behaviour of investment firms that are their members, either in client-facing areas (such as best execution, information or investment advice) or market-facing areas (such as transparency for orders executed off-exchange). Regulated exchanges have limited powers even vis-à-vis their issuers, who obtain the generic right to be admitted to trading on a Regulated Market by filing their prospectus with their supervisor.

U.S. Securities Framework

The U.S. securities regulations and oversight are organised in three different layers:

1. **Federal laws and a federal regulator**, the Securities and Exchange Commission (SEC). The SEC is responsible for protecting investors and maintaining the integrity of securities markets. Several federal statutes regulate securities, and the historical trend has been to shift powers away from the states to the federal level (see table 1.1). The SEC may issue rules interpreting the securities laws passed by Congress (for example, Reg ATS for Alternative Trading Systems, Reg NMS for equity markets). The SEC also reviews any rules proposed by SROs and has final say over whether those rules are consistent with the Securities Exchange Act of 1934. Nonetheless, there are limitations to the SEC's oversight: the SEC does not regulate the primary government bond market (Treasury and FED oversight as government securities are exempt from securities registration) but it oversees the secondary market; it does not regulate commodity futures and options (Commodity Futures Trading Commission oversight),[5] and it has only limited oversight over the OTC derivative market. Municipal bonds are dealt with by a SRO under the oversight of the SEC (see below).[6] The SEC also does not regulate sales of securities by commercial banks (banking regulators oversight): they can act as securities broker and dealers without having to register with the SEC under limited exemptions permitted by the Gramm-Leach-Bliley Act (GLB Act, see infra).
2. **States laws and regulators**: In the United States, states register and supervise broker-dealers and investment advisers that are not registered with the SEC, including investment advisers managing less than US$25 million. They are pre-empted by and must rely on the SEC rules (Section 15(h) of the Exchange Act). They tend to focus on combating fraud within their borders, and they track complaints. State law enforcers can pursue criminal prosecutions, while

the SEC is limited to civil and administrative actions and referring criminal matters to the Justice Department. So individual states often collaborate with the SEC and self-regulatory organizations (SROs) to regulate the securities industry within state borders.

3. **Self-Regulatory Organizations**: they set rules and supervise business practices for their members. Their rules supplement the SEC's rules and federal laws, although they may differ in specifics and emphasis. Any rules that SROs adopt must be reviewed and, in some cases, approved by the SEC, which has ultimate authority over them. Examples of SROs include national exchanges (such as the NYSE, Chicago Climate Exchange, Nasdaq Stock Market), and national securities associations (the current one of which, the Financial Industry Regulatory Authority (FINRA) was created in 2007 as a result of a merger between the National Association of Securities Dealers (NASD) and the regulation, enforcement and arbitration functions of the NYSE). For municipal bonds, a specific SRO called the Municipal Securities Rulemaking Board is responsible for adopting investor protection rules governing broker-dealers and banks that underwrite, trade, and sell tax-exempt bonds, college savings plans and other types of municipal securities.

In sum, the United States securities framework is tiered. The SEC oversees the SROs, which are required to enforce the federal securities laws. Generally the SROs have first line supervisory responsibility. However, in all cases, the SEC retains direct authority over brokers and dealers. The states also have oversight over brokers and dealers in some cases (capital, books and records, margin), but they are pre-empted and must rely on the SEC rules. There is nonetheless fragmentation of oversight between the SEC and the banking supervisors as regards commercial banks dealing with securities. The GLB Act repealed the blanket exemption banks had enjoyed from the definition of broker, and replaced it with a set of limited exemptions. Any securities activities that fall outside of the exceptions may no longer be handled directly in the bank, but rather must be pushed out into a SEC-supervised securities affiliate of the bank.[7]

U.S. securities laws and regulations are numerous, and were adopted mainly in reaction to catalytic events (1929 crash, 2001 Enron scandal) and the technological evolution of markets (Reg NMS).

Table 1.1: Overview of Federal Securities Laws and Regulations

1933 Securities Act "Securities Act"	It stems from the 1929 crash when the DJIA fell by nearly 30% in 6 days in October. Before that, policy makers were divided as to whether federal regulation was needed for securities, some states argued that inconsistency and limitations in state laws left investors vulnerable while others took the view that federal regulation would curb the development of the stock market. Only after the crash and the ensuing depression did the federal view prevail. First federal text to regulate securities; it regulates *new* offering of securities and prohibits fraud. It pursues a disclosure-based approach to regulation (companies must disclose material information related to their business and finances before issuing securities) with a view that fair disclosure creates a level-playing field for investors. This contrasts with earlier state laws which could prohibit the sale of investment products on the basis of merit.
1934 Securities and Exchange Act "Exchange Act"	It creates the SEC, regulates the buying and trading of *existing* securities and makes insider trading a crime.
1938 Maloney Act	It amends the 1934 Securities Exchange Act by authorizing the creation and registration of national securities associations which would supervise their members under the oversight of the SEC. It led to the creation of the NASD in 1939.
1940 Investment Companies Act "1940 Act"	It extends the fair disclosure requirement to mutual funds and investment unit trusts: they are required to publish information on their finances, fee structure, and investment policies. The EU counterpart of this act would be the Undertaking for Collective Investments in Transferable Securities (UCITS) Directives.
1940 Investment Advisers Act	It requires persons or firms that receive a fee for securities advice to register as investment advisers.
1956 Uniform Securities Act "USA"	It sets uniform standards for the registration of securities, broker-dealers and investments advisers, in line with federal laws. States are not required to pass the Act although 40 have adopted some version of it.
1970 Bank Secrecy Act	It establishes the U.S. anti-money laundering regime
1996 National Securities Market Improvement Act	First federal law to limit states' powers to regulate securities. Despite the Uniform Securities Act, duplication agencies efforts and inconsistencies remained a major problem. The Act excludes from state registration securities such as exchange-listed securities and mutual funds shares.
1998 Regulation ATS "Reg ATS"	It regulates Alternative Trading Systems, and requires them to register as either exchanges or broker-dealers.
1999 Gramm-Leach-Bliley Act or Financial Modernization Act, "GLB Act"	It repeals part of the Glass-Steagall Act of 1933 and allows commercial banks, investment banks, securities firms and investment companies to consolidate. It also repeals the blanket exemption banks had enjoyed from the registration as broker-dealer if they provided securities services, and replaced it by a set of limited exemptions.
2002 Sarbanes-Oxley Act "Sarbanes-Oxley"	It mandates new corporate governance and accounting requirements for public companies, in response to several corporate scandals.
2005 Regulation NMS "Reg NMS"	Promulgated by the SEC, it is designed to strengthen the national market system for equity securities created in 1975 (common structure to settle equity transactions in real time) in response to technological changes. It consists of four different rules: -"Order Protection Rule" (also known as "trade-through rule") requires trading centres to establish and enforce written policies designed to prevent the execution of trades at prices inferior to protected quotations displayed by automated trading centres. -"Access Rule" requires fair and non-discriminatory access to quotations, establishes a limit on access fees to harmonize the pricing of quotations across different trading centers, and require each national securities exchange and association to adopt and enforce rules that prohibit their members from displaying quotations that lock or cross automated quotations. - "Sub-Penny Rule" prohibits market participants from accepting, ranking, or displaying orders, quotations, or indications of interest in a pricing increment smaller than a penny, except for orders priced at less than $1.00 per share. - "Market Data Rules" update the requirements for consolidating, distributing, and displaying market information.

Sources: www.pathtoinvesting.org; www.sec.org.

The federal rules most comparable to MiFID are the 1934 Securities Exchange Act, the 1998 Reg ATS and the 2005 Reg NMS (for equities only). They are complemented by SRO rules from NYSE and NASD, being merged into the FINRA rules.[8] Oversight of the U.S. exchanges (NYSE-Euronext, Nasdaq, American Stock Exchange, International Securities Exchange and Chicago Climate Exchange) is carried out by the SEC, while trading in the off-exchange securities markets is overseen by the SEC and FINRA. FINRA's disciplinary action is subject to appeal to the SEC (Section 19(d)(2) of the 1934 Securities Exchange Act).

The tiered supervisory structure may result in regulatory overlaps in some instances. For example on margin requirements, the initial requirement for buying securities in a margin account is set by the Board of Governors of the Federal Reserve System, but once the investor buys on margin, the ongoing margin requirements are set by FINRA, and the investor's brokerage firm. There do not seem to be overlap in the MiFID regulations since the national supervisors are primarily responsible for oversight and enforcement, but there is a risk of differing interpretations from supervisors. This is well identified and CESR has been tasked with harmonizing national supervisors' implementation of MiFID.

Notes

[1] Communication from the European Commission, European Financial Supervision, COM(2009) 232, 27 May 2009. Council of the European Union 18/19 June, Presidency Conclusions, 19 June 2009.

[2] Securities negotiable on the capital markets with the exception of instruments of payment such as shares in partnerships and depositary receipts, bonds and securitized debt, other securities giving rise to a cash settlement determined by reference to other transferable securities, currencies, interest rates, commodities.

[3] Directive 2006/73/EC of 10 August 2006 implementing Directive 2004/39/EC of the European Parliament and the Council as regards organizational requirements and operating conditions for investment firms and defined terms for the purpose of that Directive. Commission Regulation 1287/2006 of 10 August 2006 implementing Directive 2004/39/EC as regards record-keeping obligations for investment firms, transaction reporting, market transparency, admission of financial instruments to trading, and defined terms for the purpose of that Directive.

[4] Directive 2003/71/EC of 4 November 2003 on the prospectus to be published when securities are offered to the public or admitted to trading (so called "Prospectus Directive") and Directive 2004/109/EC of 15 December 2004 on the harmonization of transparency requirements in relation to information about issuers whose securities are admitted to trading on a Regulated Market (so-called "Transparency Directive").

[5] The SEC and the CFTC have joint jurisdiction over security futures (futures contracts based on securities), therefore firms that engage in activities involving this instrument must register with the SEC and the CFTC.

[6] Nonetheless, municipal securities dealers and government securities broker and dealers have to register with the SEC pursuant section 15B and 15C of the Exchange Act.

[7] Sec, Final Rules to implement the Bank "Broker" Provisions of the Gramm-Leach-Bliley Act http://www.sec.gov/news/press/2007/2007-198.htm

[8] As a result, several NASD rules remain, for example on suitability (NASD 2310) and best execution (NASD 2320).

CHAPTER 2

Scope of the Securities Regulations

The MiFID encompasses investment firms, Regulated Markets, and MTF. It regulates investment advice as a service requiring authorization. **The U.S. regulations focus on brokers and dealers and exchanges, which are respectively the "investment firms" and the "Regulated Markets" in the sense of the MiFID.**[1] The main difference between the two regulations is that dark pools are not explicitly captured by the MiFID (the Directive is not currently applied to them) whereas they are considered as ATS in the United States and are registered as broker and dealers. They however do not display public quotes if they are below a certain trading volume threshold.

Hedge fund managers are partially captured by both regulations. In Europe, if they deal with transferable securities, hedge fund managers would be considered as investment firms but would not have to apply all the requirements of the MiFID Directive if they only had professional clients. In the United States, hedge funds managers have to register as investment advisers, but can benefit from waivers if they deal with qualified investors. Some hedge funds may also have to register with the SEC as brokers and dealers. Traditionally the SEC has distinguished "dealers" from "traders":[2] if hedge funds place quotations on both sides of the market, are known as a source of liquidity, and are a supplier of securities, they would be considered dealers. Finally, some managers or consultants of hedge funds may have to register with the SEC as brokers, if they participate in a meaningful way in any of the key phases of a securities transaction (for example, receipt of transaction-related compensation, solicitation of securities transactions and handling of funds and securities).

The outcome of both regulations, focusing either on investment firms or brokers/dealers, seems nonetheless similar: the advice, brokerage, dealing in securities has to be authorized/registered, and transparent so as to ensure investors' protection.

The EU Securities Regulations Focus on Investment Firms and Trading Venues

Article 1 of the MiFID Directive states: "this Directive shall apply to investment firms and Regulated Markets."

The Level 1 Directive encompasses three main concepts:

1. **Investment firm**: Any legal person whose regular occupation or business is the provision of investment services to third parties and/or the performance of one or more investment activities on a professional basis. Member states may include under this definition undertakings which are not legal persons, provided that (i) their legal status ensures a level of protection for third parties interest equivalent to that afforded by legal persons; and (ii) they are subject to equivalent prudential supervisions appropriate to their legal form. They can be **systematic internalizers (SI)**, which on an organized, frequent, and systematic basis deal on own account by executing client orders outside a Regulated Market or MTF. Concretely, investment firms declare themselves SI for selected equities (self-certification regime), and route most orders to other trading venues including their own platform. SI are associated with the trading in shares and regulated under article 27 of the MiFID Directive.

2. **Multilateral Trading Facility** (MTF) is a multilateral system operated by an investment firm or a market operator, which brings together multiple third-party buying and selling interests in financial instruments—in the system and in accordance to non-discretionary rules. There are basically alternative trading platforms to exchanges, often created by banks to process their trades such as Turquoise as regards equities. The MTF concept is similar to the Alternative Trading Systems (ATS) widely developed in the United States (see Section 2.2).

3. **Regulated Market** (RM) is a multilateral system (i) operated and/or managed by a market operator, (ii) which brings together multiple third-party buying and selling interests in financial instruments—in the system and in accordance with its discretionary rules—in a way that results in a contract in respect to the financial instruments admitted to trading under its rules and/or systems and (iii) which is authorized and functions regularly. RMs correspond to the major exchanges in the EU, but not all exchanges are RMs, some of them are regulated as MTFs. The main difference between a RM and a MTF remains the non-application of the Prospectus Directive (2003/71/EC), the Transparency Directive (2004/109/EC) and subsequently the IFRS to MTFs.

MiFID regulations seek to capture the execution of trading in securities irrespective of the trading methods used to conclude those transactions: thus, Regulated Markets, MTF, and systematic internalizers are all subject to transparency requirements albeit to a varying degree (waivers exist for MTF and systematic internalizers in the case of large or illiquid transactions). However, some trading venues such as dark pools are not currently captured by MiFID, although they account for a substantial amount of trading volume (up to 40 percent by some estimates).

Dark pools of liquidity are trading facilities which match anonymously large and small orders. In Europe, they may be classified in two categories: (i) dark pools operated by broker-dealers or investment banks, also called "crossing networks" and (ii) dark pools operated as MTFs. Crossing networks of the first category do not have to comply with MiFID pre-trade transparency requirements, and with other rules imposed on RMs and MTFs such as the obligation to treat investors equally, to provide fair access to the trading platform and market surveillance, and to operate a non-discretionary execution system. Dark pools operated as MTFs of the second category are regulated, but they benefit from some pre-trade transparency waivers permitted by the MiFID Level 2 Regulation (market model, large orders).[3] However in all cases, investment firms responsible for executing the order on behalf of a client will need to decide whether the submission to a dark pool complies with the order-handling and best execution obligations to which they are subject.[4]

There is an active public debate going on in Europe as to crossing networks should be regulated as MTFs. Exchanges and MTFs argue that the fact they operate outside the MiFID Directive gives them an unfair commercial advantage. Conversely, investment banks argue that their crossing networks are merely an automation of OTC services that they have always carried out to facilitate clients' orders.[5] CESR is looking at this issue and is expected to deliver a supervisory guidance in the coming months. The MiFID review by the EU Commission expected to be launched at the end of 2009 will address this issue as well.

Table 2.1 attempts to shed light on the "dark" concept. It is important to note that several types of dark pools exist, and that the distinction with exchanges and MTF is becoming more blurry since exchanges and MTF have established their own dark pools of liquidity in recent years.

As regards the MiFID's scope on financial instruments: Some dispositions are applied differently depending on the instruments and the trading venues. Certain MiFID obligations only apply to financial instruments admitted to trading on a RM. There are no pre and post-trade transparency requirements for bonds, securitized debt and derivatives; however the duty of best execution applies to all instruments including bonds; there is no obligation of transaction reporting for securities that are not admitted to trading on a Regulated Market; exemptions to the appropriateness test are possible for non-complex products but not for bonds or securitized debt that embed a derivative.

The U.S. Securities Regulations Focus on Broker-Dealers and Exchanges

The 1934 Securities Exchange Act regulates the registration, operations and integrity of brokers and dealers. At the SRO level, the FINRA rules control the organisation and business conduct of brokers and dealers (with concepts such as investment suitability and best execution). **In the United States, brokers and dealers are the "investment firms."**

The broker-dealer concept is nonetheless broader than the MiFID "investment firms": alternative trading platforms such as dark pools or Electronic Communication Networks (ECNs) register with the SEC as broker-dealers. The 1998 SEC regulation on Alternative Trading Systems (Reg ATS) requires ATS to register as broker-dealers, exchanges (if they have self-regulatory powers or trade above a certain market volume),[6] or to respect minimum requirements if they represent less than 5 percent of the trading volume for any given security they trade.[7] If an ATS accounts for more than 5 percent of the average daily volume in a security over four of the preceding six months, it (i) must establish written standards for granting access to trading on its system, and (ii) must not unreasonably prohibit or limit any person in respect to access to services offered by such system by applying these written standards in an unfair or discriminatory manner.[8]

Table 2.1: The "Dark" Concept

Concept	Definition and Example	EU regulation	U.S. regulation
Dark pool	Trading venue that provides liquidity that is not displayed on order books.	Two types of dark pools: a) dark pools operated by broker-dealers also called crossing networks, which are unregulated and are not subject to pre-trade transparency requirements; b) dark pools operated as MTFs, which do benefit from pre-trade transparency waivers but have to comply with other MTF rules. There is however a post-trade transparency requirement for equities traded on dark pools: investment firms are required to report transactions in public shares carried out outside a Regulated Market or a MTF.	Dark pools are considered as ATS and register as brokers and dealers. However, most of them do not display public quotes, because they represent less than 5 percent of the trading volume in any security they trade, or because they may have obtained an exemption from the 5 percent rule (for example, Liquidnet). Nevertheless, they must promptly report trades over 100 shares.
Independent dark pools	For example, Liquidnet Instinet, Posit, Euro-Millenium	Most are regulated as MTF in Europe.	They are considered as ATS
Broker-dealer dark pool (crossing network)	Dark pool usually operated by an investment bank for example, Credit Suisse cross finder	Investment banks do not need to apply for a waiver from MiFID's pre-trade transparency obligations as long as the platform is not registered as a MTF.	They are considered as ATS
MTF dark pool	Dark pool owned by a MTF in Europe. For example: Turquoise's dark pool	MTFs apply to their supervisor for a waiver from MiFID's pre-trade transparency obligations	They are considered as ATS
Exchange owned dark pool	Dark pool owned by a Regulated Market. For example: Baikal, the London Stock Exchange's dark pool and Neuro Dark NASDAQ-OMX's dark pool	Exchanges apply to their supervisor for a waiver from MiFID's pre-trade transparency obligations	They are considered as ATS

Source: CESR, MiFID Directive, Reg ATS.

Dark pools are regulated in the United States under Reg ATS and register as broker-dealers. As most of them are below the 5 percent threshold or have obtained exemptions (for example, Liquidnet),[9] they do not display quotes in the public data stream but they must promptly report their executed trades to the public. However, the trade report does not identify the particular pool responsible for the trade, which makes it difficult to assess the liquidity in a particular stock. As dark pools have strongly developed in the past year, there is also a debate in the United States as to whether more regulation on those pools is needed.[10]

The MiFID concept of systematic internalizer for equity trades is not regulated as such in the United States. Internalization within a broker-dealer would be considered as OTC trade, unless the trade is printed on an exchange.

As regard the instruments, the U.S. rules are similar to MiFID in the sense that bonds, securitized debt and derivatives do not bear pre and post transparency requirements (there are some exceptions: corporate and municipal bonds benefit from post-trade transparency in the United States). On national securities exchanges, traded securities must be registered, which is similar to MiFID article 40, admission of financial instruments to trading.

The following tables summarize the scope of EU and U.S. securities regulations, and give an overview of the market share of each trading venues. It seems that since the start of the global financial crisis, the share of OTC equity trading (including dark pools) in Europe has significantly increased, mainly as a result of declining trading volumes at regulated exchanges.[11] Tables 2.3 and 2.4 illustrate **the sheer difficulty to measure precisely the trading market share of dark pools given their multiple facets**. In Europe they are included in the OTC trading without the possibility to differentiate dark pools from other OTC. In the United States, OTC and ATS are grouped together, but there are independent estimates of the market share of dark pools in equities trading at around 7–9 percent, accounted for about 40 dark pools.[12]

Table 2.2: Scope of EU and U.S. Securities Regulations

MiFID	U.S. Securities Regulations
Investment Firms (IF)	Brokers and Dealers
Systematic Internalizers (SI)	No concept of Systematic Internalizer
Multilateral Trading Facilities (MTF)	Alternative Trading Systems (ATS)
Regulated Markets (RM)	Exchanges
Key provisions of MiFID are not applied to dark pools unless they are set up as MTFs; thus they do not apply to crossing networks	Dark pools regulated under Reg ATS but they may be exempted from pre-trade transparency requirements if below a certain volume threshold
Some dispositions applied differently depending on financial instruments (for example, transparency requirements)	Some dispositions applied differently depending on financial instruments (for example, transparency requirements)

Table 4: Market Shares of Trading Venues by Type of Financial Instrument

EU (MiFID)	Equities	Fixed-Income	Derivatives
Regulated Markets	49.0%	5.0%	20%
MTF	8.0%	3.1%	0%
OTC including dark pools	41.0%	89.2%	80%
SI (for equities only)	2.0%	NA	NA
Other	0.0%	2.7%	
United States	**Equities**	**Fixed-Income**	**Derivatives**
Exchanges	64.2%	<1%	20%
OTC (including ATS/dark pools)	35.8%	>99%	80%

Source: FESE, Xtrakter (http://www.xtrakter.com/ye2008fi.aspx), FINRA, European Commission and BIS (for Derivatives).
EU Equities trading as of May 2009, fixed income as of Dec. 2008.
U.S. equities as of July 2009 in exchange listed stocks, fixed income as of July 2009 (TRACE).

Notes

[1] The U.S. regulations define brokers and dealers as follows: a broker is any person engaged in the business of effecting transactions in securities for the account of others; a dealer is any person that is engaged in the business of buying and selling securities for its own account (Exchange Act section 3 (a) (4)(5)).

[2] A trader is a person that buys and sells securities not as part of a regular business and is not registered with the SEC.

[3] There are four types of pre-trade transparency waivers: (i) systems based on a trading methodology by which the price is determined with a reference price generated by another system (reference waiver price); (ii) systems that formalize negotiated transactions (negotiated trade waiver); (iii) orders that are held in an order management facility maintained by the Regulated Market or MTF pending their being disclosed to the market (order management facility waiver); (iv) orders that are large in scale compared with normal market size (large in scale waiver). Source: CESR, Impact of MiFID on equity secondary markets functioning, 10 June 2009.

[4] CESR, Questions and Answers on MiFID, May 2009.

[5] Complinet, CESR will investigate exchanges' MiFID level playing field concern about crossing networks, 12 June 2009.

[6] Reg ATS introduction part C: "any system exercising self-regulatory powers, such as regulating its members' conduct when engaged in activities outside of that trading system must register as an exchange or be operated by a national securities association". "In addition, the Commission can determine that a dominant alternative trading system should be registered as an exchange. It would first have to exceed certain volume levels (...)".

[7] They only have to file with the SEC a notice of operation and quarterly reports, maintain records, and refrain from using the words "exchanges" or "stock market". Source: Reg ATS introduction part C.

[8] "Fair Access Rule" of Reg ATS amended by Reg NMS, 17 CFR 242.301(b)(5)(ii)(B). SEC, Order Granting Exemption to Liquidnet, Inc. from Certain Provisions of Regulation ATS under the Securities Exchange Act of 1934, September 27, 2005.

[9] SEC, ibid.

[10] SEC, Speech by SEC Chairman, remarks at the IOSCO Technical Committee Conference, October 8, 2009. Wall Street Journal, NYSE Executives: More regulation of dark pools needed, May 19, 2009.

[11] Source: FESE. The market share of OTC venues in equity trading in Europe has increased from 26 percent in October 2008 to 41 percent in May 2009.

[12] Rosenblatt Securities estimates the market share of dark pools in U.S. listed stocks at 8.9 percent in December 2008. According to Tabb Group, this market share was 7.14 percent in April 2009.

CHAPTER 3

Objectives of the Securities Regulations in Europe and the United States

Securities regulations in the EU and United States have a similar emphasis on investor protection, fair and orderly markets, and price transparency, which is viewed in the United States as a tool to achieve both investor protection and fair and orderly markets. Such similarities are in line with the 2003 IOSCO Core Principles of Securities Regulation.[1] Harmonization is also an important goal in Europe for institutional reasons, but it has no equivalent in the United States, since state powers in securities regulation are pre-empted by and must rely on the SEC rules (Section 15(h) of the Exchange Act).

Objectives of the EU Securities Regulations

The introductory part of the 2004/39/EC Directive mentions three objectives: "it is necessary to provide for the degree of harmonization needed to offer investors a high level of protection and to allow investment firms to provide services throughout the Community."

Enhance competition in the single market: the 1986 Single European Act intends to create "an area without internal frontiers in which the free movement of goods, persons, services and capital is ensured." The 1999 Financial Services Action Plan (FSAP) aims to establish a single wholesale financial market and to open and secure retail financial markets in the EU. MiFID is a key component of the FSAP. Compared to its predecessor, the 1993 Investment Services Directive (ISD), **it abolishes the concentration rule** in which member states could require investment firms to route clients' orders to domestic Regulated Markets, preventing competition between national exchanges and alternative trading venues. In addition, MiFID establishes a "full passport," enabling investment firms, once authorized and supervised in a member state, to offer their services in another member state without further authorization from the host state. This implies mutual recognition.

Protect investors depending on their characteristics: MiFID distinguishes between **retail clients, professional clients** (defined as having the experience, knowledge and expertise to make their own investment decisions) and **eligible counterparties** (investment firms, credit institutions, insurance companies, governments, central banks, mutual and pension funds and their management companies, undertaking dealing on own account commodities, futures, options). **Client categorization is binding**: firms have to inform their clients how they categorize them, and this entails a different level of protection. Retail investors benefit from greater protection, in particular as regards the suitability of the investment recommendation, the information they receive on the investment firm, the information on transactions' charges. The key dispositions to ensure investor protection are fair, clear and "not misleading" information to clients; suitability; best execution; and expeditious execution of client orders (articles 19, 21 and 22 of MiFID Level 1 Directive). The Directive defines eligible counterparties to which the latter dispositions do not apply (article 24). Eligible counterparties and professional clients are roughly similar but the two concepts are used in different instances.

Harmonize member states regulations: the ISD harmonised the initial authorization and operating requirements for investment firms but featured minimal harmonization and mutual recognition. As a result, member states could enact their own rules on top of the Directive's requirements (gold-plating) which impeded the creation of a level-playing field. MiFID prohibits such gold-plating, leading to "maximum harmonization." However, the intention in the Level 1 Directive was undermined in the implementation process. The Level 2 Directive allows member states to impose additional requirements in exceptional cases and under certain circumstances.

Objectives of the U.S. Securities Regulations

According to the SEC website, "the mission of the U.S. Securities and Exchange Commission is to protect investors, maintain fair, orderly, and efficient markets, and facilitate capital formation." To this end, U.S. regulations point out the need for price discovery process. **The main difference with MiFID is that investor protection rules are not two-tiered: the system protects all investors with some carve-outs for institutional investors.** Institutional or "accredited" investors are defined in the Exchange Act as investment companies, financial institutions, and small business investments (Section 3, 54).

Maintain fair, orderly and efficient markets: this is the founding objective of securities regulation. The first Act to regulate securities at the federal level, the 1933 Securities Act states in its title "An act to provide full and fair disclosure of the character of securities sold in interstate and foreign commerce and through the mails, and to prevent frauds in the sale thereof, and for other purposes." This objective results in organizational arrangements for brokers and dealers and markets, a tight control on fraud, the facilitation of competition and a concern to maintain market liquidity. In addition, this objective requires the **SEC to consider the impact of regulation on competition**, and prohibits it from adopting rules that would impose an unnecessary burden on competition (Exchange Act Section 23(a)(2)).

Protect investors: according to the SEC, "all investors, whether large institutions or private individuals, should have access to certain basic facts about an investment prior to buying it, and so long as they hold it."[2] Therefore, public companies are required to disclose meaningful financial and other information to the public. This provides a common pool of knowledge for all investors to use to judge for themselves whether to buy, sell, or hold a particular security. The flow of information results in more transparent capital markets which facilitate capital formation. **Compared to MiFID, the categorization of investors is less binding**: brokers and dealers do not have to categorize their clients. The U.S. regulatory scheme is not two-tiered; it protects all investors, with some carve-outs for institutional investors.[3] However, the result of both systems is comparable in the sense that retail investors benefit from stronger protection than institutional or informed investors. The U.S. regulatory reform is considering the reinforcement of retail investors' protection: the Treasury White Paper on financial reform proposes to establish a fiduciary duty for broker-dealers offering investment advice, and harmonize the regulation of investment advisers and broker-dealers.[4] The paper acknowledges that although they are regulated under different frameworks, investment advisers and broker-dealers provide similar services to retail investors.

To achieve fair and orderly markets and investor protection, the **U.S. regulations emphasize** *inter alia* **the need for price discovery**. When Congress authorized the SEC to establish a national market system for equities in 1975, it stated the principle of competition among orders, enabling price discovery for orders of all sizes. In Reg NMS, the SEC indicates that if "competition among orders is lessened, the quality of price discovery for all sizes of orders can be compromised. Impaired price discovery could cause market prices to deviate from fundamental values, reduce market depth and liquidity."[5]

Notes

[1] IOSCO Core Principles put forward three objectives: the protection of investors, ensuring that markets are fair, efficient and transparent, and the reduction of systemic risk.

[2] SEC Website.

[3] Examples of carve-outs for institutional investors include: exemptions from the registration requirements of the Securities Act if an entity sells a security only to accredited investors; under Regulation R. there is an exemption from the definition of "broker" for banks that make certain institutional referrals; the suitability rule imposes less stringent requirements on firms if they are dealing with institutional investors; communications that are delivered and made available solely to institutional investors may benefit from exemptions from the advertising filing requirements (NASD Rule 2210 and 2211).

[4] U.S. Treasury Department, Financial Regulatory Reform: A New Foundation, 17 June 2009.

[5] Reg NMS, Principles and Objectives, Competition among markets and competition among orders, Section I.B.1.

CHAPTER 4

Implementation of the Different Objectives

As Regards Competition/Fair and Orderly Markets

Authorizing procedures for investments firms, brokers-dealers, and exchanges: The authorizing procedures are similar on both sides of the Atlantic. Pre-clearance is required for investment firms/broker-dealers and Regulated Markets/exchanges before they begin business, and the information needed to obtain the authorization is broad.

    Authorization of investment firms/registration of brokers and dealers: European regulators are not supposed to grant authorization until an investment firm meets a set of predefined conditions including the following: fit and proper tests for managers and shareholders and persons with qualifying holdings; organizational and initial capital requirements; and membership in authorized Investor Compensation Scheme (if required). Additionally the investment firms specify the scope of their investment services or activities. When a regulator is fully satisfied that an investment firm meets all the requirements it can grant an authorization not later than 6 months after the submission of the application. Investment firms must require an extension of the authorization if they involve in additional activities.

    In the United States, brokers and dealers must not engage in securities business until 1) they have filed an application form (Form BD) and the SEC has granted its registration; 2) they have become a member of an SRO; 3) they have become a member of the Securities Investors Protection Corporation; 4) they comply with all applicable state requirements; 5) their associated persons have satisfied applicable qualifications requirements.[1] The SEC acts on application within 45 days, provided the broker-dealer is a SRO member and the SRO has approved the application. Form BD submitted by brokers and dealers in the United States is very detailed. It requires information about the background of the broker-dealer and its associated persons (principals, controlling persons, and employees). An applicant has to disclose persons that exercise direct or indirect control over a broker-dealer and describe the nature of the control. Similar to the European requirements, broker-dealers have to specify the scope of their activities and update the form every time they involve into new or pull out from the existing activities. Within six months after the registration is granted, the Commission or a self-regulatory organization conducts an inspection in order to determine the conformity of broker-dealers with the Exchange Act and the related rules and regulations.

Authorization of Regulated Markets/Registration of Exchanges: Pre-clearance by regulators is required before Regulated Markets and exchanges engage into business. There are two major differences in pre-conditions for clearance in Europe and in the United States. The first is the **application of fit and proper tests** for managers and **persons exercising significant influence** over the management of Regulated Markets in Europe, while similar provisions do not appear in the United States. The second difference is the requirement for exchanges in the United States to demonstrate **the ability to discipline** their members for violation of both federal and SROs rules. In Europe, exchanges shall only demonstrate that they **are able to monitor compliance** of their members and report to competent authorities any violation of the rules of the Regulated Markets and other legal provisions. In particular in Europe, MiFID, and the Market Abuse Directive[2] require regulated exchanges to monitor for market abuse. Promotion of fair trading and non-discrimination by rules of the Regulated Market/exchange is present both in Europe and in the United States.

Other pre-conditions for the authorization in Europe include organizational requirements; clear and transparent rules as regard access to Regulated Markets; and admission/removal of financial instruments from trading. Similar pre-conditions are in place in the United States as well as rules on fair representation of members and investment community in the management of exchanges and rules to provide equitable principles on allocation of fees and other charges among members of the exchanges.

Fit and proper tests requirements differ markedly in Europe and in the United States: Firstly, the U.S. system is rule-based versus principle-based in the EU. Strict reputational and professional requirements are in place for broker-dealers in the United States, established under the Exchange Act (Section 15, Par. 4) and enhanced by the SROs' rules. There is a set of specific and objective criteria under which the competence and reputation of broker-dealers and their associated persons can be assessed and statutory disqualification can be imposed.[3] However, **neither the SEC or the SROs has a mandate to make a judgment, as it is the case in Europe, of whether executives of an investment firm/Regulated Market are of sufficiently good repute and sufficiently experienced to direct the business**. There is no pre-determined set of criteria in Europe. Secondly, the scope of the European fit and proper test is broader: (i) the U.S. securities regulation has not established reputational or professional requirements for exchanges and their associated persons; in Europe, MiFID requires fit and proper tests for the managers of Regulated Markets and persons who exercise significant influence over the management of Regulated Markets. (ii) According to MiFID, **a regulator has the power to assess potential acquirers of investment firms,**[4] **which is not the case in the United States**. The U.S. regulator has taken the stance that acquisitions will be assessed by the market, where potential synergies (strategic or financial) will be reflected in market price. At the same time broker-dealers will have to comply with reputational and professional tests, capital requirements, and money laundering rules at all times, before and after being acquired.

In Europe fit and proper tests are stronger for Regulated Markets than for the investment firms. In the case of investment firms a regulator has the authority to judge whether a manager of an investment firm is sufficiently experienced and of sufficiently good repute to direct the business and to assess suitability of shareholders or members, whether direct or indirect, with qualifying holdings.[5] In the case of a **Regulated Market**

a regulator goes one step further by requiring that persons that directly or indirectly exercise influence[6] over the management of Regulated Market must be suitable. A regulator imposes an obligation on a Regulated Market to disclose identity and scale of interest of persons who exercise significant influence over the management. Competent authorities will not grant authorization to investment firms if close links that exist between the firm and other natural or legal person can jeopardize effective supervision. However, there is no requirement for an investment firm to disclose those links. Instead, the burden of proof remains with the regulator.

In the United States, the Exchange Act establishes detailed reputational requirements for broker-dealers and their associated persons. The definition of an associated person is broad and includes any partner, officer, director, branch manager, employees (except when their functions are solely clerical or ministerial) and any person directly or indirectly controlling, controlled by, or under common control with a broker-dealer. The term "control"[7] contains a negative presumption that any person who does not own voting securities, participate in profits or function as an executive, shall be presumed not to have control over another person (see NYSE Rule 2f and form BD). There is no such a concept as "person who exercises significant influence over the management" as mentioned in the case of Regulated Markets in Europe, that may arise even from a tiny percentage of shareholding interest. Reputational requirements include violations or crimes related to trading, investment advising, credit rating agency business, violation of securities and investment regulation as well as general crimes. The regulator goes that far to prohibit membership to persons who failed to supervise a person subject to his/her supervision in relation to securities trading/investing.

In addition to federal regulation, each SRO can impose reputational and professional requirements for broker-dealers. Broker-dealers provide information about its associated persons to the SEC and to FINRA by submitting the Form BD, but they also have to file U-4 form with SRO (when members) for each person that effects transaction in securities. The U-4 form contains individual's employment and disciplinary history.

Professional requirements arise from the Exchange Act, but qualification tests are designed and administered by SROs. An associated person who effects transaction in securities is obliged to meet qualification requirements, which includes passing a qualification examination.

Transparency of holdings and beneficial ownership: Similar to Europe where disclosure of shareholders or members and persons with qualifying holdings and amount of those holdings is a requirement, broker-dealers have to disclose persons who exercise direct or indirect control, indicating the percentage of their ownership and describing the nature of the control. However, the requirement is weaker in the United States in the sense that beneficial owners of exchanges do not have to be disclosed to the regulator, as a result of a presumption that the market will identify reputational issues.

Organizational requirements for investment firms and broker-dealers: They are similar in Europe and the United States. MiFID lays down detailed organizational requirements that must be met by investment firms in order to receive authorization from a competent authority. Several of those requirements can be found under the U.S.

rules: 1) requirements for investment firms and broker-dealers to have in place arrangements to prevent conflict of interest; 2) adequate systems, resources and procedures in order to assure continuity in business services; 3) responsibilities when outsourcing to third parties; 4) sound accounting and administrative procedures and 5) policies and procedures on personal transactions of employees and tied agents.[8]

The organizational requirements for exchanges are broader in the United States than in Europe and are focused on the exchanges' disciplinary role, rather than on internal systems and policies which is mostly the case in Europe. The common feature in the two regulatory frameworks is the promotion of fair and orderly trading and transparency in transactions. The U.S. exchanges must demonstrate that they have in place solid disciplinary and enforcement procedures in order to exercise their complementary function in securities markets regulation (SRO role). On the other side, the main objective of the organizational requirements for Regulated Markets in Europe is the prevention of operational risks and system disruptions, and ensuring sufficient resources in order to carry on business activity. The difference between the SRO-disciplinary role of the U.S. exchanges and the more limited role of the EU exchanges is the main reason why operational requirements on EU exchanges are lighter.

Capital requirements for investment firms/brokers and dealers: Regulatory capital requirements are different in Europe and in the United States. While in Europe capital requirements are risk based, in the United States the Net Capital Rule (Rule 15c3-1) for broker-dealers is based on the concept of maintaining a highly liquid core of capital. This rule is "to oblige broker-dealers to have at all times enough liquid assets to be able to satisfy the claims of customers in the case a broker-dealer goes out of business."[9] Investment firms in Europe are required to comply with the Capital Requirement Directives for credit institutions.[10]

Under the SEC rule broker-dealers must have in place minimum capital levels, subject to the type of securities activities they are engaged in and based on certain financial ratios. For example, a broker-dealer that carries customer or broker-dealer accounts and receives or holds funds or securities for those persons is required to maintain a minimum net capital of US$250,000. Large broker-dealers that hold customer funds and securities often choose to calculate their net capital based on the alternative method. Pursuant to such method, a broker- dealer must maintain at least the greater of US$250,000 or 2 percent of aggregate debit items computed using the Formula for Determination of Reserve Requirements for Brokers and Dealers.[11] Minimum capital requirements for broker-dealers who do not carry customer accounts are smaller.

In Europe, investment firms need to have initial amount of capital in place in order to engage in the business activity. Investment firms that hold client funds or securities are required to have an initial capital of EUR 125,000. Firms that do not carry client funds can operate with an initial capital of EUR 50,000. Additionally, capital requirements rules stipulate the minimum amounts of own financial resources that credit institutions and investment firms must have in order to cover the risks to which they are exposed. The aim is to protect clients and the stability of the financial system.[12] The capital requirement rules are currently under review in the EU, to better account in particular for large exposures, securitization exposures, and risks to the trading book.[13]

Mitigation of conflict of interest: The conflict of interest requirements under MiFID are broad and general, while in the United States they appear to be focused on specific situations.

In Europe, every investment firm must establish, implement, and maintain an effective conflict of interest policy, depending on the nature and complexity of its business. The policy shall clearly identify situations that may raise conflicts of interest based on the guidelines provided by MiFID. In the United States, there is no such equivalent of a "conflict of interest policy"; there are nonetheless several provisions to mitigate conflicts of interest, which are targeted to specific situations. For example, when recommending a security a broker dealer has a duty to disclose any material conflict of interest (Exchange Act, Section 10(b)(5)); a broker dealer also has to disclose in writing to customers if he has any control, affiliation, or interest in a security that is offering or in the issuer of such security (Exchange Act 15c1-5&6). Section 15(f) of the Exchange Act requires brokers and dealers to establish and enforce procedures to prevent the misuse of material non-public information, and Section 11(a) prohibit them from effecting transactions on exchanges for their own accounts.[14]

Access to market is an important rule to foster competition and fair and orderly trading and is similar on both sides of the Atlantic: In Europe, exchanges grant access to persons who are fit and proper, have sufficient level of trading ability and competence, comply with organizational requirements and have sufficient financial resources for the role they perform.

In the United States, exchanges may provide an access to any registered broker and dealer. As discussed under the registration, brokers and dealers have to comply with reputational and professional tests in order to be registered. Additionally, exchanges are entitled to deny membership to broker-dealers who are under statutory disqualifications, do not meet standards of financial responsibility or operational capability, or a broker-dealer or any natural person associated with such broker-dealer who does not meet standards of training, experience, and competence as prescribed by the rules of the exchange.

The Access rule is featured in the United States in the Regulation NMS. The rule is designed to contribute to fair and efficient access to quotations of trading centers. This is achieved in three ways. Firstly, the Access rule promotes the use of **private linkages** offered by connectivity providers to enable market participants to get access to trading centers quotations through indirect sources. Secondly, it **limits the fees that a trading center can charge** for access to protected quotations (not more than US$0.003 per share[15]). Finally, the Access rule prohibits the display of quotations that lock or cross protected quotations of other trading centers. MiFID, on the contrary, does not establish strict rules on access to quotations. For example, a regulator requires Regulated Markets (MiFID, Article 44) to make arrangements **on reasonable commercial** and non-discriminatory basis for access to its quotations by investment firms, leaving to market forces to determine the level of fees. The same rule applies to MTF and SI, but there is no requirement for OTC orders if not traded on a MTF or SI.

Verification of funds (AML): AML rules are similar in Europe and the United States. In Europe the AML rules are set in the three AML Directives (91/308/EEC, 2001/97/EC, 2001/97/EC, 2005/60/EC), and in the United States in the 1970 Bank and Secrecy Act.

The three Directives establish detailed rules on record keeping of transactions, customer due diligence, including enhanced due diligence for high-risk customers or business relationships. The third anti-money laundering Directive (2005/60/EC) introduces substantial changes in the European regime, including:

- a new risk-based approach so that financial institutions must identify criteria to assess the potential money-laundering risks their business face
- a new requirement to identify a beneficial owner of a customer (defined as the natural person who ultimately owns or controls the customer and/or the natural person on whose behalf a transaction is being conducted)
- appropriate procedures to identify politically exposed persons (defined as natural persons who have been entrusted with prominent public functions and immediate family members or close relatives of those persons)
- ongoing monitoring checks on business relationships.

MiFID requires investment firms to comply at all times with the dispositions on the prevention of the use of the financial system for the purpose of money laundering.

Similarly, the NASD Rule 3011 requires all the NASD members to develop and implement anti-money laundering programs which should be designed to achieve members' compliance with the Bank and Secrecy Act. Broker-dealers have broad obligations under the Bank and Secrecy Act to prevent money laundering and terrorist financing through their firms. The Act requires them to file and keep records related to suspicious transactions, customer identity, large transactions, cross-border currency movement, foreign banks accounts, and wire transfers, among other things. They also have to determine for foreign customers whether they are "senior political figures" whose definition is as broad as in Europe.[16]

As Regards Investors' Protection

Three major concepts *inter alia* exist in the United States and Europe to ensure investors' protection: **fair dealing, suitability, and best execution. Those concepts are similar in both regulatory frameworks, a difference being the best execution principle:** in the United States, it covers a number of factors, with price being typically the most important; in Europe price is one factor among others to assess whether the client has obtained the best possible result for the execution of its trade.

Conduct of business/fair dealing: This concept is very similar in Europe and in the United States. In the United States broker-dealers owe their customers a duty of fair dealing arising from the Act anti-fraud provisions and SRO just and equitable principles of trade. In Europe, investment firms are required to act honestly, fairly and professionally, when providing investment services to clients. An important difference is related to customer categorization. In Europe an investment firm is obliged to make a categorization between retail and professional clients and eligible counterparties and inform clients about their respective categories. A firm also informs client about his right to request a different categorization and what that may entail in terms of the level of protection. In the United States, brokers and dealers also differentiate clients: some products are only available to certain investors based on factors such as net worth, assets, trading experience. However categorization is less biding than in Europe, in the sense that a client does not have to be informed about its categorization.

The NASD Rule on fair dealing requires all its members and registered representatives to deal with clients fairly; fairly means treating clients in an equitable manner depending on their circumstances, but it does not mean equally. In addition, the NASD rule on suitability covers situations that might involve violations of fair treatment. These include, for example, recommending securities to customers without attempting to obtain information about customers' financial situation, excessive trading, fraudulent activity, and recommending purchase beyond customer capability.

Suitability requirements: Suitability is recognized as a principle in the European and United States regulatory environments (article 19(4) of MiFID Level 1, and NASD rule 2310). In both cases it is triggered by a recommendation provided by an investment firm/broker-dealer. While the suitability rule can allow for more exemptions in Europe, it is restricted to investment advice and portfolio management: for services other than investment advice and portfolio management, investment firms are required to apply an appropriateness test to assess suitability. There is no such equivalent in the United States.

Both in Europe and in the United States under the suitability requirement an investment firm/broker-dealer will have an obligation to obtain relevant information about a product and a customer in order to make judgments about whether a product is suitable for a particular customer based on his investment objectives, financial situation, knowledge, and experience. In Europe, an investment firm has a right to assume that a professional client has the necessary knowledge and experience for a product for which it is qualified. Similarly, an investment firm is entitled to assume that a professional client is able to bear investment risks consistent with his investment objectives. It the United States, there is a separate suitability rule for institutional clients, which establishes guidelines on assessing a client's competence to understand investment risk. This rule does not permit broker-dealers to assume that institutional clients will be competent to understand risk (as in Europe) for products for which they are qualified.

When the appropriateness test is applied for execution and transmission services in Europe, an investment firm does not need to obtain as much information as under the suitability test and only has to determine whether a client can understand risks associated with a particular product/service. Again, a firm can assume that professional clients will have a solid risk understanding for products for which they are qualified. Appropriateness test can be waived in certain circumstances including transactions in non-complex products when executed on exchanges at a client's request.

Finally, in Europe, neither suitability nor appropriateness tests must be applied to eligible counterparties.

Duty of Best Execution: The best execution principle is broad in Europe and is defined as obtaining the best possible result that can be judged in terms of price, speed, likelihood of execution and settlement, size, nature of the order. In the United States, the concept covers also a number of factors,[17] but with price being typically the most important.

However, the application of best execution is broader in the United States, where there is no exemption in terms of asset classes or clients. In Europe, transactions executed with eligible counterparties can be exempted from the best execution rule.

When applying best execution in Europe, an investment firm also takes into account criteria such as the categorization of a client (retail or professional), the characteristics of the client order, the type of a financial instrument, and the characteristics of the trading venues. When an order comes from a retail client, the investment firm is obliged to take into account a total consideration, representing the price of a financial instruments and transaction costs. CESR supervisory guidance recognizes the total consideration as the most relevant factor for best execution also for professional customers unless there are other reasons to think otherwise.

Under MiFID, each investment firm is required to adopt a best execution policy and obtain clients' consent with the policy before the execution. Every time there is a possibility that an order can be executed outside a Regulated Market or an MTF, an investment firm is required to inform a client about that possibility and shall not execute the order without a client's consent. Similarly, in the United States a broker-dealer obligation to its client under the best execution is "generally not fulfilled when he channels transactions through another broker-dealer, unless he can show that by so doing he reduced the costs of the transactions to the client."[18]

In the United States, a broker should use **reasonable** diligence to obtain the best trading venue for the security so that the **resultant price** to the customer is **as favorable as possible under prevailing market conditions**. Criteria taken into account include the character of the market for a security (price, liquidity, volatility), the size and type of the transaction, the number of markets checked, accessibility of quotation and terms and conditions of the order.

NMS Regulation provides an additional enforcement of best execution principle for the NMS stocks. The order protection rule requires trading venues to route an order to competing venues with better top of the book automated quotes. Additionally, investors in the United States are in situation to constantly evaluate the best execution of their order against quotations (obtained under the Access rule) because post-trade transparency rules require all equity trades to be centrally reported and disseminated in real time.

Best execution rule is complemented in both regulations by the client order handling rules which require prompt and expeditious execution of client order depending on their characteristics.

As Regards Price Discovery: Pre and Post-Trade Transparency Requirements

Price discovery process is an important component to foster efficient markets; both regulations therefore have pre and post-trade transparency requirements on investment firms and broker-dealers for equity markets. We consider two types of market transparency: pre-trade transparency, which allows investors to have access to quote information before trading and post-trade transparency, which requires the dissemination of information about completed trades to the public (see Appendix 1).

There are two main differences in the **pre-trade transparency requirements for equities** in Europe and the United States. First, according to MiFID, trading venues are required to provide pre-trade transparency information for shares admitted to trading on Regulated Markets. Definition of trading venues includes Regulated Markets, MTFs, and SIs but leaves out crossing networks (dark pools operated by broker-dealers/investment banks). As a result, a large share of equity trading is conducted without public quotes (about 40 percent, see table 4 page 17). The U.S. regulation captures pre-trade transparency on all the trading venues through the obligation of broker-dealers (ATS are registered as broker-dealers), national exchanges, and associations to make available quotations to data-vendors. As discussed earlier in section 2.2, ATS that display quotes to more than one person are required to make their quotes available to the public for each stock in which they exceed a 5 percent trading volume threshold.[19] Therefore, to be truly "dark", dark pools have to remain under the 5 percent trading volume threshold.

A second difference is the consolidation of best quotes and trades in a single coordinator in the United States,[20] while in Europe, quotes and trades are fragmented among multiple trading venues and investment firms, and no consolidation is required. Under Reg NMS, best execution requires trading centers to execute the orders at the best—wherever available—price (National "Best Bid and Offer"), which implies that market centers in the United States need to link and route orders to one another. By contrast, under MiFID, investment firms (and not trading centers) are responsible for the best execution of client orders; consequently, markets do not need to be interconnected.[21] There is no equivalent of a mandated "Best Bid and Offer" in Europe. A number of commercial offerings of a BBO have been launched in Europe. The investor community considers the current level of data consolidation unsatisfactory, but there are divergent views on how best to achieve a higher degree of consolidation while meeting multiple investor needs.

Post trade transparency requirements for equities also differ in the existence of trade data consolidation in the United States, whereas this is not required in Europe. However, in both regions, post-trade transparency requirements are applied across all the trading venues: in particular, trades in public shares via dark pools in Europe will be reported, since investment firms are required to report transactions in public shares carried out outside a Regulated Market or a MTF.

A common feature of the European and U.S. securities regulations is that pre and post-trade transparency requirements are heavier for equities given that most of them are admitted to trading on Regulated Markets, and more limited or absent for bonds and derivatives.

As regards fixed income trading: nearly all the trading in bonds in Europe and the United States takes place on OTC markets. A small number of bonds, mostly corporate, are listed on exchanges. In both regions, there are no regulatory pre-trade transparency requirements for bonds or other fixed income securities; however, in practice, transparency is automatically provided by exchanges for those securities which are listed. Similarly to bonds, trading in asset-backed securities is not subject to any transparency regime at present and trading information is limited given that these securities are less liquid and rarely standardized. As for post-trade transparency requirements in fixed-income securities, the major difference in the United States versus Europe is the obligation for corporate and municipal bonds reporting. In the United States, NASD implemented in 2002 a system for post-trade transparency in corporate bonds called TRACE (Trade Reporting and Compliance Engine) which has no equivalent in Europe. Municipal bonds benefit from post-trade transparency through the Municipal Securities Rulemaking Board. Markets participants claim in Europe that despite the absence of trade transparency requirements, a large amount of information in bond market is already available through data vendors, private, and other sources.[22]

As for derivatives: Many are traded over-the-counter and are not subject to pre and post-trade transparency requirements either in Europe or the United States. This is the case with CDSs, and other complex credit derivatives, although price information on CDSs might be available through data providers (for example in the United States through the Trade Information Warehouse of the Depositary Trust and Clearing Corporation[23]). However, exchanges do provide pre and post-trade transparency for the derivatives traded on-exchange (for example, futures). The issue of low transparency for off-exchange derivatives is being debated in the two regions (see infra).

Notes

[1] SEC: Guide to Broker-Dealer Registration (April 2008).

[2] Directive 2003/6/EC of 28 January 2003 on insider dealing and market manipulation (market abuse).

[3] Exchange Act, Section 3(a) (39). The form BD contains several reputational criteria and the Guide to Broker-Dealer Registration indicates that broker-dealers are subject to examination and inspection by the SEC and SROs.

[4] Five tests for the assessment of a potential acquirer (Directive 44/2007/EC which amends the MiFID Directive among others):

1) the reputation of the proposed acquirer;
2) the reputation and experience on any person who will direct the business of the investment firm as a result of proposed acquisition;
3) the financial soundness of the proposed acquirer;
4) whether the investment firm will be able to continue to apply with the prudential requirements based on MiFID and other directives, in particular, whether a new corporate structure will allow for effective supervision;
5) whether there are reasonable grounds to suspect that in relation to proposed acquisition money laundering activities might be attempted, or there might be a high risk thereof.

[5] Qualifying holding means any direct or indirect holding in an investment firm which represents 10 percent or more of the capital or of the voting rights, as set out in Articles 9 and 10 of Directive 2004/109/EC(2).

[6] A proposed acquirer is considered to exercise a *"significant influence"* when its shareholding, although below the 10 percent threshold, allows it to exercise a significant influence over the management of the institution (for example, allows it to have a representative on the board of directors). Holdings are subject to the full notification requirements if the Member State concerned demonstrates, on a case-by-case basis, that the ownership structure of the target financial institution and the concrete involvement of the acquirer in the management create a significant influence even at this low level (Guidelines for the implementation of Directive 2007/44/EC).

[7] SEC Rule 12b-2: The term "control" (including the terms "controlling," "controlled by" and "under common control with") means the possession, direct or indirect, of the power to direct or

cause the direction of the management and policies of a person, whether through the ownership of voting securities, by contract, or otherwise (Sec Rule 12b-2)

NYSE Rule 2f: The term "control" means the power to direct or cause the direction of the management or policies of a person whether through ownership of securities, by contract or otherwise. A person shall be presumed to control another person if such person, directly or indirectly,

- has the right to vote 25 percent or more of the voting securities,
- is entitled to receive 25 percent or more of the net profits, or
- is a director, general partner or principal executive (or person occupying a similar status or performing similar functions) of the other person.

NYSE Rule 2f and Form BD: Any person who does not so own voting securities, participate in profits or function as a director, general partner or principal executive of another person shall be presumed not to control such other person. Any presumption may be rebutted by evidence, but shall continue until a determination to the contrary has been made by the Exchange.

[8] Additionally record keeping requirements for broker-dealers in the United States are covered under section 17 of the Exchange Act, as well as the Rules 17a-3, 17a-4, 17a-5, 17a-11 on Required Books, Records, and Reports. Arrangements for safeguarding clients' funds in Europe are equivalent to the SEC Rule 15c3-3 on Customer Protection. There are also few rules in the United States (Rules 17h-1T and 17h-2T) on Risk Assessment but they are narrower in scope compared to the MiFID requirements on risk assessment mechanism.

[9] SEC: Guide to Broker-Dealer Registration (April 2008).

[10] Directive 2006/49/EC of 14 June 2006 on the capital adequacy of investment firms and credit institutions; Directive 2006/48/EC relating to the taking up and pursuit of the business of credit institutions.

[11] Exhibit A to Rule 15c3-3 (http://www.law.uc.edu/CCL/34ActRls/rule15c3-3a.html).

[12] Directive 2006/49/EC of 14 June 2006 on the capital adequacy of investment firms and credit institutions.

[13] http://ec.europa.eu/internal_market/bank/regcapital/index_en.htm, June 2008.

[14] There are other examples: Section 11(d) of the Exchange Act generally prohibits a broker dealer that participate in the distribution of a new issue of securities from extending credit to customers in connection with the new issue during the distribution period and for 30 days thereafter. Regulation M is aimed at preventing persons having an interest in an offering from influencing the market price in the offered security; SRO rules generally limit how a member may participate in the public offering of its own or its affiliates' public debt or equity securities.

[15] Except for shares priced less than US$1.

[16] It includes members of the executive legislative, administrative, military and judicial branches of a foreign government, executives of state-owned enterprises, official of major political parties and their close associates (31 CFR 103.175 and EC Directive 2006/70/EC of 1 August 2006 on the definition of politically exposed person).

[17] Other factors include: the character of the market for a security -price, liquidity, volatility, the size and type of the transaction, the number of markets checked, accessibility of quotation and terms and conditions of the order. See NASD Rule 2320.

[18] NASD Rule 2320, Best Execution and Interpositioning.

[19] Securities and Exchange Commission, Keynote Speech by Erik Sirri, Director, Division of Trading and Markets, at the SIFMA 2008 Dark Pools Symposium, February 1, 2008.

[20] For securities listed on the NYSE, AMEX or a regional exchange, data distribution is governed by the Consolidated Tape Association Plan and the Consolidated Quotation Plan, For Nasdaq securities, data distribution is governed by the Nasdaq UTP Plan (Petrella, 2009).

[21] Giovanni Petrella: Mifid, Reg NMS and Competition Across Trading Venues in Europe and United States, Milan Catholic University, January 2009.

[22] Biais, Declerck, Dow, Portes: European Corporate Bonds Market: Transparency, Liquidity Efficiency, 2006.

[23] DTCC is a market-neutral, member-owned, and member-governed organization. It is regulated by the Securities and Exchange Commission (SEC), the Federal Reserve Board of Governors, and the New York State Banking Department.

CHAPTER 5

Post-Financial Crisis Lessons

The international financial crisis has revealed some gaps in the securities regulations on both sides of the Atlantic. Main issues have focused on the imperfect oversight of large interconnected institutions, the low transparency of OTC markets, especially derivatives, and the insufficient liquidity and capital across financial institutions. Regulators on both sides have announced plans to address them.

Better Supervision of Large and Interconnected Financial Institutions

The financial crisis has shown that some institutions could pose a significant risk to the financial system, while not being tightly regulated. This marks a shift from the traditional thinking that banks ought to be more regulated than other financial institutions because they take deposits from the public.

Under the U.S. regulatory reform plans, the Federal Reserve would have the power to conduct consolidated supervision and regulation of all large interconnected financial firms,[1] which are identified as Tier 1 Financial Holding Companies (Tier 1 FHCs). These firms will be subject to the non-financial activities restrictions of the Bank Holding Company Act, regardless of whether they own insured depositary institutions.[2] The U.S. regulatory reform would shift the policy of separating banking and commerce to protect banks from the risk of commercial activities, to a separation of finance and commerce. As a result, regulatory requirements on U.S. securities firms identified as Tier 1 FHC are likely to increase. In addition Tier 1 FHCs would have to respect stricter and more conservative prudential standards than those that apply to other bank holding companies (including higher standards on capital, liquidity and risk management); they would also be subject to a prompt corrective action regime that would require them and their supervisory agencies to take corrective actions as their regulatory capital levels decline. The draft legislation sent to Congress also includes the creation of a Financial Services Oversight Council to identify emerging risks in financial markets.

In the EU, the Commission communication of 27 May 2009[3] envisions the creation of a European Risk Systemic Council to identify risks in the financial system, and a European System of Financial Supervisors so as to enhance supervision of cross-border institutions. Plans to enhance the powers of CESR are also being discussed. However, the European and American approaches differ: the United States plans to separate financial from commercial activities, while this is not currently considered in Europe.

Hedge funds and their managers, which are important players in securities markets and frequently engage in short-selling of stocks, would be registered, according to a G20 initiative.[4] However, the EU and U.S. proposals feature a different approach, with the EU focusing on the leverage of the funds and the United States on the registration of the managers.

Increase Market Transparency

The comparison between MiFID and corresponding U.S. regulations has shown that OTC derivatives such as Credit Default Swaps (CDS) are largely exempted from regulation. The collapse of Lehman and the difficulties of AIG were to some extent related to extensive trading in OTC derivatives, and showed the sheer difficulty of accurately assessing exposures in the absence of transparency and central repository.[5]

In the United States, the Treasury unveiled a comprehensive reform of OTC derivatives in May 2009: all "standardized" OTC derivatives would be cleared, dealers and firms who create large exposures to counterparties would be subject to tough regulation (with conservative capital requirements, business conduct standards, margin requirements), and un-cleared trades would be reported to a regulated trade repository.[6] It remains unclear at the moment how standardization will be defined, although it is a critical feature to enable clearing.

The EU Commission is examining several courses of action: standardization, central data repository, central counterparty clearing and moving trading to more public venues.[7] CDS have started to clear at the end of July 2009, and the European Commission is consulting informally on whether broadening the scope of OTC instruments subject to central counterparty clearing.

In both regions, there is a risk of adding carve-outs to the regulation of derivatives. Industrial firms claim that clearing would incur significant costs (because they would have to post margins), while they mostly use derivatives for hedging purposes. They argue that the clearing of derivatives should only apply to financial institutions trading with each other. However, creating a loophole for industrial companies may nullify the very idea of regulating derivatives: companies such as Enron and Metallgesellschaft, the German energy group that collapsed in 1993 under derivative liabilities, were sizeable participants in the financial markets despite not being financial institutions. In addition, banks could set up industrial subsidiaries to evade clearing requirements.[8] The more contracts are cleared, the more liquid the derivatives market, and the lower the price of trades. Derivative clearing may be in the interest of all participants in the long run.

Transparency is also an issue in OTC equity markets. Section 2 has shown that some dark pools are not subject to pre-trade transparency requirements, which makes it difficult for participants to assess the liquidity in a given stock, and raises concerns of market fragmentation. As part of increasing transparency of capital markets, the SEC and CESR are investigating whether dark pools should be subject to stricter regulation.

Enhance Capital and Liquidity Requirements

Reportedly, at the end of 2008, the liquid core of capital of U.S. securities firms was largely eroded. Some claim that the 2004 SEC amendments to the broker-dealer net capital rule allowed large securities firms to increase their leverage to unsafe levels although this is debated.[9] The U.S. draft systemic risk legislation proposes to raise capital and management requirements for all Financial Holding Companies (including

Tier 1 FHCs), as well as rigorous liquidity risk requirements and a robust process to continuously monitor the liquidity profiles of these institutions. The White Paper further promotes the integration of the liquidity risk management into the overall risk management of Tier 1 FHCs and establishment of explicit internal liquidity risk exposures and risk management policies.

In the EU, a comprehensive reform of the Capital Requirement Directives is currently under review. The first package in October 2008 focuses mainly on improving the management of large exposures, strengthening supervision of cross-border banking groups, and improving liquidity risk management; the second package of proposals issued in July 2009 involves higher capital requirements for re-securitization, tighter disclosure of securitization exposures, higher capital requirements for the trading book, and sound remuneration policies that do not encourage excessive risk-taking.[10] Further proposals on bank capital and liquidity as well as to implement a new leverage ratio considered by the Basel Committee are expected this autumn.

A common approach is to consider stricter capital requirements to address the exposure to securitization: Under proposals both in Europe and the United States, originators of the securitized products would retain on their books 5 percent of the financial interest in issued securitized products.

Notes

[1] According to draft legislation released in July 2009, Tier 1 financial holding companies are defined depending on the following set of criteria: (i) the amount and nature of the company's financial assets; (ii) the amount and types of the company's liabilities, including the degree of reliance on short-term funding; (iii) the extent of the company's off-balance sheet exposures; (iv) the extent of the company's transactions and relationships with other major financial companies; (v) the company's importance as a source of credit for households, businesses and State and local governments and as a source of liquidity for the financial system; (vi) the recommendation, if any, of the Financial Services Oversight Council; and (vii) any other factors that the Board deems appropriate. See http://www.treas.gov/press/releases/tg227.htm.

[2] Under the Bank Holding Company (BHC) Act, the companies that control banks can only engage in the activities of managing or controlling banks unless an exception from the "nonbanking prohibitions" of the BHC Act applies. The exceptions permit activities that are "closely related to banking", and certain passive and non-controlling investments. If a bank holding company meets certain heightened management and capital requirements, it can also make "merchant banking" investments and conduct a broader range of financial—but not commercial—activities.

[3] Communication from the European Commission, European Financial Supervision, COM (2009) 232, May 27, 2009.

[4] G20, "Declaration on Strengthening the Financial System," London, April 2, 2009.

[5] When Lehman Brother collapsed, the market initially speculated that the credit derivative exposure was around US$400 billion. The DTCC informed that based on its records the net exposure was of about US$6 billion; the actual value turned out to be US$5.2 billion when the Lehman exposure was closed out.

[6] See Article: http://www.securitiesindustry.com/news/-23476-1.html, May 2009.

[7] European Commission, "Communication on Ensuring Efficient, Safe and Sound Derivatives Markets," July 3, 2009.

[8] *Financial Times*, "Clearing Up the Future of Futures," October 1, 2009.

[9] Statement by Senator Carl Levin (D-Mich) Before Homeland Security and Governmental Affairs Committee: "Where Were the Watchdogs? The Financial Crisis and the Breakdown of Financial Governance," January 21, 2009

[10] Europa Press Releases, Commission proposes revision of bank capital requirement rules to reinforce financial stability, October 1, 2008; Commission proposes further revision of banking regulation to strengthen rules on bank capital and remuneration in the banking sector, July 13, 2009.

CHAPTER 6

Conclusion and Areas for Future Research

There are differences in securities rules and approaches on both sides of the Atlantic:

- **Regarding the trading venues**, MiFID is not currently applied to dark pools, while in the United States, dark pools are considered as ATS and register as broker-dealers. They have to make their quotes available to the public above a certain trading volume threshold.

- **EU regulators have more discretion in authorizing investment firms and intervening in their management** since they can judge whether the managers of investment firms or Regulated Markets are sufficiently experienced and reputable, while the U.S. regulator can only control their reputation and competences. The EU regulations go one step further in allowing supervisors to control the integrity of ultimate controllers of Regulated Markets regardless of their ownership, while the U.S. rules generally base the notion of control on ownership.

- **Organizational requirements** are broader in scope for exchanges in the United States and focus on disciplinary powers. This is explained by the self-regulatory role of exchanges in the United States versus a more limited role in the EU.

- **Capital requirements** are risk-based in the EU and based on the concept of maintaining a highly liquid core of capital in the United States.

- **The mitigation of conflicts of interest** is a broad and general obligation for investment firms in Europe while it is focused on more specific situations in the United States.

- **Investor protection rules** in Europe are two-tiered between retail and professional investors (client categorization is binding), while the U.S. regulatory scheme protects all investors, with some carve-outs for institutional investors.

- **Best execution** in the United States covers a number of factors, with price being typically the most important; in Europe price is one factor among others to assess whether the client has obtained the best possible result for the execution of its trade. In addition, under MiFID, investment firms are responsible for the best execution of client orders, while in the United States, the responsibility rests with trading centers. This provision implies that market centers in the United States need to link and route orders to one another.

▨ **Data consolidation on equity trades exists in the United States and not in the EU**: in the United States, quotes and transaction data reported by national exchanges and associations are consolidated into a single system and disseminated to market participants, whereas in Europe, quotes and trades are fragmented between multiple trading venues and no consolidation is required.

But the objectives of the two regulations are similar, and some outcomes are comparable:

▨ Both regulatory systems aim to maintain fair and orderly markets, protect investors, and provide price transparency.

▨ **Equity securities are subject to more scrutiny** and transparency requirements than bonds or derivatives. In the two regions, pre and post-trade transparency requirements apply to equities while there is currently no or limited transparency requirements for derivatives and bonds. Reg NMS only applies to equities. Internalization is regulated solely are regards equity trades in Europe (concept of Systematic Internalizer).

▨ **Investor protection regimes are broad** and offer better protection to individual investors, whether the rules to achieve such protection are strictly tiered or not.

▨ **Competition has increased in Europe**. New MTF entrants such as Chi-X, Turquoise and BATS Europe are estimated to hold about 16 percent of share trading.[1] There is a question as to whether MiFID has led to a situation which pre-existed before the implementation of Reg NMS since trading has become more fragmented and liquidity has moved from exchanges. In both regions, consolidation between exchanges stepped up (NYSE-Euronext, Nasdaq-OMX, and LSE-Borsa Italiana mergers), and dark pools have become more visible (either because their market share has increased over exchanges' in Europe or because dark ATS have gained market share over broker-dealer platforms in the United States[2]).

▨ **There are concerns on both sides regarding the fragmentation of oversight**. The U.S. SEC does not oversee futures and government bonds; it also shares supervisory responsibility with the banking supervisors, which supervise commercial banks dealing with securities. In Europe, MiFID is implemented by 27 national supervisors which may lead to different interpretations. For instance, a recent report by CESR emphasizes that pre-trade transparency waivers which exclude trading platforms from transparency requirements are interpreted differently across Europe; the report also hints at different interpretations of the concept of SI, given the few firms that have registered as SI (13 so far).[3]

A discussion on the outcomes cannot really be achieved without looking at the implementation of the securities regulations. Thus the study suggests some directions for future research:

- **Assess enforcement** on both sides, at the SEC and SRO level in the United States, and at the level of the 27 supervisors in the EU.
- **Deepen the knowledge of dark pools** on both sides and examine how to improve disclosure and price discovery.
- In Europe in particular, examine ways to achieve **quotes and trades consolidation**.

Notes

[1] Reuters, "IOSCO-EU Regulators Eye Shares Shuffling into the Dark," June 10, 2009.
[2] Securities and Exchange Commission, Keynote Speech by Erik Sirri, Director, Division of Trading and Markets, at the SIFMA 2008 Dark Pools Symposium, February 1, 2008.
[3] CESR, "Impact of MiFID on Equity Secondary Markets Functioning," June 10, 2009.

Appendixes

Technical Appendix 1: Pre and Post Trade Transparency Requirements, Europe and the United States

	Trading Venues	Equities		Fixed Income: Bonds and Securitized Debt (Government, Corporate, and Municipal Bonds, Asset Backed Securities, Structured Notes, Asset Backed Commercial paper)		Derivatives (Option, Futures, Credit Derivatives, Interest Rare Derivatives, Other)	
		Europe	United States	Europe	United States	Europe	United States
Pre-Trade Transparency	RMs/	YES for shares admitted to trading on RMs.	YES. National exchanges collect quotations in NMS stocks from broker-dealers and make them available to data vendors.	NO requirements imposed by regulators. Transparency is automatically provided by RMs, but a **small number** of bonds and securitized debt are traded on exchanges.	NO requirements imposed by regulators. Transparency automatically provided by exchanges, but a **small number** of bonds and securitized debt are traded on exchanges.	Transparency automatically provided by RMs.	Transparency automatically provided by exchanges.
	Exchanges	Can apply for waivers based on criteria such as large order, reference price, order management system.	Broker-dealers are responsible to report quotations to exchanges.			However only 20% of derivatives are traded on exchanges.	However only 20% of derivatives are traded on exchanges.
	MTFs/ATSs	YES for shares admitted to trading on Regulated Markets.	YES. ATSs report quotations in NMS stocks to national exchanges or national securities associations.	NO transparency imposed by regulators.	NO transparency imposed by regulators.		
	Can apply for waivers based on criteria such as large order, reference price, order management system.	If registered as exchanges ATS make quotations available to vendors. ?	Market participants can get quotes from trading platforms. For example up to 6 quotes from the biggest corporate bond platform in Europe MarketAxess	Market participants can get quotes from trading platforms. For example NYSE Bonds. Currently for 1,000 corporate bonds traded on NYSE but is to be expanded to trade the unlisted corporate debt issues of all NYSE listed equites (about 6,000 additional bonds)			
	SI	YES for shares admitted to trading on RMs.	Not Applicable	Not Applicable	Not Applicable	Not Applicable	Not Applicable
	Exemptions for illiquid shares and sizes above standard market size.						
	OTC	NO	YES	NO requirements imposed by regulators.	NO requirements imposed by regulators.	NO	NO
		Broker-Dealers and ATSs communicate quotations in NMS stocks to national securities associations. The latter make them available to vendors.	Market participants may get indicative quotes for actively trading bonds through data vendors such as Bloomberg.	Market participants may get indicative quotes for actively trading bonds through data vendors such as Bloomberg.			
		Exemptions (dark pools if trading less than 5% in all securities)					

| | Trading Venues | Equities | | Fixed Income: Bonds and Securitized Debt (Government, Corporate, and Municipal Bonds, Asset Backed Securities, Structured Notes, Asset Backed Commercial paper) | | Derivatives (Option, Futures, Credit Derivatives, Interest Rare Derivatives, Other) | |
		Europe	United States	Europe	United States	Europe	United States
Post-Trade Transparency	RMs/	YES for shares admitted to trading on RMs.	YES. National exchanges collect last sale data and report them to Processor to be Included in Consolidated Tape. Data from different sources are then consolidated and made available to market participants.	NO transparency requirements imposed by regulators. Transparency is automatically provided by RMs, but a **small number** of bonds and securitized debt are traded on exchanges.	NO transparency requirements imposed by regulators. Transparency automatically provided by exchanges, but a **small number** of bonds and securitized debt are traded on exchanges.	Transparency automatically provided by RMs.	Transparency automatically provided by exchanges.
	Exchanges					However only 20% of derivatives are traded on exchanges.	However only 20% of derivatives are traded on exchanges.
	MTFs/ATSs	YES for shares admitted to trading on RMs.	YES	NO requirements by regulator	NO requirements by regulator	NO	
		ATSs report transactions to national securities associations, or directly to Processors if registered as exchanges.					
	SI in Europe	YES. Investment firms required to make public transactions (for shares admitted to trading on RMs) outside RMs and MTFs	Not Applicable	Not Applicable	Not Applicable	Not Applicable	Not Applicable
	OTC	YES. Investment firms required to make public transactions (for shares admitted to trading on RMs) outside RMs and MTFs.	YES. Broker dealers report transaction to OTC Reporting Facility Operated by Finra. Finra makes data available to Processors.	NO	NO, except YES for corporate bonds through NASD TRACE (Trade Reporting and Compliance Engine) introduced in 2002; and YES for municipal bonds through the Municipal Securities Rulemaking Board	NO	NO

Technical Appendix 2: Detailed Comparative Analysis

European Regulatory Framework for Financial Instruments	U.S. Regulatory Framework for Financial Instruments
Relevant Texts	**Relevant Texts**
Directive 2004/39/EC on Markets in Financial Instruments (MiFID or "MiFID Level 1") Directive 2006/73/EC implementing Directive 2004/39/EC Commission Regulation 1287/2006 implementing Directive 2004/39/EC (both latter texts referred to as "MiFID Level 2")	1934 Securities Exchange Act FINRA Rules (including NASD rules not yet codified into the FINRA manual) NYSE Rules SEC Regulation NMS SEC Regulation ATS
• Scope of Activities for investment firms MiFID, Article 6 1. The authorization must specify the investment services or activities which the investment firm is authorized to provide. Authorization shall in no case be granted solely for provision of ancillary services. 2. An investment firm seeking to extend its business to additional activities must submit a request for extension of its authorization.	• Scope of Activities for brokers and dealers Application: Form BD, http://www.sec.gov/about/forms/formbd.pdf 1. When submitting the application for registration brokers and dealers specify types of businesses they are engaged in or are to be engaged in (if not yet active). This applies only to businesses that account for more than 1% of annual revenue from the securities or investment advisory business. By law, the applicant must promptly update Form BD (Application for registration) information by submitting amendments whenever the information on file becomes inaccurate or incomplete for any reason.
• Procedures for granting and refusing request for the authorization MiFID, Article 7 1. The competent authority shall not grant authorization unless and until it is fully satisfied that the applicant complies with all requirements under the provisions adopted pursuant to Directive 2004/39/EC (fit and proper requirements for managers shareholders and persons with qualifying holdings, capital	• Manner of registration of brokers and dealers Section 15(b) of the Securities Exchange Act. 1. Broker or dealer may be registered by filing with the Commission an application for registration. Within **45 days** of the date of the filing of application (or within such longer period as to which the applicant consents), the Commission shall – a) By order grant registration, or b) Institute

European Regulatory Framework for Financial Instruments	U.S. Regulatory Framework for Financial Instruments
requirements, organizational requirements, membership in investor compensation schemes if required).	proceedings to determine whether registration should be denied. The proceedings shall include notice of the grounds for denial and opportunity for hearing and shall be concluded within 120 days of the date of the filing of the application for registration. At the conclusion of such proceedings, the Commission, by order, shall grant or deny registration. **The order granting registration shall not be effective until a broker or dealer has become a member of a registered securities association, or until a broker or dealer has become a member of a national securities exchange if a broker or dealer effects transactions solely on that exchange**, unless the Commission has exempted a broker or dealer, by rule or order, from the membership.
2. The investment firm shall provide all information, including a programme of operations setting out the types of business envisaged and the organizational structure, necessary to enable the competent authority to satisfy itself that the investment firm has established, at the time of initial authorization, all the necessary arrangements to meet its obligations under the provisions of this Chapter.	2. The Commission shall grant registration if it finds that the requirements of the section 15 (see reputational and professional requirements in Paragraph 4) are satisfied. The Commission shall deny registration if it finds that the requirements of this section are not satisfied or if it estimates that in the case the applicant were registered, its registration would be subject to suspension under paragraph 4 (see below).
3. An applicant shall be informed, **within 6 months** of the submission of a complete application, whether or not authorization has been granted.	
• Withdrawal of authorizations MiFID, Article 8	• Censure on activities of Brokers and Dealers Section 15 (b) of the Securities Exchange Act.
The competent authority may withdraw the authorization issued to an investment firm where such an investment firm:	**Paragraph 4)** The Commission shall censure, place limitations on the activities, functions, or operations of, suspend for a period not exceeding 12 months, or revoke the registration of any broker or dealer if it finds (on the record after notice and opportunity for hearing), that such **broker or dealer**, whether prior or subsequent to becoming such, **or any person associated** with such broker or dealer, whether prior or subsequent to becoming so associated -
1. **does not make use of the authorization within 12 months**, expressly renounces the authorization or has provided no investment services or performed no investment activity for the preceding six months, unless the Member State concerned has provided for authorization to lapse in such cases;	1. has willfully **made** or caused to be made in any application for registration or report required to be filed with the Commission or with any other appropriate
2. has obtained the authorization by making **false statements** or by any other	

European Regulatory Framework for Financial Instruments	U.S. Regulatory Framework for Financial Instruments
irregular means; 3. **no longer meets the conditions** under which authorization was granted, such as compliance with the conditions set out in Directive 93/6/EEC; 4. **has seriously and systematically infringed the provisions** adopted pursuant to this Directive governing the operating conditions for investment firms	regulatory agency under Securities Exchange Act, or in any proceeding before the Commission with respect to registration, any **statement** which was *false or misleading* with respect to any material fact, or has omitted to state in any such application or report any material fact which is required to be stated therein. 2. has been **convicted within 10 years** preceding the filing of any application for registration or at any time thereafter of any **crime** or of a substantially equivalent crime by a foreign court of competent jurisdiction which the Commission finds – • **involves the purchase or sale of any security, the taking of a false oath, the making of a false report, bribery, perjury, burglary**, any substantially equivalent activity however denominated by the laws of the relevant foreign government, or conspiracy to commit any similar offense; • **arises out of the conduct of the business of a broker, dealer, municipal securities dealer, government securities broker, government securities dealer, investment adviser, bank, insurance company, fiduciary, transfer agent, nationally recognized statistical rating organization, foreign person performing a function substantially** equivalent to any of the above, or entity or person required to be registered under the Commodity Exchange Act or any substantially equivalent foreign statute or regulation; • involves the **larceny, theft, robbery, extortion, forgery, counterfeiting, fraudulent concealment, embezzlement, fraudulent conversion, or misappropriation of funds, or securities**, or substantially equivalent activity however denominated by the laws of the relevant foreign government; or • involves the violation of Section 152, 1341, 1342, or 1343 or chapter 25 or 47 of *title 18* (crimes and criminal procedures) or a

European Regulatory Framework for Financial Instruments	U.S. Regulatory Framework for Financial Instruments
	violation of a substantially equivalent foreign statute. 3. is permanently or temporarily **enjoined by order, judgment, or decree of any court of competent jurisdiction from acting as an investment adviser, underwriter, broker, dealer, municipal securities dealer, government securities broker, government securities dealer, transfer agent, nationally recognized statistical rating organization, foreign person performing a function substantially equivalent to any of the above,** or entity or person required to be registered under the Commodity Exchange Act or any substantially equivalent foreign statute or regulation, or as an affiliated person or employee of any investment company, bank, insurance company, foreign entity substantially equivalent to any of the above, or entity or person required to be registered under the Commodity Exchange Act or any substantially equivalent foreign statute or regulation, or from engaging in or continuing any conduct or practice in connection with any such activity, or in connection with the purchase or sale of any security. 4. has wilfully **violated** any provision of the Securities Act, the Investment Advisers Act, the Investment Company Act, the Commodity Exchange Act, the Securities Exchange Act, the rules or regulations under any of such statutes, or the rules of the Municipal Securities Rulemaking Board, or is unable to comply with any such provision. 5. has wilfully **aided, abetted, counseled, commanded, induced,** or procured the violation by any other person or any provision of the Securities Act, the Investment Advisers Act, the Investment Company Act, the Commodity Exchange Act, the Securities Exchange Act, the rules or regulations under any of such statutes, or the rules of the Municipal Securities Rulemaking Board, or has **failed reasonably to supervise**, with a view to preventing violations of the provisions of such statutes, rules, and regulations, another person who commits such a violation, if such other person is subject to his supervision. For the purposes of this subparagraph (5) **no person shall be deemed to have failed to supervise any other person,** if – • there have been established procedures, and a system for

European Regulatory Framework for Financial Instruments	U.S. Regulatory Framework for Financial Instruments
	applying such procedures, which would reasonably be expected to prevent and detect any such violation by such other person, and • such person has reasonably discharged the duties and obligations incumbent upon without reasonable cause to believe that such procedures and system were not being complied with. 6. is subject to any order of the Commission barring or suspending the right of the person to be associated with a broker or dealer. 7. has been found by a foreign financial regulatory authority to have – • made or caused to be made in any application for registration or report required to be filed with a foreign financial regulatory authority, or in any proceeding before a foreign financial regulatory authority any statement that was false or misleading with respect to any material fact, or has omitted to state in any application or report to the foreign financial regulatory authority any material fact that is required to be stated therein; • **violated** any **foreign statute or regulation regarding transactions in securities**, or contracts of sale of a commodity for future delivery, traded on or subject to the rules of a contract market or any board of trade; • **aided, abetted, counseled, commanded, induced,** or procured the violation by any person of any provision of **any statutory provisions** enacted by a foreign government, or rules or regulations thereunder, empowering a foreign financial regulatory authority regarding transactions in securities, or contracts of sale of a commodity for future delivery, traded on or subject to the rules of a contract market or any board of trade, or has been found, by a foreign financial regulatory authority, to have **failed to supervise**, with a view to preventing violations of such statutory provisions, rules, and regulations, another person who commits such a violation, if such other person is subject to his supervision; or

European Regulatory Framework for Financial Instruments	U.S. Regulatory Framework for Financial Instruments

	8. **is subject to any final order** of a State securities commission (or any agency or officer performing like functions), State authority that supervises or examines banks, savings associations, or credit unions, State insurance commission (or any agency or office performing like functions), an appropriate Federal banking agency (as defined in Section 3 of the Federal Deposit Insurance Act, or the National Credit Union Administration, **that -**
	
	    • **bars such person from association** with an entity regulated by such commission, authority, agency, or officer, or from engaging in the business of securities, insurance, banking, savings association activities, or credit union activities; or
	
	    • constitutes a final order based on violations of any laws or regulations that prohibit fraudulent, manipulative, or deceptive conduct.
	
	Paragraph 5) Pending final determination whether any registration under this subsection shall be revoked, the Commission, by order, may suspend such registration, if such suspension appears to the Commission, after notice and opportunity for hearing, to be necessary or appropriate in the public interest or for the protection of investors. **Any registered broker or dealer may**, upon such terms and conditions as the Commission deems necessary or appropriate in the public interest or for the protection of investors, **withdraw from registration** by filing a written notice of withdrawal with the Commission. If the Commission finds that any registered broker or dealer is no longer in existence or has ceased to do business as a broker or dealer, the Commission, by order, shall cancel the registration of such broker or dealer.

• Fit and Proper Tests MiFID Article 9, **Management Requirements** 1. Member States shall require **the persons who effectively direct the**	• Reputational and professional tests for Associated Persons Section 15(b) of the Securities Exchange Act, Paragraph 6 1. With respect to any **person who is associated**, who is seeking to become associated, or, at the time of the alleged misconduct, who was associated or

European Regulatory Framework for Financial Instruments	U.S. Regulatory Framework for Financial Instruments
business of an investment firm to be of sufficiently good repute and sufficiently experienced as to ensure the sound and prudent management of the investment firm. 2. Member States shall require the investment firm to notify the competent authority of any changes to its management, along with all information needed to assess whether the new staff appointed to manage the firm are of sufficiently good repute and sufficiently experienced. 3. The competent authority shall refuse authorization if it is not satisfied that the persons who will effectively direct the business of the investment firm are of sufficiently good repute or sufficiently experienced, or if there are objective and demonstrable grounds for believing that proposed changes to the management of the firm pose a threat to its sound and prudent management. 4. Member States shall require that the management of investment firms is undertaken by **at least 2 persons** meeting the requirements laid down in paragraph 1. MiFID Article 10, **Shareholders and members with qualifying holdings** 1. The competent authorities shall not authorize the performance of investment services or activities by an investment firm until they have been informed of the identities of the shareholders or members, whether direct or indirect, natural or legal persons, that have qualifying holdings and the amounts of those holdings. The competent authorities shall refuse authorization if, taking into account the need to ensure the sound and prudent management of an investment firm, they are not satisfied as to the suitability of the shareholders or members that have qualifying holdings. Where **close links** exist between the investment firm and other natural or legal persons, **the competent authority shall grant authorization only if those links do not prevent the effective exercise of the supervisory functions of the competent authority**.	was seeking to become associated with a broker or dealer, or any person participating, or, at the time of the alleged misconduct, who was participating, in an offering of any penny stock, the Commission, by order, shall censure, place limitations on the activities or functions of such person, or suspend for a period not exceeding 12 months, or bar such person from being associated with a broker or dealer, or from participating in an offering of **penny stock** (, if the Commission finds, on the record after notice and opportunity for a hearing, that such censure, placing of limitations, suspension, or bar is in the public interest and that such person - • has committed or omitted any act, or is subject to an order or finding, enumerated in subparagraph 1, 4 and 5 of paragraph (4) of Section 15.. • has been convicted of any offense specified in subparagraph 2 of paragraph (4) within 10 years of the commencement of the proceedings under this paragraph; or • is enjoined from any action, conduct, or practice specified in subparagraph 3 of paragraph (4). 2. It shall be unlawful – • for any person as to whom an order under subparagraph 1. is in effect, without the consent of the Commission, willfully to become, or to be, associated with a broker or dealer in contravention of such order, or to participate in an offering of penny stock in contravention of such order; • for any broker or dealer to permit such a person, without the consent of the Commission, to become or remain, a **person associated with the broker** or dealer in contravention of such order, if such broker or dealer knew, or in the exercise of reasonable care should have known, of such order; or • for any broker or dealer to permit such a person, without the consent of the Commission, to participate in an offering of penny

European Regulatory Framework for Financial Instruments	U.S. Regulatory Framework for Financial Instruments
2. The competent authority shall refuse authorization if the laws, regulations or administrative provisions of a third country governing one or more natural or legal persons with which the undertaking has close links, or difficulties involved in their enforcement, prevent the effective exercise of its supervisory functions. 3. Member States shall require any natural or legal person or such persons acting in concert (hereinafter referred to as the proposed acquirer), who have taken a decision either **to acquire, directly or indirectly, a qualifying holding in an investment firm or to further increase,** directly or indirectly, such **a qualifying holding** in an investment firm as a result of which the proportion of the voting rights or of the capital held would reach or exceed **20 %, 30 % or 50 %** or so that the investment firm would become its subsidiary (hereinafter referred to as the proposed acquisition), first to notify in writing the competent authorities of the investment firm in which they are seeking to acquire or increase a qualifying holding, indicating the size of the intended holding and relevant information, as referred to in Article 10b(4). Member States shall require any natural or legal person who has taken a decision to dispose, directly or indirectly, of a qualifying holding in an investment firm first to notify in writing the competent authorities, indicating the size of the intended holding. Such a person shall likewise notify the competent authorities if he has taken a decision to reduce his qualifying holding so that the proportion of the voting rights or of the capital held would fall below 20 %, 30 % or 50 % or so that the investment firm would cease to be his subsidiary. Member States need not apply the 30 % threshold where, in accordance with Article 9(3)(a) of Directive **2004/109/EC,** they apply a threshold of **one-third.** In determining whether the criteria for a qualifying holding referred to in this Article are fulfilled, Member States shall not take into account voting rights or shares which investment firms or credit institutions may hold as a result of providing the underwriting of financial instruments and/or placing of financial instruments on a firm commitment basis included under point 6 of Section A of Annex I, provided that those rights are, on the one hand, not exercised or otherwise used to intervene in the management of the issuer and, on the other, disposed	stock in contravention of such order, if such broker or dealer knew, or in the exercise of reasonable care should have known, of such order and of such participation. 3. For purposes of this paragraph, the term "person participating in an offering of penny stock" includes any person acting as any promoter, finder, consultant, agent, or other person who engages in activities with a broker, dealer, or issuer for purposes of the issuance or trading in any penny stock, or inducing or attempting to induce the purchase or sale of any penny stock. **Professional test for Brokers and Dealers and Associated Persons:** 1. No registered broker or dealer **shall effect any transaction** in, or induce the purchase or sale of, any security unless such broker or dealer meets such standards of operational capability and such **broker or dealer** and **all natural persons associated** with such broker or dealer **meet such standards of training, experience, competence, and such other qualifications as the Commission finds necessary or appropriate** in the public interest or for the protection of investors. The Commission shall establish such standards by rules and regulations, which may - • specify that all or any portion of such standards shall be applicable to any class of brokers and dealers and persons associated with brokers and dealers; • require persons in any such class to pass tests prescribed in accordance with such rules and regulations, which tests shall, with respect to any class of **partners, officers, or supervisory** employees (which latter term may be defined by the Commission's rules and regulations and as so defined shall include branch managers of brokers or dealers) **engaged in the management of the broker or dealer,** include questions relating to bookkeeping, accounting, internal control over cash and securities, supervision of

European Regulatory Framework for Financial Instruments	U.S. Regulatory Framework for Financial Instruments
of within one year of acquisition. 4. The relevant competent authorities shall work in full consultation with each other when carrying out the assessment if the proposed acquirer is one of the following: • a credit institution, assurance undertaking, insurance undertaking, reinsurance undertaking, investment firm or UCITS management company authorized in another Member State or in a sector other than that in which the acquisition is proposed; • the parent undertaking of a credit institution, assurance undertaking, insurance undertaking, reinsurance undertaking, investment firm or UCITS management company authorized in another Member State or in a sector other than that in which the acquisition is proposed; or • (c) a natural or legal person controlling a credit institution, assurance undertaking, insurance undertaking, reinsurance undertaking, investment firm or UCITS management company authorized in another Member State or in a sector other than that in which the acquisition is proposed. The competent authorities shall, without undue delay, provide each other with any information which is essential or relevant for the assessment. In this regard, the competent authorities shall communicate to each other upon request all relevant information and shall communicate on their own initiative all essential information. A decision by the competent authority that has authorized the investment firm in which the acquisition is proposed shall indicate any views or reservations expressed by the competent authority responsible for the proposed acquirer. 5. Member States shall require that, if an investment firm becomes aware of any acquisitions or disposals of holdings in its capital that cause holdings to exceed or fall below any of the thresholds referred to in the first subparagraph	employees, maintenance of records, and other appropriate matters; and • provide that persons in any such class other than brokers and dealers and partners, officers, and supervisory employees of brokers or dealers, may be qualified solely on the basis of compliance with such standards of training and such other qualifications as the Commission finds. NYSE Rule 311. Formation and Approval of Member Organizations 1. Any person who proposes to form a member organization and any member organization which proposes to **admit therein any approved person shall notify the Exchange** in writing before any such formation or admission and shall submit such information as may be required by the Rules of the Exchange. **No such member organization shall become or remain a member organization unless all persons required to be approved are so approved** and execute such agreements with the Exchange as the Rules of the Exchange may prescribe. 2. The Board of Directors shall not approve a partnership or corporation as a member organization unless: • each director of such corporation is a member, principal executive or an approved person; and • **every person who controls such corporation is a member, principal executive or approved person;** and • every natural person who is a general partner in such partnership is a member or principal executive and every other person who controls such partnership is a member, principal executive or approved person; and • every person who engages in a securities or kindred business and **is controlled by or under common control with such partnership or corporation is an approved person;** and

European Regulatory Framework for Financial Instruments	U.S. Regulatory Framework for Financial Instruments
of paragraph 3, that investment firm is to inform the competent authority without delay. At least once a year, investment firms shall also inform the competent authority of the names of shareholders and members possessing qualifying holdings and the sizes of such holdings as shown, for example, by the information received at annual general meetings of shareholders and members or as a result of compliance with the regulations applicable to companies whose transferable securities are admitted to trading on a Regulated Market. 6. Member States shall require that, where the influence exercised by the persons referred to in the first subparagraph of paragraph 1 is likely to be prejudicial to the sound and prudent management of an investment firm, the competent authority take appropriate measures to put an end to that situation. Such measures may consist in applications for judicial orders and/or the imposition of sanctions against directors and those responsible for management, or suspension of the exercise of the voting rights attaching to the shares held by the shareholders or members in question. Similar measures shall be taken in respect of persons who fail to comply with the obligation to provide prior information in relation to the acquisition or increase of a qualifying holding. If a holding is acquired despite the opposition of the competent authorities, the Member States shall, regardless of any other sanctions to be adopted, provide either for exercise of the corresponding voting rights to be suspended, for the nullity of the votes cast or for the possibility of their annulment. **Assessment of potential acquirers** (5 tests, Directive 2007/44/EC) In assessing the notification provided for in Article 10(3) and the information referred to in	• The Board of Directors of such corporation designates "principal executives"; and • such partnership or corporation complies with such additional requirements as the rules of the Exchange may prescribe. 3. In the case of existing corporations making application to become member corporations, there shall be submitted to the Exchange: • **A certified list of all holders of record of each class of stock, giving the name and address of the holder and the number of shares of each class of such stock held;** • **A certified list of all persons who are to become members, principal executives, directors or approved persons,** • **A certified list of all persons designated as principal executives** of the corporation. **Rule 312. of NYSE states that** In the case of a member corporation, such member corporation 1. shall give written notice (1) **of any material change in the stockholdings of any member, principal executive or approved person** of such member corporation, (2) of any proposed change in the directors or officers, or (3) of any proposed change in the charter, certificate of incorporation, by-laws or other documents on file with the Exchange, or (4) of the failure to comply with all the conditions of approval specified in Rule 311. 2. Each member, principal executive and approved person of a member corporation shall promptly notify his member corporation of any **material acquisition or disposition** of shares of stock of such corporation. Whenever a person **who is required to be approved by the Board** as a member, principal executive or approved person fails or ceases to be so approved, **each member corporation shall promptly redeem or convert to a fixed income security such of its outstanding voting stock as may be necessary to reduce such party's ownership of voting stock in the member corporation below that level which enables such party to exercise**

European Regulatory Framework for Financial Instruments	U.S. Regulatory Framework for Financial Instruments
Article 10a(2), the competent authorities shall, in order to ensure the sound and prudent management of the investment firm in which an acquisition is proposed, and having regard to the likely influence of the proposed acquirer on the investment firm, appraise the suitability of the proposed acquirer and the financial soundness of the proposed acquisition against all of the following criteria: 1. the reputation of the proposed acquirer; 2. the reputation and experience of any person who will direct the business of the investment firm as a result of the proposed acquisition; 3. the financial soundness of the proposed acquirer, in particular in relation to the type of business pursued and envisaged in the investment firm in which the acquisition is proposed; 4. whether the investment firm will be able to comply and continue to comply with the prudential requirements based on this Directive and, where applicable, other Directives, notably, Directives 2002/87/EC (1) and 2006/49/EC (2), in particular, whether the group of which it will become a part has a structure that makes it possible to exercise effective supervision, effectively exchange information among the competent authorities and determine the allocation of responsibilities among the competent authorities; 5. whether there are reasonable grounds to suspect that, in connection with the proposed acquisition, money laundering or terrorist financing within the meaning of Article 1 of Directive 2005/60/ EC (3) is being or has been committed or attempted, or that the proposed acquisition could increase the risk thereof. • Initial capital requirements (link to Directive 93/6/EEC) MiFID, level 1, Article 12 Member States shall ensure that the competent authorities do not grant authorization	controlling influence over the management or policies of such member corporation. SEC Rule 12b-2: The term "control" (including the terms "controlling," "controlled by" and "under common control with") means the possession, direct or indirect, of the power to direct or cause the direction of the management and policies of a person, whether through the ownership of voting securities, by contract, or otherwise (Sec Rule 12b-2) NYSE Rule 2f: The term "control" means the power to direct or cause the direction of the management or policies of a person whether through ownership of securities, by contract or otherwise. A person shall be presumed to control another person if such person, directly or indirectly, • has the right to vote 25 percent or more of the voting securities, • is entitled to receive 25 percent or more of the net profits, or • is a director, general partner or principal executive (or person occupying a similar status or performing similar functions) of the other person. NYSE Rule 2f and Form BD: Any person who does not so own voting securities, participate in profits or function as a director, general partner or principal executive of another person shall be presumed not to control such other person. Any presumption may be rebutted by evidence, but shall continue until a determination to the contrary has been made by the Exchange. • Minimum Capital Requirements for Brokers and Dealers – • Rule 15c3-1 Net Capital Requirements for Brokers or Dealers a. Every broker or dealer shall at all times have and maintain net capital no less than the greater of the highest minimum requirement applicable to its

European Regulatory Framework for Financial Instruments	U.S. Regulatory Framework for Financial Instruments
unless the investment firm has sufficient initial capital in accordance with the requirements of Directive 93/6/EEC (this has now been updated in Directive 2006/48/EC, Article 11, Annex VII) having regard to the nature of the investment service or activity in question. Provisions from Directive 2006/49/EC on the capital adequacy of investment firms and credit institutions, Chapter 2, Initial capital Article 5 1. An investment firm that **does not deal in any financial instruments for its own account** or underwrite issues of financial instruments on a firm commitment basis, but which **holds clients' money and/or securities** and which offers one or more of the following services, shall have initial capital of **EUR 125,000:** a) the reception and transmission of investors' orders for financial instruments; b) the execution of investors' orders for financial instruments; or c) the management of individual portfolios of investments in financial instruments. The competent authorities may allow an investment firm which executes investors' orders for financial instruments to hold such instruments for its own account if the following conditions are met: a) such positions arise only as a result of the firm's failure to match investors' orders precisely; b) the total market value of all such positions is subject to a ceiling of 15 % of the firm's initial capital; c) the firm meets the requirements laid down in Articles 18, 20 and 28; and d) such positions are incidental and provisional in nature and strictly	**ratio requirement** under paragraph (a)(1) of this section, or to any of its activities under paragraph (a)(2) of this section. In lieu of applying paragraphs (a)(1) and (a)(2) of this section, an OTC derivatives dealer shall maintain net capital pursuant to paragraph (a)(5) of this section. Each broker or dealer also shall comply with the supplemental requirements of paragraphs (a)(4) and (a)(9) of this section, to the extent either paragraph is applicable to its activities. In addition, a broker or dealer shall maintain net capital of not less than its own net capital requirement plus the sum of each broker's or dealer's subsidiary or affiliate minimum net capital requirements, which is consolidated pursuant to Appendix C. **Ratio Requirements** **Aggregate Indebtedness Standard** 1. i. No broker or dealer, other than one that elects the provisions of paragraph (a)(1)(ii) of this section, shall permit its aggregate indebtedness to all other persons to exceed 1500 percent of its net capital (or 800 percent of its net capital for 12 months after commencing business as a broker or dealer). **Alternative Standard** ii. A broker or dealer may elect not to be subject to the Aggregate Indebtedness Standard of paragraph (a)(1)(i) of this section. That broker or dealer shall not permit its net capital to be **less than the greater of $250,000 or 2 percent of aggregate debit items** computed in accordance with the Formula for Determination of Reserve Requirements for Brokers and Dealers (Exhibit A to Rule 15c3-3). Such broker or dealer shall notify its Examining Authority, in writing, of its election to operate under this paragraph (a)(1)(ii). Once a broker or dealer has notified its Examining Authority, it shall continue to operate under this paragraph unless a change

European Regulatory Framework for Financial Instruments	U.S. Regulatory Framework for Financial Instruments
limited to the time required to carry out the transaction in question. The holding of non-trading-book positions in financial instruments in order to invest own funds shall not be considered as dealing in relation to the services set out in paragraph 1 or for the purposes of paragraph 3. 2. **Member States may reduce the amount referred to in paragraph 1 to EUR 50,000 where a firm is not authorized to hold clients' money or securities, to deal for its own account, or to underwrite issues on a firm commitment basis.** Article 6 Local firms shall have initial capital of EUR 50 000 insofar as they benefit from the freedom of establishment or to provide services specified in Articles 31 and 32 of Directive 2004/39/EC. Article 7 Coverage for the firms referred to in Article 3(1)(b)(iii) (those that **do not hold clients funds or securities**) shall take one of the following forms: a) initial capital of EUR 50 000; b) professional indemnity insurance covering the whole territory of the Community or some other comparable guarantee against liability arising from professional negligence, representing at least EUR 1,000,000 applying to each claim and in aggregate EUR 1,000,000 per year for all claims; or c) a combination of initial capital and professional indemnity insurance in a form resulting in a level of coverage equivalent to that referred to in points (a) or (b). The amounts referred to in the first sub-paragraph shall be periodically reviewed by the Commission in order to take account of changes in the European Index of Consumer Prices as published by Eurostat, in line with and at the same time as the adjustments made under Article 4(7) of Directive 2002/92/EC of the European Parliament and of the Council of 9 December 2002 on insurance mediation (1). All investment firms other than those referred to in Articles 5 to 8 (Art. 8 is on insurance	is approved upon application to the Commission. A broker or dealer that elects this standard and is not exempt from Rule 15c3-3 shall: 1. *Make the computation required by Rule 15c3-3(e) and set forth in Exhibit A, Rule 15c3-3a, on a weekly basis and, in lieu of the 1 percent reduction of certain debit items required by Note E(3) in the computation of its Exhibit A requirement, reduce aggregate debit items in such computation by 3 percent;* 2. *Include in Items 7 and 8 of Exhibit A, Rule 15c3-3a, the market value of items specified therein more than 7 business days old;* 3. *Exclude credit balances in accounts representing amounts payable for securities not yet received from the issuer or its agent which securities are specified in paragraphs (c)(2)(vi)(A) and (E) of this section and any related debit items from the Exhibit A requirement for 3 business days; and* 4. *Deduct from net worth in computing net capital 1 percent of the contract value of all failed to deliver contracts or securities borrowed that were allocated to failed to receive contracts of the same issue and which thereby were excluded from Items 11 or 12 of Exhibit A, Rule 15c3-3a.* 2. **Brokers or Dealers That Carry Customer Accounts 1.** i. A broker or dealer shall maintain net capital of not less than $250,000 if it carries customer or broker or dealer accounts and receives or holds funds or securities for those persons, ii. A broker or dealer that is exempt from the provisions of Rule 15c3-3 pursuant to paragraph (k)(2)(i) (no thereof shall maintain net capital of not less than $100,000.

European Regulatory Framework for Financial Instruments	U.S. Regulatory Framework for Financial Instruments
firms) shall have initial capital of EUR 730 000. **Article 11, Trading book** 1. The trading book of an institution shall consist of all positions in financial instruments and commodities held either with trading intent or in order to hedge other elements of the trading book and which are either free of any restrictive covenants on their tradability or able to be hedged. 2. Positions held with trading intent are those held intentionally for short-term resale and/or with the intention of benefiting from actual or expected short-term price differences between buying and selling prices or from other price or interest rate variations. The term 'positions' shall include proprietary positions and positions arising from client servicing and market making. 3. Trading intent shall be evidenced on the basis of the strategies, policies and procedures set up by the institution to manage the position or portfolio in accordance with Part A of Annex VII. 4. Institutions shall establish and maintain systems and controls to manage their trading book in accordance with Parts B and D of Annex VII of this Directive. 5. Internal hedges may be included in the trading book, in which case Part C of Annex VII shall apply. **Article 18, Provisions against risk** 1. Institutions shall have own funds which are always more than or equal to the sum of the following: (a) the capital requirements, calculated in accordance with the methods and options laid down in Articles 28 to 32 and Annexes I, II and VI and, as appropriate, **Annex V, for their trading-book business;** Annex VII Trading Intent 1. Positions/portfolios held with trading intent shall comply with the following	paragraph (k)(2)(i): Who carries no margin accounts, promptly transmits all customer funds and delivers all securities received in connection with his activities as a broker or dealer, does not otherwise hold funds or securities for, or owe money or securities to, customers and effectuates all financial transactions between the broker or dealer and his customers through one or more bank accounts, each to be designated as "Special Account for the Exclusive Benefit of Customers of (name of the broker or dealer)"; or **Dealers** iii. A dealer shall maintain net capital of not less than $100,000. The term "dealer" includes: iv. Any broker or dealer that endorses or writes options otherwise than on a registered national securities exchange or a facility of a registered national securities association; and v. Any broker or dealer that effects more than ten transactions in any one calendar year for its own investment account. This section shall not apply to those persons engaging in activities described in paragraphs 1.5., 1.6. municipal brokers brokers, or to those persons whose underwriting activities are limited solely to acting as underwriters in best efforts or all or none underwritings in conformity with paragraph (b)(2) of Rule 15c2-4, so long as those persons engage in no other dealer activities. **Brokers or Dealers That Introduce Customer Accounts And Receive Securities** vi. A broker or dealer shall maintain net capital of not less than $50,000 if it introduces transactions and accounts of customers or other brokers or dealers to another registered broker or dealer that carries such accounts on a fully disclosed basis, and if the broker or dealer receives but does not hold customer or other broker or dealer securities. A broker or dealer operating under this paragraph may participate in a firm commitment underwriting without being subject to the provisions of paragraph 1.3, but may not enter into a commitment for the purchase of shares related to that underwriting.

European Regulatory Framework for Financial Instruments	U.S. Regulatory Framework for Financial Instruments
	Brokers or Dealers Engaged in the Sale of Redeemable Shares of Registered Investment Companies and Certain Other Share Accounts vii. A broker or dealer shall maintain net capital of not less than $25,000 if it acts as a broker or dealer with respect to the purchase, sale and redemption of redeemable shares of registered investment companies or of interests or participations in an insurance company separate account directly from or to the issuer on other than a subscription way basis. A broker or dealer operating under this section may sell securities for the account of a customer to obtain funds for the immediate reinvestment in redeemable securities of registered investment companies. A broker or dealer operating under this paragraph must promptly transmit all funds and promptly deliver all securities received in connection with its activities as a broker or dealer, and may not otherwise hold funds or securities for, or owe money or securities to, customers. **Other Brokers or Dealers** viii. A broker or dealer that does not receive, directly or indirectly, or hold funds or securities for, or owe funds or securities to, customers and does not carry accounts of, or for, customers and does not engage in any of the activities described in paragraphs 1.1. through (1.5.) of this section shall maintain net capital of not less than $5,000. A broker or dealer operating under this paragraph may engage in the following dealer activities without being subject to the requirements of paragraph 2.3. of this section: a. In the case of a buy order, prior to executing such customer's order, it purchases as principal the same number of shares or purchases shares to accumulate the number of shares necessary to complete the order, which shall be cleared through another registered broker or dealer or b. In the case of a sell order, prior to executing such customer's order, it sells as principal the same number of shares or a portion thereof, which shall be cleared through another registered broker or dealer.
requirements: (a) there must be a clearly documented trading strategy for the position/instrument or portfolios, approved by senior management, which shall include expected holding horizon; (b) there must be clearly defined policies and procedures for the active management of the position, which shall include the following: (i) positions entered into on a trading desk; (ii) position limits are set and monitored for appropriateness; (iii) dealers have the autonomy to enter into/manage the position within agreed limits and according to the approved strategy; (iv) positions are reported to senior management as an integral part of the institution's risk management process; and (v) positions are actively monitored with reference to market information sources and an assessment made of the marketability or hedge ability of the position or its component risks, including the assessment of, the quality and availability of market inputs to the valuation process, level of market turnover, sizes of positions traded in the market; and (c) there must be a clearly defined policy and procedures to monitor the position against the institution's trading strategy including the monitoring of turnover and stale positions in the institution's trading book. Systems and Controls 1. Institutions shall establish and maintain systems and controls sufficient to provide prudent and reliable valuation estimates. 2. Systems and controls shall include at least the following elements: (a) documented policies and procedures for the process of valuation. This includes clearly defined responsibilities of the various areas involved in the determination of the valuation, sources of market information and review of their appropriateness, frequency of independent valuation, timing of closing prices, procedures for adjusting valuations, month end and ad hoc verification procedures; and (b) reporting lines for the department accountable for the valuation process that are clear	

European Regulatory Framework for Financial Instruments	U.S. Regulatory Framework for Financial Instruments
and independent of the front office. The reporting line shall ultimately be to a main board executive director. **Prudent Valuation Methods** 3. Marking to market is the at least daily valuation of positions at readily available close out prices that are sourced independently. Examples include exchange prices, screen prices, or quotes from several independent reputable brokers. 4. When marking to market, the more prudent side of bid/offer shall be used unless the institution is a significant market maker in the particular type of financial instrument or commodity in question and it can close out at mid market. 5. Where marking to market is not possible, institutions must mark to model their positions/portfolios before applying trading book capital treatment. Marking to model is defined as any valuation which has to be benchmarked, extrapolated or otherwise calculated from a market input. 6. The following requirements must be complied with when marking to model: (a) senior management shall be aware of the elements of the trading book which are subject to mark to model and shall understand the materiality of the uncertainty this creates in the reporting of the risk/performance of the business; (b) market inputs shall be sourced, where possible, in line with market prices, and the appropriateness of the market inputs of the particular position being valued and the parameters of the model shall be assessed on a frequent basis; (c) where available, valuation methodologies which are accepted market practice for particular financial instruments or commodities shall be used; (d) where the model is developed by the institution itself, it shall be based on appropriate assumptions, which have been assessed and challenged by suitably qualified parties independent of the development process; (e) there shall be formal change control procedures in place and a secure copy of the model shall be held and periodically used to check valuations; (f) risk management shall be aware of the weaknesses of the models used and how best to reflect those in the valuation output; and	3. Reserved: **Capital Requirements for Market Makers** 4. broker or dealer engaged in activities as a market maker shall maintain net capital in an amount not less than $2,500 for each security in which it makes a market (unless a security in which it makes a market has a market value of $5 or less, in which event the amount of net capital shall be not less than $1,000 for each such security) based on the average number of such markets made by such broker or dealer during the 30 days immediately preceding the computation date. Under no circumstances shall it have net capital less than that required by the provisions of paragraph 1 of this section, or be required to maintain net capital of more than $1,000,000 unless required by paragraph (a) of this section. 5. In accordance with Appendix F to this section, the Commission may grant an application by an OTC derivatives dealer when calculating net capital to use the market risk standards of Appendix F as to some or all of its positions in lieu of the provisions of paragraph (c)(2)(vi) of this section and the credit risk standards of Appendix F to its receivables (including counterparty net exposure) arising from transactions in eligible OTC derivative instruments in lieu of the requirements of paragraph (c)(2)(iv) of this section. An OTC derivatives dealer shall at all times maintain tentative net capital of not less than $100 million and net capital of not less than $20 million. **Market Makers, Specialists and Certain Other Dealers** 6. i. A dealer who meets the conditions of paragraph (a)(6)(ii) of this section may elect to operate under this paragraph (a)(6) and thereby not apply, except to the extent required by this paragraph (a)(6), the provisions of paragraphs (c)(2)(vi) or Appendix A (Rule 15c3-1a) of this section to market maker and specialist transactions and, in lieu thereof, apply thereto the provisions of paragraph (a)(6)(iii) of this section.

European Regulatory Framework for Financial Instruments	U.S. Regulatory Framework for Financial Instruments
(g) the model shall be subject to periodic review to determine the accuracy of its performance (for example, assessing the continued appropriateness of assumptions, analysis of profit and loss versus risk factors, comparison of actual close out values to model outputs). For the purposes of point (d), the model shall be developed or approved independently of the front office and shall be independently tested, including validation of the mathematics, assumptions and software implementation. 7. Independent price verification should be performed in addition to daily marking to market or marking to model. This is the process by which market prices or model inputs are regularly verified for accuracy and independence. While daily marking to market may be performed by dealers, verification of market prices and model inputs should be performed by a unit independent of the dealing room, at least monthly (or, depending on the nature of the market/trading activity, more frequently). Where independent pricing sources are not available or pricing sources are more subjective, prudent measures such as valuation adjustments may be appropriate. Valuation adjustments or reserves 8. Institutions shall establish and maintain procedures for considering valuation adjustments/reserves. General standards 9. The competent authorities shall require the following valuation adjustments/reserves to be formally considered: unearned credit spreads, close out costs, operational risks, early termination, investing and funding costs, future administrative costs and, where relevant, model risk. Standards for less liquid positions 10. Less liquid positions could arise from both market events and institution-related situations, for example concentrated positions and/or stale positions. 11. Institutions shall consider several factors when determining whether a valuation reserve is necessary for less liquid positions. These factors include the amount of time it would take to hedge out the position/risks within the position, the volatility and average of	ii. This paragraph (a)(6) shall be available to a dealer who does not effect transactions with other than brokers or dealers, who does not carry customer accounts, who does not effect transactions in unlisted options, and whose market maker or specialist transactions are effected through and carried in a market maker or specialist account cleared by another broker or dealer as provided in paragraph (a)(6)(iv) of this section. iii. A dealer who elects to operate pursuant to this paragraph (a)(6) shall at all times maintain a liquidating equity in respect of securities positions in his market maker or specialist account at least equal to: A. An amount equal to 25 percent (5 percent in the case of exempted securities) of the market value of the long positions and 30 percent of the market value of the short positions; provided, however, in the case of long or short positions in options and long or short positions in securities other than options which relate to a bona fide hedged position as defined in paragraph (c)(2)(x)(C) of this section, such amount shall equal the deductions in respect of such positions specified by paragraph (c)(2)(x)(A)(1)-(9) of this section. B. Such lesser requirement as may be approved by the Commission under specified terms and conditions upon written application of the dealer and the carrying broker or dealer. C. For purposes of this paragraph (a)(6)(iii), equity in such specialist or market maker account shall be computed by 1. marking all securities positions long or short in the account to their respective current market values, 2. adding (deducting in the case of a debit balance) the credit balance carried in such specialist or market maker account, and 3. adding (deducting in the case of short positions) the market value of positions long in such account. iv. The dealer shall obtain from the broker or dealer carrying the market maker or specialist account a written undertaking which shall be designated

European Regulatory Framework for Financial Instruments	U.S. Regulatory Framework for Financial Instruments
bid/offer spreads, the availability of market quotes (number and identity of market makers) and the volatility and average of trading volumes, market concentrations, the aging of positions, the extent to which valuation relies on marking-to-model, and the impact of other model risks. 12. When using third party valuations or marking to model, institutions shall consider whether to apply a valuation adjustment. In addition, institutions shall consider the need for establishing reserves for less liquid positions and on an ongoing basis review their continued suitability. 13. When valuation adjustments/reserves give rise to material losses of the current financial year, these shall be deducted from an institution's original own funds according to point (k) of Article 57 of Directive 2006/48/EC 14. Other profits/losses originating from valuation adjustments/reserves shall be included in the calculation of 'net trading book profits' mentioned in point (b) of Article 13(2) and be added to/deducted from the additional own funds eligible to cover market risk requirements according to such provisions. 15. Valuation adjustments/reserves which exceed those made under the accounting framework to which the institution is subject shall be treated in accordance with point 13 if they give rise to material losses, or point 14 otherwise. Internal Hedges 1. An internal hedge is a position that materially or completely offsets the component risk element of a non-trading book position or a set of positions. Positions arising from internal hedges are eligible for trading book capital treatment, provided that they are held with trading intent and that the general criteria on trading intent and prudent valuation specified in Parts A and B are met. In particular: (a) internal hedges shall not be primarily intended to avoid or reduce capital requirements; (b) internal hedges shall be properly documented and subject to particular internal approval and audit procedures; (c) the internal transaction shall be dealt with at market conditions; (d) the bulk of the market risk that is generated by the internal hedge shall be dynamically	"Notice Pursuant to Rule 15c3-1(a)(6) of Intention to Carry Specialist or Market Maker Account." Said undertaking shall contain the representations required by paragraph (a)(6) and shall be filed with the Commission's Washington, DC, Office, the regional office of the Commission for the region in which the broker or dealer has its principal place of business and the Designated Examining Authorities of both firms prior to effecting any transactions in said account. The broker or dealer carrying such account: A. Shall mark the account to the market not less than daily and shall issue appropriate calls for additional equity which shall be met by noon of the following business day; B. Shall notify by telegraph the Commission and the Designated Examining Authorities pursuant to Rule 17a-11, if the market maker or specialist fails to deposit any required equity within the time prescribed in paragraph (a)(6)(iv)(A) above; said telegraphic notice shall be received by the Commission and the Designated Examining Authorities not later than the close of business on the day said call is not met; C. Shall not extend further credit in the account if the equity in the account falls below that prescribed in paragraph (a)(6)(iii) above, and D. Shall take steps to liquidate promptly existing positions in the account in the event of a failure to meet a call for equity. v. No such carrying broker or dealer shall permit the sum of A. the deductions required by paragraph (c)(2)(x)(A) of this section in respect of all transactions in market maker accounts guaranteed, indorsed or carried by such broker or dealer pursuant to paragraph (c)(2)(x) of this section and B. the equity required by paragraph (iii) of this paragraph (a)(6) in respect of all transactions in the accounts of specialists of market makers in options carried by such broker or dealer pursuant to this paragraph (a)(6) to exceed 1,000 percent of such broker's or dealer's net capital as defined in paragraph (c)(2) of this section for any period exceeding five business

European Regulatory Framework for Financial Instruments	U.S. Regulatory Framework for Financial Instruments
	days; *Provided*, That solely for purposes of this paragraph (a)(6)(v), deductions or equity required in a specialist or market maker account in respect of positions in fully paid securities (other than options), which do not underlie options listed on the national securities exchange or facility of a national securities association of which the specialist or market maker is a member, need not be recognized. *Provided further*, That if at any time such sum exceeds 1,000 percent of such broker's or dealer's net capital, then the broker or dealer shall immediately transmit telegraphic notice of such event to the principal office of the Commission in Washington, DC, the regional office of the Commission for the region in which the broker or dealer maintains its principal place of business, and such broker's or dealer's Designated Examining Authority. *Provided further*, That if at any time such sum exceeds 1,000 percent of such broker's or dealer's net capital, then such broker or dealer shall be subject to the prohibitions against withdrawal of equity capital set forth in paragraph (e) of this section, and to the prohibitions against reduction, prepayment and repayment of subordination agreements set forth in paragraph (b)(11) of Rule 15c3-1d, as if such broker or dealer's net capital were below the minimum standards specified by each of the aforementioned paragraphs.

European Regulatory Framework for Financial Instruments	U.S. Regulatory Framework for Financial Instruments
managed in the trading book within the authorized limits; and (e) internal transactions shall be carefully monitored. Monitoring must be ensured by adequate procedures. 2. The treatment referred to in point 1 applies without prejudice to the capital requirements applicable to the 'non-trading book leg' of the internal hedge. 3. Notwithstanding points 1 and 2, when an institution hedges a non-trading book credit risk exposure using a credit derivative booked in its trading book (using an internal hedge), the non-trading book exposure is not deemed to be hedged for the purposes of calculating capital requirements unless the institution purchases from an eligible third party protection provider a credit derivative meeting the requirements set out in point 19 of Part 2 of Annex VIII to Directive 2006/48/EC with regard to the non-trading book exposure. Where such third party protection is purchased and is recognized as a hedge of a non-trading book exposure for the purposes of calculating capital requirements, neither the internal nor external credit derivative hedge shall be included in the trading book for the purposes of calculating capital requirements. Inclusion In The Trading Book 1. Institutions shall have clearly defined policies and procedures for determining which position to include in the trading book for the purposes of calculating their capital requirements, consistent with the criteria set out in Article 11 and taking into account the institution's risk management capabilities and practices. Compliance with these policies and procedures shall be fully documented and subject to periodic internal audit. 2. Institutions shall have clearly defined policies and procedures for overall management of the trading book. At a minimum these policies and procedures shall address: (a) the activities the institution considers to be trading and as constituting part of the trading book for capital requirement purposes; (b) the extent to which a position can be marked to market daily by reference to an active, liquid two-way market; (c) for positions that are marked to model, the extent to which the institution can: (i) identify all material risks of the position;	

European Regulatory Framework for Financial Instruments	U.S. Regulatory Framework for Financial Instruments
(ii) hedge all material risks of the position with instruments for which an active, liquid two-way market exists; and (iii) derive reliable estimates for the key assumptions and parameters used in the model; (d) the extent to which the institution can, and is required to, generate valuations for the position that can be validated externally in a consistent manner; (e) the extent to which legal restrictions or other operational requirements would impede the institution's ability to effect a liquidation or hedge of the position in the short term; (f) the extent to which the institution can, and is required to, actively risk manage the position within its trading operation; and (g) the extent to which the institution may transfer risk or positions between the non-trading and trading books and the criteria for such transfers. 3. Competent authorities may allow institutions to treat positions that are holdings in the trading book as set out in Article 57(l), (m) and (n) of Directive 2006/48/EC as equity or debt instruments, as appropriate, where an institution demonstrates that it is an active market maker in these positions. In this case, the institution shall have adequate systems and controls surrounding the trading of eligible own funds instruments. 4. Term trading-related repo-style transactions that an institution accounts for in its non-trading book may be included in the trading book for capital requirement purposes so long as all such repo-style transactions are included. For this purpose, trading-related repo-style transactions are defined as those that meet the requirements of Article 11(2) and of Annex VII, Part A, and both legs are in the form of either cash or securities includable in the trading book. Regardless of where they are booked, all repo-style transactions are subject to a non-trading book counterparty credit risk charge. • Organizational Requirements for Investment Firms MiFID, level 1, Article 13 1. An investment firm shall establish **adequate policies and procedures**	• Organizational Requirements for Brokers and Dealers NASD 3012 Supervisory Control System (a) **General Requirements**

European Regulatory Framework for Financial Instruments	U.S. Regulatory Framework for Financial Instruments
sufficient to ensure **compliance of the firm including its managers, employees and tied agents with its obligations** under the provisions of Directive **2004/39/EC** as well as appropriate rules governing personal transactions by such persons.	(1) Each member shall designate and specifically identify to NASD one or more principals who shall establish, maintain, and enforce a system of supervisory control policies and procedures that (A) test and verify that the member's supervisory procedures are reasonably designed with respect to the activities of the member and its registered representatives and associated persons, to achieve compliance with applicable securities laws and regulations, and with applicable NASD rules and (B) create additional or amend supervisory procedures where the need is identified by such testing and verification. The designated principal or principals must submit to the member's senior management no less than annually, a report¹ detailing each member's system of supervisory controls, the summary of the test results and significant identified exceptions, and any additional or amended supervisory procedures created in response to the test results.
2. An investment firm shall maintain and **operate effective organizational and administrative arrangements** with a view to taking all reasonable steps designed to **prevent conflicts of interest** as defined in Article 18 of Directive **2004/39/EC** from adversely affecting the interests of its clients.	(2) The establishment, maintenance, and enforcement of written supervisory control policies and procedures pursuant to paragraph (a) shall include:
3. An investment firm shall take reasonable steps **to ensure continuity and regularity in the performance of investment services and activities.** To this end the investment firm shall employ appropriate and proportionate systems, resources and procedures.	(A) procedures that are reasonably designed to review and supervise the customer account activity conducted by the member's branch office managers, sales managers, regional or district sales managers, or any person performing a similar supervisory function.
4. An investment firm shall ensure, when relying on a third party for the performance of operational functions which are critical for the provision of continuous and satisfactory service to clients and the performance of investment activities on a continuous and satisfactory basis, that it takes reasonable steps to avoid undue additional operational risk. **Outsourcing of important operational functions may not be undertaken in such a way as to impair materially the quality of its internal control and the ability of the supervisor to monitor the firm's compliance with all obligations.** An investment firm shall have sound administrative and accounting procedures, internal control mechanisms, effective procedures for risk assessment, and effective control and safeguard arrangements for information processing systems.	(i) General Supervisory Requirement. A person who is either senior to, or otherwise independent of, the producing manager must perform such supervisory reviews. For purposes of this Rule, an "otherwise independent" person: may not report either directly or indirectly to the producing manager under review; must be situated in an office other than the office of the producing manager; must not otherwise have supervisory responsibility over the activity being reviewed (including not being directly compensated based in whole or in part on the revenues accruing for those activities); and must alternate such review responsibility with another qualified person every two years or less.
5. An investment firm shall arrange for records to be kept of all services and transactions undertaken by it which shall be sufficient to enable the competent authority to monitor compliance with the requirements under this Directive, and in particular **to ascertain that the investment firm has complied with all obligations with respect to clients or potential clients.**	(ii) "Limited Size and Resources" Exception. If a member is so limited in size and resources that there is no qualified person senior to, or otherwise independent of, the producing manager to conduct the reviews pursuant to (i) above (e.g., a member has only one office or an insufficient number of qualified personnel who can conduct reviews on a two-year rotation), the reviews may be conducted by a principal who is sufficiently knowledgeable of the member's supervisory control procedures, provided that the reviews
6. An investment firm shall, when holding financial instruments belonging to clients, **make adequate arrangements so as to safeguard clients'**	

European Regulatory Framework for Financial Instruments	U.S. Regulatory Framework for Financial Instruments
ownership rights, especially in the event of the investment firm's insolvency, and to prevent the use of a client's instruments on own account except with the client's express consent. 7. An investment firm shall, **when holding funds belonging to clients, make adequate arrangements to safeguard the clients' rights** and, except in the case of credit institutions, prevent the use of client funds for its own account. 8. In the case of branches of investment firms, the competent authority of the Member State in which the branch is located shall, without prejudice to the possibility of the competent authority of the home Member State of the investment firm to have direct access to those records, enforce the obligation laid down in paragraph 6 with regard to transactions undertaken by the branch. Implementing Measures specified in Directive **2006/73/EC (MiFID level 2):** **Article 5** 6. Member States shall require investment firms to comply with the following requirements: a) **to establish, implement and maintain decision-making procedures** and an organisational structure which clearly and in documented **manner specifies reporting lines and allocates functions and responsibilities;** b) to ensure that their relevant persons are aware of the procedures which must be followed for the proper discharge of their responsibilities; c) to establish, implement and **maintain adequate internal control mechanisms** designed to secure compliance with decisions and procedures at all levels of the investment firm; d) to employ personnel with the skills, knowledge and expertise necessary for the discharge of the responsibilities allocated to them; e) to establish, implement and maintain effective **internal reporting** and communication of information at all relevant levels of the investment	are in compliance with (i) to the extent practicable. (iii) Notification Requirement. If a member determines that it must rely on the "limited size and resources" exception set forth in (ii) above to conduct any of its producing managers' supervisory reviews, the member must notify NASD through an electronic process (or any other process prescribed by NASD) within 30 days of the date on which the member first relies on the exception,[2] and annually thereafter.[3] If a member subsequently determines that it no longer needs to rely on the exception to conduct any of its producing managers' supervisory reviews, the member must, within 30 days of ceasing to rely on the exception, notify NASD by using the electronic process or any other process prescribed by NASD. (iv) Documentation Requirement. A member relying on (ii) above must document in its supervisory control procedures the factors used to determine that complete compliance with all of the provisions of (i) is not possible and that the required supervisory systems and procedures in place with respect to any producing manager comply with the provisions of (i) above to the extent practicable. (B) procedures that are reasonably designed to review and monitor the following activities: (i) all transmittals of funds (e.g., wires or checks, etc.) or securities from customers to third party accounts (i.e., a transmittal that would result in a change of beneficial ownership); from customer accounts to outside entities (e.g., banks, investment companies, etc.); from customer accounts to locations other than a customer's primary residence (e.g., post office box, "in care of" accounts, alternate address, etc.); and between customers and registered representatives, including the hand-delivery of checks; (ii) customer changes of address and the validation of such changes of address; and (iii) customer changes of investment objectives and the validation of such changes of investment objectives. The policies and procedures established pursuant to paragraph (a)(2)(B) must include a means or method of customer confirmation, notification, or follow-up that can be documented. If a member does not engage in all of the activities enumerated above, the member must identify those activities in which it does not engage in its written supervisory control policies and procedures and document in those policies and procedures that

European Regulatory Framework for Financial Instruments	U.S. Regulatory Framework for Financial Instruments
firm; f) to maintain adequate and orderly records of their business and internal organization; g) to ensure that the performance of multiple functions by their relevant persons does not and is not likely to prevent those persons from discharging any particular function soundly, honestly, and professionally. Member States shall ensure that, for those purposes, investment firms take into account the nature, scale and complexity of the business of the firm, and the nature and range of investment services and activities undertaken in the course of that business. 7. Member States shall require investment firms to establish, implement and maintain systems and procedures that are adequate to safeguard the security, integrity and confidentiality of information, taking into account the nature of the information in question. 8. Member States shall require investment firms to establish, implement and maintain an adequate business continuity policy aimed at ensuring, in the case of an interruption to their systems and procedures, the preservation of essential data and functions, and the maintenance of investment services and activities, or, where that is not possible, the timely recovery of such data and functions and the timely resumption of their investment services and activities. 9. Member States shall require investment firms to establish, implement and maintain accounting policies and procedures that enable them, at the request of the competent authority, to deliver in a timely manner to the competent authority financial reports which reflect a true and fair view of their financial position and which comply with all applicable accounting standards and rules. 10. Member States shall require investment firms to monitor and, on a regular basis, to evaluate the adequacy and effectiveness of their systems, internal control mechanisms and arrangements established in accordance with paragraphs 1 to 4, and to take appropriate measures to address any	additional supervisory policies and procedures for such activities must be in place before the member can engage in them; and (C) procedures that are reasonably designed to provide heightened supervision over the activities of each producing manager who is responsible for generating 20% or more of the revenue of the business units supervised by the producing manager's supervisor. For the purposes of this subsection only, the term "heightened supervision" shall mean those supervisory procedures that evidence supervisory activities that are designed to avoid conflicts of interest that serve to undermine complete and effective supervision because of the economic, commercial, or financial interests that the supervisor holds in the associated persons and businesses being supervised. In addition, for the purpose of this section only, when calculating the 20% threshold, all of the revenue generated by or credited to the producing manager or the producing manager's office shall be attributed as revenue generated by the business units supervised by the producing manager's supervisor irrespective of a member's internal allocation of such revenue. A member must calculate the 20% threshold on a rolling, twelve-month basis. **(b) Dual Member** Any member in compliance with substantially similar requirements of the New York Stock Exchange, Inc. shall be deemed to be in compliance with the provisions of this Rule. • As regard personal transactions: **Securities and Exchange Act, Sec. 11: Trading by members of exchanges, brokers, and dealers** a) Trading for own account or account of associated person; exceptions 1) It shall be unlawful for any member of a national securities exchange to effect any transaction on such exchange for its own account, the account of an associated person, or an account with respect to which it or an associated person thereof exercises investment discretion: Provided, however, That this paragraph shall not make unlawful - A) any transaction by a dealer acting in the capacity of market maker; B) any transaction for the account of an odd-lot dealer in a security in which he

European Regulatory Framework for Financial Instruments	U.S. Regulatory Framework for Financial Instruments
deficiencies. Article 6 Compliance 1. Member States shall ensure that investment firms establish, implement and maintain adequate policies and procedures designed to detect any risk of failure by the firm to comply with its obligations under Directive 2004/39/EC, as well as the associated risks, and put in place adequate measures and procedures designed to minimize such risk and to enable the competent authorities to exercise their powers effectively under that Directive. Member States shall ensure that, for those purposes, investment firms take into account the nature, scale and complexity of the business of the firm, and the nature and range of investment services and activities undertaken in the course of that business. 2. Member States shall require investment firms to establish and maintain a permanent and effective compliance function which operates independently and which has the following responsibilities: h) to monitor and, on a regular basis, to assess the adequacy and effectiveness of the measures and procedures put in place in accordance with the first subparagraph of paragraph 1, and the actions taken to address any deficiencies in the firm's compliance with its obligations; i) to advise and assist the relevant persons responsible for carrying out investment services and activities to comply with the firm's obligations under Directive 2004/39/EC. 3. In order to enable the compliance function to discharge its responsibilities properly and independently, Member States shall require investment firms to ensure that the following conditions are satisfied: the compliance function must have the necessary authority, resources, expertise and access to all relevant information; a) a compliance officer must be appointed and must be responsible for the	is so registered; C) any stabilizing transaction effected in compliance with rules under section 78j(b) (on Manipulative and deceptive devices) of this title to facilitate a distribution of a security in which the member effecting such transaction is participating; D) any bona fide arbitrage transaction, any bona fide hedge transaction involving a long or short position in an equity security and a long or short position in a security entitling the holder to acquire or sell such equity security, or any risk arbitrage transaction in connection with a merger, acquisition, tender offer, or similar transaction involving a recapitalization; E) any transaction for the account of a natural person, the estate of a natural person, or a trust created by a natural person for himself or another natural person; F) any transaction to offset a transaction made in error; G) any other transaction for a member's own account provided that (i) such member is primarily engaged in the business of underwriting and distributing securities issued by other persons, selling securities to customers, and acting as broker, or any one or more of such activities, and whose gross income normally is derived principally from such business and related activities and (ii) such transaction is effected in compliance with rules of the Commission which, as a minimum, assure that the transaction is not inconsistent with the maintenance of fair and orderly markets and yields priority, parity, and precedence in execution to orders for the account of persons who are not members or associated with members of the exchange; H) any transaction for an account with respect to which such member or an associated person thereof exercises investment discretion if such member - (i) has obtained, from the person or persons authorized to transact business for the account, express authorization for such member or associated person to effect such transactions prior to engaging in the practice of effecting such transactions; (ii) furnishes the

European Regulatory Framework for Financial Instruments	U.S. Regulatory Framework for Financial Instruments
compliance function and for any reporting as to compliance required by Article 9(2); b) the relevant persons involved in the compliance function must not be involved in the performance of services or activities they monitor; c) the method of determining the remuneration of the relevant persons involved in the compliance function must not compromise their objectivity and must not be likely to do so. However, an investment firm shall not be required to comply with point (c) or point (d) if it is able to demonstrate that in view of the nature, scale and complexity of its business, and the nature and range of investment services and activities, the requirement under that point is not proportionate and that its compliance function continues to be effective. **Article 7** **Risk management** 1. Member States shall require investment firms to take the following actions: a) to establish, implement and maintain adequate risk management policies and procedures which identify the risks relating to the firm's activities, processes and systems, and where appropriate, set the level of risk tolerated by the firm; b) to adopt effective arrangements, processes and mechanisms to manage the risks relating to the firm's activities, processes and systems, in light of that level of risk tolerance; c) to monitor the following: i) the adequacy and effectiveness of the investment firm's risk management policies and procedures; ii) the level of compliance by the investment firm and its relevant persons with the arrangements, processes and mechanisms adopted in accordance with point (b);	person or persons authorized to transact business for the account with a statement at least annually disclosing the aggregate compensation received by the exchange member in effecting such transactions; and (iii) complies with any rules the Commission has prescribed with respect to the requirements of clauses (i) and (ii); and (I) any other transaction of a kind which the Commission, by rule, determines is consistent with the purposes of this paragraph, the protection of investors, and the maintenance of fair and orderly markets. 2) The Commission, by rule, as it deems necessary or appropriate in the public interest and for the protection of investors, to maintain fair and orderly markets, or to assure equal regulation of exchange markets and markets occurring otherwise than on an exchange, may regulate or prohibit: A) transactions on a national securities exchange not unlawful under paragraph (1) of this subsection effected by any member thereof for its own account (unless such member is acting in the capacity of market maker or odd-lot dealer), the account of an associated person, or an account with respect to which such member or an associated person thereof exercises investment discretion; B) transactions otherwise than on a national securities exchange effected by use of the mails or any means or instrumentality of interstate commerce by any member of a national securities exchange, broker, or dealer for the account of such member, broker, or dealer (unless such member, broker, or dealer is acting in the capacity of a market Maker) on the account of an associated person, or an account with respect to which such member, broker, or dealer or associated person thereof exercises investment discretion; and C) transactions on a national securities exchange effected by any broker or dealer not a member thereof for the account of such broker or dealer (unless such broker or dealer is acting in the capacity of market maker), the account of an associated person, or an account with respect to which such broker or dealer or associated person thereof exercises investment

European Regulatory Framework for Financial Instruments	U.S. Regulatory Framework for Financial Instruments
iii) the adequacy and effectiveness of measures taken to address any deficiencies in those policies, procedures, arrangements, processes and mechanisms, including failures by the relevant persons to comply with such arrangements, processes and mechanisms or follow such policies and procedures. 2. Member States shall require investment firms, where appropriate and proportionate in view of the nature, scale and complexity of their business and the nature and range of the investment services and activities undertaken in the course of that business, to establish and maintain a risk management function that operates independently and carries out the following tasks: a) implementation of the policy and procedures referred to in paragraph 1; b) provision of reports and advice to senior management in accordance with Article 9(2). Where an investment firm is not required under the first sub-paragraph to establish and maintain a risk management function that functions independently, it must nevertheless be able to demonstrate that the policies and procedures which it is has adopted in accordance with paragraph 1 satisfy the requirements of that paragraph and are consistently effective. Article 8 Internal audit Member States shall require investment firms, where appropriate and proportionate in view of the nature, scale and complexity of their business and the nature and range of investment services and activities undertaken in the course of that business, to establish and maintain an internal audit function which is separate and independent from the other functions and activities of the investment firm and which has the following responsibilities: a) to establish, implement and maintain an audit plan to examine and evaluate the adequacy and effectiveness of the investment firm's systems, internal control mechanisms and arrangements; b) to issue recommendations based on the result of work carried out in	discretion. c) Exemptions from provisions of section and rules and regulations: If because of the limited volume of transactions effected on an exchange, it is in the opinion of the Commission impracticable and not necessary or appropriate in the public interest or for the protection of investors to apply any of the foregoing provisions of this section or the rules and regulations thereunder, the Commission shall have power, upon application of the exchange and on a showing that the rules of such exchange are otherwise adequate for the protection of investors, to exempt such exchange and its members from any such provision or rules and regulations. d) Prohibition on extension of credit by broker-dealer. It shall be unlawful for a member of a national securities exchange who is both a dealer and a broker, or for any person who both as a broker and a dealer transacts a business in securities through the medium of a member or otherwise, to effect through the use of any facility of a national securities exchange or of the mails or of any means or instrumentality of interstate commerce, or otherwise in the case of a member, (1) any transaction in connection with which, directly or indirectly, he extends or maintains or arranges for the extension or maintenance of credit to or for a customer on any security (other than an exempted security) which was a part of a new issue in the distribution of which he participated as a member of a selling syndicate or group within thirty days prior to such transaction: Provided, That credit shall not be deemed extended by reason of a bona fide delayed delivery of (i) any such security against full payment of the entire purchase price thereof upon such delivery within thirty-five days after such purchase or (ii) any mortgage related security or any small business related security against full payment of the entire purchase price thereof upon such delivery within one hundred and eighty days after such purchase, or within such shorter period as the Commission may prescribe by rule or regulation, or (2) any transaction with respect to any security (other than an exempted security) unless, if the transaction is with a customer, he discloses to such customer

European Regulatory Framework for Financial Instruments	U.S. Regulatory Framework for Financial Instruments
accordance with point (a); c) to verify compliance with those recommendations; d) to report in relation to internal audit matters in accordance with Article 9(2). **Article 9** Responsibility of senior management 1. Member States shall require investment firms, when allocating functions internally, to ensure that senior management, and, where appropriate, the supervisory function, are responsible for ensuring that the firm complies with its obligations under Directive 2004/39/EC. In particular, senior management and, where appropriate, the supervisory function shall be required to assess and periodically to review the effectiveness of the policies, arrangements and procedures put in place to comply with the obligations under Directive 2004/39/EC and to take appropriate measures to address any deficiencies. 2. Member States shall require investment firms to ensure that their senior management receive on a frequent basis, and at least annually, written reports on the matters covered by Articles 6, 7 and 8 indicating in particular whether the appropriate remedial measures have been taken in the event of any deficiencies. 3. Member States shall require investment firms to ensure that the supervisory function, if any, receives on a regular basis written reports on the same matters. 4. For the purposes of this Article, "supervisory function" means the function within an investment firm responsible for the supervision of its senior management. **Article 10** Complaints handling Member States shall require investment firms to establish, implement and maintain	in writing at or before the completion of the transaction whether he is acting as a dealer for his own account, as a broker for such customer, or as a broker for some other person. • NASD Conduct Rule 3040. Private Securities Transactions of an Associated Person a) **Applicability** No person associated with a member shall participate in any manner in a private securities transaction except in accordance with the requirements of this Rule. b) **Written Notice** **Prior to participating in any private securities transaction, an associated person shall provide written notice to the member with which he is associated** describing in detail the proposed transaction and the person's proposed role therein and stating whether he has received or may receive **selling compensation in connection with the transaction**; provided however that, in the case of a series of related transactions in which no selling compensation has been or will be received, an associated person may provide a single written notice. c) **Transactions for Compensation** 1. In the case of a transaction in which an associated person has received or may receive selling compensation, a member which has received notice pursuant to paragraph (b) shall advise the associated person in writing stating whether the member: A) approves the person's participation in the proposed transaction; or B) disapproves the person's participation in the proposed transaction. 2. If the member approves a person's participation in a transaction pursuant to paragraph (c)(1), the transaction shall be recorded on the books and records of the member and the member shall supervise the person's participation in the transaction as if the transaction were executed on behalf of the member. 3. If the member disapproves a person's participation pursuant to paragraph

European Regulatory Framework for Financial Instruments	U.S. Regulatory Framework for Financial Instruments

effective and transparent procedures for the reasonable and prompt handling of complaints received from retail clients or potential retail clients, and to keep a record of each complaint and the measures taken for its resolution.
 	
Article 11
 	
Meaning of personal transaction
 	
For the purposes of Article 12 and Article 25, personal transaction means a trade in a financial instrument effected by or on behalf of a relevant person, where at least one of the following criteria are met:
 	
a) that relevant person is acting outside the scope of the activities he carries out in that capacity;
 	
b) the trade is carried out for the account of any of the following persons:
  i) the relevant person;
  ii) any person with whom he has a family relationship, or with whom he has close links;
  iii) a person whose relationship with the relevant person is such that the relevant person has a direct or indirect material interest in the outcome of the trade, other than a fee or commission for the execution of the trade.
 	
Article 12
 	
Personal transactions
 	
1. Member States shall require investment firms to establish, implement and maintain adequate arrangements aimed at preventing the following activities in the case of any relevant person who is involved in activities that may give rise to a conflict of interest, or who has access to inside information within the meaning of Article 1(1) of Directive 2003/6/EC or to other confidential information relating to clients or transactions with or for clients by virtue of an activity carried out by him on behalf of the firm:
 	
a) entering into a personal transaction which meets at least one of the following criteria:
	(c)(1), the person shall not participate in the transaction in any manner, directly or indirectly.
	
	d) **Transactions Not for Compensation**
	
	In the case of a transaction or a series of related transactions in which an associated person has not and will not receive any selling compensation, a member which has received notice pursuant to paragraph (b) shall provide the associated person prompt written acknowledgment of said notice and may, at its discretion, require the person to adhere to specified conditions in connection with his participation in the transaction.
	
	e) **Definitions**
	
	For purposes of this Rule, the following terms shall have the stated meanings:
	
	1. "Private securities transaction" shall mean any securities transaction outside the regular course or scope of an associated person's employment with a member, including, though not limited to, new offerings of securities which are not registered with the Commission, provided however that transactions subject to the notification requirements of Rule 3050 on (transactions for or by associated persons), transactions among immediate family members (as defined in Rule 2790), for which no associated person receives any selling compensation, and personal transactions in investment company and variable annuity securities, shall be excluded.
	
	2. "Selling compensation" shall mean any compensation paid directly or indirectly from whatever source in connection with or as a result of the purchase or sale of a security, including, though not limited to, commissions; finder's fees; securities or rights to acquire securities; rights of participation in profits, tax benefits, or dissolution proceeds, as a general partner or otherwise; or expense reimbursements.
	
	Securities and Exchange Act
	Rule 15c3-3 -- Customer Protection--Reserves and Custody of Securities

European Regulatory Framework for Financial Instruments	U.S. Regulatory Framework for Financial Instruments
i) that person is prohibited from entering into it under Directive 2003/6/EC; ii) it involves the misuse or improper disclosure of that confidential information; iii) it conflicts or is likely to conflict with an obligation of the investment firm under Directive 2004/39/EC; b) advising or procuring, other than in the proper course of his employment or contract for services, any other person to enter into a transaction in financial instruments which, if a personal transaction of the relevant person, would be covered by point (a) or Article 25(2)(a) (see investment research) or (b) or Article 47(3) (see client order handling); c) without prejudice to Article 3(a) of Directive 2003/6/EC, disclosing, other than in the normal course of his employment or contract for services, any information or opinion to any other person if the relevant person knows, or reasonably ought to know, that as a result of that disclosure that other person will or would be likely to take either of the following steps: i) to enter into a transaction in financial instruments which, if a personal transaction of the relevant person, would be covered by point (a) or Article 25(2)(a)(see part on investment research) or (b) or Article 47(3) (see client order handling rules); ii) to advise or procure another person to enter into such a transaction. 2. The arrangements required under paragraph 1 must in particular be designed to ensure that: a) each relevant person covered by paragraph 1 is aware of the restrictions on personal transactions, and of the measures established by the investment firm in connection with personal transactions and disclosure, in accordance with paragraph 1;	a. *Physical possession or control of securities.* 1. A broker or dealer shall promptly obtain and shall thereafter maintain the physical possession or control of all fully-paid securities and excess margin securities carried by a broker or dealer for the account of customers. 2. A broker or dealer shall not be deemed to be in violation of the provisions of paragraph (b)(1) of this section regarding physical possession or control of customers' securities if, solely as the result of normal business operations, temporary lags occur between the time when a security is required to be in the possession or control of the broker or dealer and the time that it is placed in his physical possession or under his control, provided that the broker or dealer takes timely steps in good faith to establish prompt physical possession or control. The burden of proof shall be on the broker or dealer to establish that the failure to obtain physical possession or control of securities carried for the account of customers as required by paragraph (b)(1) of this section is merely temporary and solely the result of normal business operations including same day receipt and redelivery (turnaround), and to establish that he has taken timely steps in good faith to place them in his physical possession or control. 3. A broker or dealer shall not be deemed to be in violation of the provisions of paragraph (b)(1) of this section regarding physical possession or control of fully-paid or excess margin securities borrowed from any person, provided that the broker or dealer and the lender, at or before the time of the loan, enter into a written agreement that, at a minimum; i. Sets forth in a separate schedule or schedules the basis of compensation for any loan and generally the rights and liabilities of the parties as to the borrowed securities; ii. Provides that the lender will be given a schedule of the securities actually borrowed at the time of the borrowing of the securities; iii. Specifies that the broker or dealer:

U.S. Regulatory Framework for Financial Instruments

a. Must provide to the lender, upon the execution of the agreement or by the close of the business day of the loan if the loan occurs subsequent to the execution of the agreement, collateral, which fully secures the loan of securities, consisting exclusively of cash or United States Treasury bills and Treasury notes or an irrevocable letter of credit issued by a bank as defined in section 3(a)(6)(A)–(C) of the Act or such other collateral as the Commission designates as permissible by order as necessary or appropriate in the public interest and consistent with the protection of investors after giving consideration to the collateral's liquidity, volatility, market depth and location, and the issuer's creditworthiness; and

b. Must mark the loan to the market not less than daily and, in the event that the market value of all the outstanding securities loaned at the close of trading at the end of the business day exceeds 100 percent of the collateral then held by the lender, the borrowing broker or dealer must provide additional collateral of the type described in paragraph (b)(3)(iii)(A) of this section to the lender by the close of the next business day as necessary to equal, together with the collateral then held by the lender, not less than 100 percent of the market value of the securities loaned; and

iv. Contains a prominent notice that the provisions of the Securities Investor Protection Act of 1970 may not protect the lender with respect to the securities loan transaction and that, therefore, the collateral delivered to the lender may constitute the only source of satisfaction of the broker's or dealer's obligation in the event the broker or dealer fails to return the securities.

4.

i. Notwithstanding paragraph (k)(2)(i) of this section, a broker or dealer that retains custody of securities that are the subject of a repurchase agreement between the broker or dealer and a counterparty shall:

European Regulatory Framework for Financial Instruments

b) the firm is informed promptly of any personal transaction entered into by a relevant person, either by notification of that transaction or by other procedures enabling the firm to identify such transactions;

In the case of outsourcing arrangements the investment firm must ensure that the firm to which the activity is outsourced maintains a record of personal transactions entered into by any relevant person and provides that information to the investment firm promptly on request.

c) a record is kept of the personal transaction notified to the firm or identified by it, including any authorization or prohibition in connection with such a transaction.

3. Paragraphs 1 and 2 shall not apply to the following kinds of personal transaction:

a) personal transactions effected under a discretionary portfolio management service where there is no prior communication in connection with the transaction between the portfolio manager and the relevant person or other person for whose account the transaction is executed;

b) personal transactions in units in collective undertakings that comply with the conditions necessary to enjoy the rights conferred by Directive 85/611/EEC or are subject to supervision under the law of a Member State which requires an equivalent level of risk spreading in their assets, where the relevant person and any other person for whose account the transactions are effected are not involved in the management of that undertaking.

Section 2
Outsourcing

Meaning of critical and important operational functions

1. For the purposes of the first subparagraph of Article 13(5) of Directive 2004/39/EC, an operational function shall be regarded as critical or important if a defect or failure in its performance would materially impair the continuing

European Regulatory Framework for Financial Instruments	U.S. Regulatory Framework for Financial Instruments
compliance of an investment firm with the conditions and obligations of its authorization or its other obligations under Directive 2004/39/EC, or its financial performance, or the soundness or the continuity of its investment services and activities. 2. Without prejudice to the status of any other function, the following functions shall not be considered as critical or important for the purposes of paragraph 1: a) the provision to the firm of advisory services, and other services which do not form part of the investment business of the firm, including the provision of legal advice to the firm, the training of personnel of the firm, billing services and the security of the firm's premises and personnel; b) the purchase of standardised services, including market information services and the provision of price feeds. Article 14 Conditions for outsourcing critical or important operational functions or investment services or activities 1. Member States shall ensure that, when investment firms outsource critical or important operational functions or any investment services or activities, the firms remain fully responsible for discharging all of their obligations under Directive 2004/39/EC and comply, in particular, with the following conditions: a) the outsourcing must not result in the delegation by senior management of its responsibility; b) the relationship and obligations of the investment firm towards its clients under the terms of Directive 2004/39/EC must not be altered; c) the conditions with which the investment firm must comply in order to be authorised in accordance with Article 5 of Directive 2004/39/EC, and to remain so, must not be undermined; d) none of the other conditions subject to which the firm's authorisation was granted must be removed or modified. 2. Member States shall require investment firms to exercise due skill, care and	a. Obtain the repurchase agreement in writing; b. Confirm in writing the specific securities that are the subject of a repurchase transaction pursuant to such agreement at the end of the trading day on which the transaction is initiated and at the end of any other day during which other securities are substituted if the substitution results in a change to issuer, maturity date, par amount or coupon rate as specified in the previous confirmation; c. Advise the counterparty in the repurchase agreement that the Securities Investor Protection Corporation has taken the position that the provisions of the Securities Investor Protection Act of 1970 do not protect the counterparty with respect to the repurchase agreement; d. Maintain possession or control of securities that are the subject of the agreement. ii. For purpose of this paragraph (b)(4), securities are in the broker's or dealer's control only if they are in the control of the broker or dealer within the meaning of Rule 15c3-3 (c)(1), (c)3, (c)(5) or (c)(6) of this title. iii. A broker or dealer shall not be in violation of the requirement to maintain possession or control pursuant to paragraph (b)(4)(i)(D) during the trading day if: a. In the written repurchase agreement, the counterparty grants the broker or dealer the right to substitute other securities for those subject to the agreement; and iv. The provision in the written repurchase agreement governing the right, if any, to substitute is immediately preceded by the following disclosure statement, which must be prominently displayed: Control of securities. Securities under the control of a broker or dealer shall be deemed to be securities which:

European Regulatory Framework for Financial Instruments	U.S. Regulatory Framework for Financial Instruments
diligence when entering into, managing or terminating any arrangement for the outsourcing to a service provider of critical or important operational functions or of any investment services or activities. Investment firms shall in particular take the necessary steps to ensure that the following conditions are satisfied: a) the service provider must have the ability, capacity, and any authorisation required by law to perform the outsourced functions, services or activities reliably and professionally; b) the service provider must carry out the outsourced services effectively, and to this end the firm must establish methods for assessing the standard of performance of the service provider; c) the service provider must properly supervise the carrying out of the outsourced functions, and adequately manage the risks associated with the outsourcing; d) appropriate action must be taken if it appears that the service provider may not be carrying out the functions effectively and in compliance with applicable laws and regulatory requirements; e) the investment firm must retain the necessary expertise to supervise the outsourced functions effectively and manage the risks associated with the outsourcing and must supervise those functions and manage those risks; f) the service provider must disclose to the investment firm any development that may have a material impact on its ability to carry out the outsourced functions effectively and in compliance with applicable laws and regulatory requirements; g) the investment firm must be able to terminate the arrangement for outsourcing where necessary without detriment to the continuity and quality of its provision of services to clients; h) the service provider must cooperate with the competent authorities of the investment firm in connection with the outsourced activities;	5. Are represented by one or more certificates in the custody or control of a clearing corporation or other subsidiary organization of either national securities exchanges or of a registered national securities association, or of a custodian bank in accordance with a system for the central handling of securities complying with the provisions of Rule 8c-1(g) and Rule 15c2-1(g) the delivery of which certificates to the broker or dealer does not require the payment of money or value, and if the books or records of the broker or dealer identify the customers entitled to receive specified quantities or units of the securities so held for such customers collectively; or 6. Are carried for the account of any customer by a broker or dealer and are carried in a special omnibus account in the name of such broker or dealer with another broker or dealer in compliance with the requirements of section 4(b) of Regulation T under the Act, such securities being deemed to be under the control of such broker or dealer to the extent that he has instructed such carrying broker or dealer to maintain physical possession or control of them free of any charge, lien, or claim of any kind in favor of such carrying broker or dealer or any persons claiming through such carrying broker or dealer; or 7. Are the subject of bona fide items of transfer; provided that securities shall be deemed not to be the subject of bona fide items of transfer if, within 40 calendar days after they have been transmitted for transfer by the broker or dealer to the issuer or its transfer agent, new certificates conforming to the instructions of the broker or dealer have not been received by him, he has not received a written statement by the issuer or its transfer agent acknowledging the transfer instructions and the possession of the securities or he has not obtained a revalidation of a window ticket from a transfer agent with respect to the certificate delivered for transfer; or 8. Are in the custody of a foreign depository, foreign clearing agency or foreign custodian bank which the Commission upon application from a broker or dealer, a registered national securities exchange or a registered national securities association, or upon its own motion shall designate as a

European Regulatory Framework for Financial Instruments	U.S. Regulatory Framework for Financial Instruments
i) the investment firm, its auditors and the relevant competent authorities must have effective access to data related to the outsourced activities, as well as to the business premises of the service provider; and the competent authorities must be able to exercise those rights of access; j) the service provider must protect any confidential information relating to the investment firm and its clients; k) the investment firm and the service provider must establish, implement and maintain a contingency plan for disaster recovery and periodic testing of backup facilities, where that is necessary having regard to the function, service or activity that has been outsourced. 3. Member States shall require the respective rights and obligations of the investment firms and of the service provider to be clearly allocated and set out in a written agreement. 4. Member States shall provide that, where the investment firm and the service provider are members of the same group, the investment firm may, for the purposes of complying with this Article and Article 15, take into account the extent to which the firm controls the service provider or has the ability to influence its actions. 5. Member States shall require investment firms to make available on request to the competent authority all information necessary to enable the authority to supervise the compliance of the performance of the outsourced activities with the requirements of this Directive. Article 15 Service providers located in third countries 1. In addition to the requirements set out in Article 14, Member States shall require that, where an investment firm outsources the investment service of portfolio management provided to retail clients to a service provider located in a third country, that investment firm ensures that the following conditions are satisfied: a) the service provider must be authorized or registered in its home	satisfactory control location for securities; or 9. Are in the custody or control of a bank as defined in section 3(a)(6) of the Act, the delivery of which securities to the broker or dealer does not require the payment of money or value and the bank having acknowledged in writing that the securities in its custody or control are not subject to any right, charge, security interest, lien or claim of any kind in favor of a bank or any person claiming through the bank; or 10. i. Are held in or are in transit between offices of the broker or dealer; or ii. are held by a corporate subsidiary if the broker or dealer owns and exercises a majority of the voting rights of all of the voting securities of such subsidiary, assumes or guarantees all of the subsidiary's obligations and liabilities, operates the subsidiary as a branch office of the broker or dealer, and assumes full responsibility for compliance by the subsidiary and all of its associated persons with the provisions of the Federal securities laws as well as for all of the other acts of the subsidiary and such associated persons; or 11. Are held in such other locations as the Commission shall upon application from a broker or dealer find and designate to be adequate for the protection of customer securities. SEC Rules 17h-1T and 17h-2T require brokers and dealers to file risk assessment forms. Rules 17a-3, 17a-4, 17a-5, 17a-11 on Required Books, Records, and Reports as arise from the Act's section on record and reports (Section 17). FINRA Guidance 05-48 Members' Responsibilities When Outsourcing Activities to Third-Party Service Providers (http://finra.complinet.com/en/display/display.html?rbid=2403&record_id=3647&element_id=3199&highlight=outsourcing#r3647)

European Regulatory Framework for Financial Instruments	U.S. Regulatory Framework for Financial Instruments
country to provide that service and must be subject to prudential supervision; b) there must be an appropriate cooperation agreement between the competent authority of the investment firm and the supervisory authority of the service provider. 2. Where one or both of those conditions mentioned in paragraph 1 are not satisfied, an investment firm may outsource investment services to a service provider located in a third country only if the firm gives prior notification to its competent authority about the outsourcing arrangement and the competent authority does not object to that arrangement within a reasonable time following receipt of that notification. 3. Without prejudice to paragraph 2, Member States shall publish or require competent authorities to publish a statement of policy in relation to outsourcing covered by paragraph 2. That statement shall set out examples of cases where the competent authority would not, or would be likely not to, object to an outsourcing under paragraph 2 where one or both of the conditions in points (a) and (b) of paragraph 1 are not met. It shall include a clear explanation as to why the competent authority considers that in such cases outsourcing would not impair the ability of investment firms to fulfill their obligations under Article 14. 4. Nothing in this article limits the obligations on investment firms to comply with the requirements in Article 14. 5. Competent authorities shall publish a list of the supervisory authorities in third countries with which they have cooperation agreements that are appropriate for the purposes of point (b) of paragraph 1. Section 3 Safeguarding of client assets Article 16 Safeguarding of client financial instruments and funds 1. Member States shall require that, for the purposes of safeguarding clients'	

European Regulatory Framework for Financial Instruments	U.S. Regulatory Framework for Financial Instruments
rights in relation to financial instruments and funds belonging to them, investment firms comply with the following requirements:	
a) they must keep such records and accounts as are necessary to enable them at any time and without delay to distinguish assets held for one client from assets held for any other client, and from their own assets;	
b) they must maintain their records and accounts in a way that ensures their accuracy, and in particular their correspondence to the financial instruments and funds held for clients;	
c) they must conduct, on a regular basis, reconciliations between their internal accounts and records and those of any third parties by whom those assets are held;	
d) they must take the necessary steps to ensure that any client financial instruments deposited with a third party, in accordance with Article 17, are identifiable separately from the financial instruments belonging to the investment firm and from financial instruments belonging to that third party, by means of differently titled accounts on the books of the third party or other equivalent measures that achieve the same level of protection;	
e) they must take the necessary steps to ensure that client funds deposited, in accordance with Article 18, in a central bank, a credit institution or a bank authorised in a third country or a qualifying money market fund are held in an account or accounts identified separately from any accounts used to hold funds belonging to the investment firm;	
f) they must introduce adequate organisational arrangements to minimize the risk of the loss or diminution of client assets, or of rights in connection with those assets, as a result of misuse of the assets, fraud, poor administration, inadequate record-keeping or negligence.	
2. If, for reasons of the applicable law, including in particular the law relating to property or insolvency, the arrangements made by investment firms in compliance with paragraph 1 to safeguard clients' rights are not sufficient to	

European Regulatory Framework for Financial Instruments	U.S. Regulatory Framework for Financial Instruments
satisfy the requirements of Article 13(7) and (8) of Directive 2004/39/EC, Member States shall prescribe the measures that investment firms must take in order to comply with those obligations.	
3. If the applicable law of the jurisdiction in which the client funds or financial instruments are held prevents investment firms from complying with points (d) or (e) of paragraph 1, Member States shall prescribe requirements which have an equivalent effect in terms of safeguarding clients' rights.	
Article 17	
Depositing client financial instruments	
1. Member States shall permit investment firms to deposit financial instruments held by them on behalf of their clients into an account or accounts opened with a third party provided that the firms exercise all due skill, care and diligence in the selection, appointment and periodic review of the third party and of the arrangements for the holding and safekeeping of those financial instruments. In particular, Member States shall require investment firms to take into account the expertise and market reputation of the third party as well as any legal requirements or market practices related to the holding of those financial instruments that could adversely affect clients' rights.	
2. Member States shall ensure that, if the safekeeping of financial instruments for the account of another person is subject to specific regulation and supervision in a jurisdiction where an investment firm proposes to deposit client financial instruments with a third party, the investment firm does not deposit those financial instruments in that jurisdiction with a third party which is not subject to such regulation and supervision.	
3. Member States shall ensure that investment firms do not deposit financial instruments held on behalf of clients with a third party in a third country that does not regulate the holding and safekeeping of financial instruments for the account of another person unless one of the following conditions is met:	
a) the nature of the financial instruments or of the investment services connected with those instruments requires them to be deposited with a	

European Regulatory Framework for Financial Instruments	U.S. Regulatory Framework for Financial Instruments
third party in that third country; b) where the financial instruments are held on behalf of a professional client, that client requests the firm in writing to deposit them with a third party in that third country. Article 18 Depositing client funds 1. Member States shall require investment firms, on receiving any client funds, promptly to place those funds into one or more accounts opened with any of the following: a) a central bank; b) a credit institution authorised in accordance with Directive 2000/12/EC; c) a bank authorised in a third country; d) a qualifying money market fund. The first subparagraph shall not apply to a credit institution authorised under Directive 2006/48/EC of the European Parliament and of the Council of 14 June 2006 relating to the taking up and pursuit of the business of credit institutions (recast) [10] 0 in relation to deposits within the meaning of that Directive held by that institution. 2. For the purposes of point (d) of paragraph 1, and of Article 16(1)(e), a "qualifying money market fund" means a collective investment undertaking authorised under Directive 85/611/EEC, or which is subject to supervision and, if applicable, authorised by an authority under the national law of a Member State, and which satisfies the following conditions: a) its primary investment objective must be to maintain the net asset value of the undertaking either constant at par (net of earnings), or at the value of the investors' initial capital plus earnings; b) it must, with a view to achieving that primary investment objective, invest exclusively in high quality money market instruments with a maturity or residual maturity of no more than 397 days, or regular yield	

European Regulatory Framework for Financial Instruments	U.S. Regulatory Framework for Financial Instruments
adjustments consistent with such a maturity, and with a weighted average maturity of 60 days. It may also achieve this objective by investing on an ancillary basis in deposits with credit institutions; c) it must provide liquidity through same day or next day settlement. For the purposes of point (b), a money market instrument shall be considered to be of high quality if it has been awarded the highest available credit rating by each competent rating agency which has rated that instrument. An instrument that is not rated by any competent rating agency shall not be considered to be of high quality. For the purposes of the second subparagraph, a rating agency shall be considered to be competent if it issues credit ratings in respect of money market funds regularly and on a professional basis and is an eligible ECAI within the meaning of Article 81(1) of Directive 2006/48/EC. 3. Member States shall require that, where investment firms do not deposit client funds with a central bank, they exercise all due skill, care and diligence in the selection, appointment and periodic review of the credit institution, bank or money market fund where the funds are placed and the arrangements for the holding of those funds. Member States shall ensure, in particular, that investment firms take into account the expertise and market reputation of such institutions or money market funds with a view to ensuring the protection of clients' rights, as well as any legal or regulatory requirements or market practices related to the holding of client funds that could adversely affect clients' rights. Member States shall ensure that clients have the right to oppose the placement of their funds in a qualifying money market fund. Article 19 Use of client financial instruments 1. Member States shall not allow investment firms to enter into arrangements for securities financing transactions in respect of financial instruments held by them on behalf of a client, or otherwise use such financial instruments for their	

European Regulatory Framework for Financial Instruments	U.S. Regulatory Framework for Financial Instruments
own account or the account of another client of the firm, unless the following conditions are met: a) the client must have given his prior express consent to the use of the instruments on specified terms, as evidenced, in the case of a retail client, by his signature or equivalent alternative mechanism; b) the use of that client's financial instruments must be restricted to the specified terms to which the client consents. 2. Member States may not allow investment firms to enter into arrangements for securities financing transactions in respect of financial instruments which are held on behalf of a client in an omnibus account maintained by a third party, or otherwise use financial instruments held in such an account for their own account or for the account of another client unless, in addition to the conditions set out in paragraph 1, at least one of the following conditions is met: a) each client whose financial instruments are held together in an omnibus account must have given prior express consent in accordance with point (a) of paragraph 1; b) the investment firm must have in place systems and controls which ensure that only financial instruments belonging to clients who have given prior express consent in accordance with point (a) of paragraph 1 are so used. The records of the investment firm shall include details of the client on whose instructions the use of the financial instruments has been effected, as well as the number of financial instruments used belonging to each client who has given his consent, so as to enable the correct allocation of any loss. Article 20 Reports by external auditors Member States shall require investment firms to ensure that their external auditors report at least annually to the competent authority of the home Member State of the firm on the adequacy of the firm's arrangements under Articles 13(7) and (8) of	

European Regulatory Framework for Financial Instruments	U.S. Regulatory Framework for Financial Instruments
Directive 2004/39/EC and this Section.	
• Obligation for on-going supervision MiFID, Article 17 1. Member States shall ensure that the competent authorities monitor the activities of investment firms so as to assess compliance with the operating conditions provided for in Directive 2004/39/EC. Member States shall ensure that the appropriate measures are in place to enable the competent authorities to obtain the information needed to assess the compliance of investment firms with those obligations. 2. In the case of investment firms which provide only investment advice, Member States may allow the competent authority to delegate administrative, preparatory or ancillary tasks related to the regular monitoring of operational requirements, in accordance with the conditions laid down in Article 48(2).	• Obligation for on-going supervision Section 15(b) of the Securities Exchange Act. Within 6 months of the date of the granting of registration to a broker or dealer, the Commission, or upon the authorization and direction of the Commission, a registered securities association or national securities exchange of which such broker or dealer is a member, shall conduct an inspection of the broker or dealer to determine whether it is operating in conformity with the provisions of the Securities and Exchange Act and the rules and regulations thereunder. Additionally please see organizational requirements for Regulated Markets. Exchanges in the United States must be able at all the times to ensure compliance of members with rules and regulation of the SEC and exchange and enforce those rules and regulation.
• Obligation to identify Conflict of Interest MiFID, Article 18 1. Member States shall require investment firms to take all reasonable steps to identify conflicts of interest between themselves, including their managers, employees and tied agents, or any person directly or indirectly linked to them by control and their clients or between one client and another that arise in the course of providing any investment and ancillary services, or combinations thereof. 2. Where organisational or administrative arrangements made by the investment firm in accordance with Article 13(3) to manage conflicts of interest are not sufficient to ensure, with reasonable confidence, that risks of damage to client interests will be prevented, the investment firm shall clearly disclose the general nature and/or sources of conflicts of interest to the client before	• Obligation to identify Conflict of Interest Sec 10b(5) of the Securities Exchange Act General. The "manipulative and deceptive devices" prohibited by Section 10(b) of the Act and Rule 10b-5 thereunder include, among other things, the purchase or sale of a security of any issuer, on the basis of material nonpublic information about that security or issuer, in breach of a duty of trust or confidence that is owed directly, indirectly, or derivatively, to the issuer of that security or the shareholders of that issuer, or to any other person who is the source of the material nonpublic information. Rule 15c1-5 and Rule 15c1-6 of the Securities Exchange Act The term "manipulative, deceptive, or other fraudulent device or contrivance," as used in

European Regulatory Framework for Financial Instruments	U.S. Regulatory Framework for Financial Instruments
undertaking business on its behalf. **Implementing measures - MiFID level 2Directive 2006/73/EC Article 21** Member States shall ensure that, for the purposes of identifying the types of conflict of interest that arise in the course of providing investment and ancillary services or a combination thereof and whose existence may damage the interests of a client, investment firms take into account, by way of minimum criteria, the question of whether the investment firm or a relevant person, or a person directly or indirectly linked by control to the firm, is in any of the following situations, whether as a result of providing investment or ancillary services or investment activities or otherwise: 1. the firm or that person is likely to make a financial gain, or avoid a financial loss, at the expense of the client; 2. the firm or that person has an interest in the outcome of a service provided to the client or of a transaction carried out on behalf of the client, which is distinct from the client's interest in that outcome; 3. the firm or that person has a financial or other incentive to favor the interest of another client or group of clients over the interests of the client; 4. the firm or that person carries on the same business as the client; the firm or that person receives or will receive from a person other than the client an inducement in relation to a service provided to the client, in the form of monies, goods or services, other than the standard commission or fee for that service. **Conflicts of interest policy** 1. Member States shall require investment firms to establish, implement and maintain an effective conflicts of interest policy set out in writing and appropriate to the size and organization of the firm and the nature, scale and complexity of its business. Where the firm is a member of a group, the policy must also take into account any circumstances, of which the firm is or should be aware, which may give rise to a conflict of interest arising as a result of the structure and business activities of other members of the group.	Section 15(c)(1) of the Act, is hereby defined to include any act of any broker, dealer or municipal securities dealer controlled by, controlling, or under common control with, the issuer of any security, designed to effect with or for the account of a customer any transaction in, or to induce the purchase or sale by such customer of, such security unless such broker, dealer or municipal securities dealer, before entering into any contract with or for such customer for the purchase or sale of such security, discloses to such customer the existence of such control, and unless such disclosure, if not made in writing, is supplemented by the giving or sending of written disclosure at or before the completion of the transaction. The term "manipulative, deceptive, or other fraudulent device or contrivance," as used in Section 15(c)(1) of the Act, is hereby defined to include any act of any broker who is acting for a customer or for both such customer and some other person, or of any dealer or municipal securities dealer who receives or has promise of receiving a fee from a customer for advising such customer with respect to securities, designed to effect with or for the account of such customer any transaction in, or to induce the purchase or sale by such customer of, any security in the primary or secondary distribution of which such broker, dealer or municipal securities dealer is participating or is otherwise financially interested unless such broker, dealer or municipal securities dealer, at or before the completion of each such transaction gives or sends to such customer written notification of the existence of such participation or interest. Sec. 15D of the Securities Exchange Act. Securities analysts and research reports 1. Analysts protections. The Commission, or upon the authorization and direction of the Commission, a registered securities association or national securities exchange, shall have adopted, not later than 1 year after July 30, 2002, rules reasonably designed **to address conflicts of interest that can arise when securities analysts recommend equity securities in research reports** and public appearances, in order to improve the objectivity of research and provide

European Regulatory Framework for Financial Instruments	U.S. Regulatory Framework for Financial Instruments
2. The conflicts of interest policy established in accordance with paragraph 1 shall include the following content: a) it must identify, with reference to the specific investment services and activities and ancillary services carried out by or on behalf of the investment firm, the circumstances which constitute or may give rise to a conflict of interest entailing a material risk of damage to the interests of one or more clients; b) it must specify procedures to be followed and measures to be adopted in order to manage such conflicts. 3. Member States shall ensure that the procedures and measures provided for in paragraph 2(b) are designed to ensure that relevant persons engaged in different business activities involving a conflict of interest of the kind specified in paragraph 2(a) carry on those activities at a level of independence appropriate to the size and activities of the investment firm and of the group to which it belongs, and to the materiality of the risk of damage to the interests of clients. For the purposes of paragraph 2(b), the procedures to be followed and measures to be adopted shall include such of the following as are necessary and appropriate for the firm to ensure the requisite degree of independence: a) effective procedures to prevent or control the exchange of information between relevant persons engaged in activities involving a risk of a conflict of interest where the exchange of that information may harm the interests of one or more clients; b) the separate supervision of relevant persons whose principal functions involve carrying out activities on behalf of, or providing services to, clients whose interests may conflict, or who otherwise represent different interests that may conflict, including those of the firm; c) the removal of any direct link between the remuneration of relevant	investors with more useful and reliable information, including rules designed • to foster greater public confidence in securities research, and to protect the objectivity and independence of securities analysts, by - 1. restricting the prepublication clearance or approval of research reports by persons employed by the broker or dealer who are engaged in investment banking activities, or persons not directly responsible for investment research, other than legal or compliance staff; 2. limiting the supervision and compensatory evaluation of securities analysts to officials employed by the broker or dealer who are not engaged in investment banking activities; and 3. requiring that a broker or dealer and persons employed by a broker or dealer who are involved with investment banking activities may not, directly or indirectly, retaliate against or threaten to retaliate against any securities analyst employed by that broker or dealer or its affiliates as a result of an adverse, negative, or otherwise unfavorable research report that may adversely affect the present or prospective investment banking relationship of the broker or dealer with the issuer that is the subject of the research report, except that such rules may not limit the authority of a broker or dealer to discipline a securities analyst for causes other than such research report in accordance with the policies and procedures of the firm; • to define periods during which brokers or dealers who have participated, or are to participate, in a public offering of securities as underwriters or dealers should not publish or otherwise distribute research reports relating to such securities or to the issuer of such

European Regulatory Framework for Financial Instruments	U.S. Regulatory Framework for Financial Instruments
persons principally engaged in one activity and the remuneration of, or revenues generated by, different relevant persons principally engaged in another activity, where a conflict of interest may arise in relation to those activities; d) measures to prevent or limit any person from exercising inappropriate influence over the way in which a relevant person carries out investment or ancillary services or activities; e) measures to prevent or control the simultaneous or sequential involvement of a relevant person in separate investment or ancillary services or activities where such involvement may impair the proper management of conflicts of interest. If the adoption or the practice of one or more of those measures and procedures does not ensure the requisite degree of independence, Member States shall require investment firms to adopt such alternative or additional measures and procedures as are necessary and appropriate for those purposes. 4. Member States shall ensure that disclosure to clients, pursuant to Article 18(2) of Directive 2004/39/EC, is made in a durable medium and includes sufficient detail, taking into account the nature of the client, to enable that client to take an informed decision with respect to the investment or ancillary service in the context of which the conflict of interest arises. **Article 23** **Record of services or activities giving rise to detrimental conflict of interest** Member States shall require investment firms to keep and regularly to update a record of the kinds of investment or ancillary service or investment activity carried out by or on behalf of the firm in which a conflict of interest entailing a material risk of damage to the interests of one or more clients has arisen or, in the case of an ongoing service or activity,	securities; • to establish structural and institutional safeguards within registered brokers or dealers to assure that securities analysts are separated by appropriate informational partitions within the firm from the review, pressure, or oversight of those whose involvement in investment banking activities might potentially bias their judgment or supervision; and • to address such other issues as the Commission, or such association or exchange, determines appropriate. 2. Disclosure. The Commission, or upon the authorization and direction of the Commission, a registered securities association or national securities exchange, shall have adopted, not later than 1 year after July 30, 2002, rules reasonably designed to require each securities analyst to disclose in public appearances, and each registered broker or dealer to disclose in each research report, as applicable, conflicts of interest that are known or should have been known by the securities analyst or the broker or dealer, to exist at the time of the appearance or the date of distribution of the report, including • the extent to which the securities analyst has debt or equity investments in the issuer that is the subject of the appearance or research report; • whether any compensation has been received by the registered broker or dealer, or any affiliate thereof, including the securities analyst, from the issuer that is the subject of the appearance or research report, subject to such exemptions as the Commission may determine appropriate and necessary to prevent disclosure by virtue of this paragraph of material non-public information regarding specific potential future investment banking transactions of such issuer, as is appropriate in the public interest and consistent with the protection of investors;

European Regulatory Framework for Financial Instruments	U.S. Regulatory Framework for Financial Instruments
may arise. **Article 24** **Investment research** 1. For the purposes of Article 25, 'investment research' means research or other information recommending or suggesting an investment strategy, explicitly or implicitly, concerning one or several financial instruments or the issuers of financial instruments, including any opinion as to the present or future value or price of such instruments, intended for distribution channels or for the public, and in relation to which the following conditions are met: a) it is labeled or described as investment research or in similar terms, or is otherwise presented as an objective or independent explanation of the matters contained in the recommendation; b) if the recommendation in question were made by an investment firm to a client, it would not constitute the provision of investment advice for the purposes of Directive 2004/39/EC. 2. A recommendation of the type covered by Article 1(3) of Directive 2003/125/EC but relating to financial instruments as defined in Directive 2004/39/EC that does not meet the conditions set out in paragraph 1 shall be treated as a marketing communication for the purposes of Directive 2004/39/EC and Member States shall require any investment firm that produces or disseminates the recommendation to ensure that it is clearly identified as such. Additionally, Member States shall require those firms to ensure that any such recommendation contains a clear and prominent statement that (or, in the case of an oral recommendation, to the effect that) it has not been prepared in accordance with legal requirements designed to promote the independence of investment research, and that it is not subject to any prohibition on dealing ahead of the dissemination of investment research. **Article 25**	• whether an issuer, the securities of which are recommended in the appearance or research report, currently is, or during the 1-year period preceding the date of the appearance or date of distribution of the report has been, a client of the registered broker or dealer, and if so, stating the types of services provided to the issuer; • whether the securities analyst received compensation with respect to a research report, based upon (among any other factors) the investment banking revenues (either generally or specifically earned from the issuer being analyzed) of the registered broker or dealer; and • such other disclosures of conflicts of interest that are material to investors, research analysts, or the broker or dealer as the Commission, or such association or exchange, determines appropriate. **NASD Rule 2711. Research Analysts and Research Reports** **(a) Definitions** For purposes of this rule, the following terms shall be defined as provided. (1) "Equity security" has the same meaning as defined in Section 3(a)(11) of the Securities Exchange Act of 1934. (2) "Investment banking department" means any department or division, whether or not identified as such, that performs any investment banking service on behalf of a member. (3) "Investment banking services" include, without limitation, acting as an underwriter or participating in a selling group in an offering for the issuer; acting as a financial adviser in a merger or acquisition; providing venture capital, equity lines of credit, private investment, public equity transactions (PIPEs) or similar investments; or serving as placement agent for the issuer. (4) "Member of a research analyst's household" means any individual whose principal residence is the same as the research analyst's principal residence. This term does not include an unrelated person who shares the same residence as a research analyst provided that the research analyst and unrelated person are financially independent of one another.

European Regulatory Framework for Financial Instruments	U.S. Regulatory Framework for Financial Instruments
Additional organizational requirements where a firm produces and disseminates investment research 1. Member States shall require investment firms which produce, or arrange for the production of, investment research that is intended or likely to be subsequently disseminated to clients of the firm or to the public, under their own responsibility or that of a member of their group, to ensure the implementation of all the measures set out in Article 22(3) in relation to the financial analysts involved in the production of the investment research and other relevant persons whose responsibilities or business interests may conflict with the interests of the persons to whom the investment research is disseminated. 2. Member States shall require investment firms covered by paragraph 1 to have in place arrangements designed to ensure that the following conditions are satisfied: • financial analysts and other relevant persons must not undertake personal transactions or trade, other than as market makers acting in good faith and in the ordinary course of market making or in the execution of an unsolicited client order, on behalf of any other person, including the investment firm, in financial instruments to which investment research relates, or in any related financial instruments, with knowledge of the likely timing or content of that investment research which is not publicly available or available to clients and cannot readily be inferred from information that is so available, until the recipients of the investment research have had a reasonable opportunity to act on it; • in circumstances not covered by point (a), financial analysts and any other relevant persons involved in the production of investment research must not undertake personal transactions in financial instruments to which the investment research relates, or in any related financial instruments, contrary to current recommendations, except in exceptional circumstances and with the prior approval of a member of the firm's legal or compliance	(5) "Public appearance" means any participation in a conference call, seminar, forum (including an interactive electronic forum) or other public speaking activity before 15 or more persons or before one or more representatives of the media, radio, television or print media interview, or the writing of a print media article, in which a research analyst makes a recommendation or offers an opinion concerning an equity security. This term does not include a password protected Webcast, conference call or similar event with 15 or more existing customers, provided that all of the event participants previously received the most current research report or other documentation that contains the required applicable disclosures, and that the research analyst appearing at the event corrects and updates during the public appearance any disclosures in the research report that are inaccurate, misleading or no longer applicable. (6) "Research analyst" means the associated person who is primarily responsible for, and any associated person who reports directly or indirectly to such a research analyst in connection with, preparation of the substance of a research report, whether or not any such person has the job title of "research analyst." (7) "Research analyst account" means any account in which a research analyst or member of the research analyst's household has a financial interest, or over which such analyst has discretion or control, other than an investment company registered under the Investment Company Act of 1940. This term does not include a "blind trust" account that is controlled by a person other than the research analyst or member of the research analyst's household where neither the research analyst nor a member of the research analyst's household knows of the account's investments or investment transactions. (8) "Research department" means any department or division, whether or not identified as such, that is principally responsible for preparing the substance of a research report on behalf of a member. (9) "Research Report" means any written (including electronic) communication that includes an analysis of equity securities of individual companies or industries, and that provides information reasonably sufficient upon which to base an investment decision. This term does not include: (A) communications that are limited to the following:

European Regulatory Framework for Financial Instruments	U.S. Regulatory Framework for Financial Instruments

function;
 	
• the investment firms themselves, financial analysts, and other relevant persons involved in the production of the investment research must not accept inducements from those with a material interest in the subject-matter of the investment research;
 	
• the investment firms themselves, financial analysts, and other relevant persons involved in the production of the investment research must not promise issuers favorable research coverage;
 	
• issuers, relevant persons other than financial analysts, and any other persons must not before the dissemination of investment research be permitted to review a draft of the investment research for the purpose of verifying the accuracy of factual statements made in that research, or for any other purpose other than verifying compliance with the firm's legal obligations, if the draft includes a recommendation or a target price.
 	
  • For the purposes of this paragraph, 'related financial instrument' means a financial instrument the price of which is closely affected by price movements in another financial instrument which is the subject of investment research, and includes a derivative on that other financial instrument.Member States shall exempt investment firms which disseminate investment research produced by another person to the public or to clients from complying with paragraph 1 if the following criteria are met: the person that produces the investment research is not a member of the group to which the investment firm belongs;
 	
  • the investment firm does not substantially alter the recommendations within the investment research;
 	
  • the investment firm does not present the investment research as having been produced by it;
 	
  • the investment firm verifies that the producer of the research is subject to requirements equivalent to the requirements under this
	(i) discussions of broad-based indices;
	
	(ii) commentaries on economic, political or market conditions;
	
	(iii) technical analyses concerning the demand and supply for a sector, index or industry based on trading volume and price;
	
	(iv) statistical summaries of multiple companies' financial data, including listings of current ratings;
	
	(v) recommendations regarding increasing or decreasing holdings in particular industries or sectors; or
	
	(vi) notices of ratings or price target changes, provided that the member simultaneously directs the readers of the notice to the most recent research report on the subject company that includes all current applicable disclosures required by this rule and that such research report does not contain materially misleading disclosure, including disclosures that are outdated or no longer applicable;
	
	(B) the following communications, even if they include an analysis of an individual equity security and information reasonably sufficient upon which to base an investment decision:
	
	(i) any communication distributed to fewer than 15 persons;
	
	(ii) periodic reports or other communications prepared for investment company shareholders or discretionary investment account clients that discuss individual securities in the context of a fund's or account's past performance or the basis for previously made discretionary investment decisions; or
	
	(iii) internal communications that are not given to current or prospective customers; and
	
	(C) communications that constitute statutory prospectuses that are filed as part of the registration statement.
	
	(10) "Subject company" means the company whose equity securities are the subject of a research report or a public appearance.
	
	(b) Restrictions on Relationship with Research Department
	
	(1) No research analyst may be subject to the supervision or control of any employee of the member's investment banking department, and no personnel engaged in investment banking activities may have any influence or control over the compensatory evaluation of

European Regulatory Framework for Financial Instruments	U.S. Regulatory Framework for Financial Instruments
Directive in relation to the production of that research, or has established a policy setting such requirements.	a research analyst. (2) Except as provided in paragraph (b)(3), no employee of the investment banking department or any other employee of the member who is not directly responsible for investment research ("non-research personnel"), other than legal or compliance personnel, may review or approve a research report of the member before its publication. (3) Non-research personnel may review a research report before its publication as necessary only to verify the factual accuracy of information in the research report or identify any potential conflict of interest, provided that: (A) any written communication between non-research personnel and research department personnel concerning the content of a research report must be made either through authorized legal or compliance personnel of the member or in a transmission copied to such personnel; and (B) any oral communication between non-research personnel and research department personnel concerning the content of a research report must be documented and made either through authorized legal or compliance personnel acting as intermediary or in a conversation conducted in the presence of such personnel. **(c) Restrictions on Communications with the Subject Company** (1) Except as provided in paragraphs (c)(2) and (c)(3), a member may not submit a research report to the subject company before its publication. (2) A member may submit sections of such a research report to the subject company before its publication for review as necessary only to verify the factual accuracy of information in those sections, provided that: (A) the sections of the research report submitted to the subject company do not contain the research summary, the research rating or the price target; (B) a complete draft of the research report is provided to legal or compliance personnel before sections of the report are submitted to the subject company; and (C) if after submitting the sections of the research report to the subject company the research department intends to change the proposed rating or price target, it must first provide written justification to, and receive written authorization from, legal or compliance personnel for the change. The member must retain copies of any draft and the final

European Regulatory Framework for Financial Instruments	U.S. Regulatory Framework for Financial Instruments
	version of such a research report for three years following its publication.
	(3) The member may notify a subject company that the member intends to change its rating of the subject company's securities, provided that the notification occurs on the business day before the member announces the rating change, after the close of trading in the principal market of the subject company's securities.
	(4) No research analyst may participate in efforts to solicit investment banking business. Accordingly, no research analyst may, among other things, participate in any "pitches" for investment banking business to prospective investment banking clients, or have other communications with companies for the purpose of soliciting investment banking business.
	(5) A research analyst is prohibited from directly or indirectly:
	(A) participating in a road show related to an investment banking services transaction; and
	(B) engaging in any communication with a current or prospective customer in the presence of investment banking department personnel or company management about an investment banking services transaction.
	(6) Investment banking department personnel are prohibited from directly or indirectly:
	(A) directing a research analyst to engage in sales or marketing efforts related to an investment banking services transaction; and
	(B) directing a research analyst to engage in any communication with a current or prospective customer about an investment banking services transaction.
	(7) Any written or oral communication by a research analyst with a current or prospective customer or internal personnel related to an investment banking services transaction must be fair, balanced and not misleading, taking into consideration the overall context in which the communication is made.
	(d) Restrictions on Research Analyst Compensation
	(1) No member may pay any bonus, salary or other form of compensation to a research analyst that is based upon a specific investment banking services transaction.
	(2) The compensation of a research analyst who is primarily responsible for the

European Regulatory Framework for Financial Instruments	U.S. Regulatory Framework for Financial Instruments
	preparation of the substance of a research report must be reviewed and approved at least annually by a committee that reports to the member's board of directors, or when the member has no board of directors, to a senior executive officer of the member. This committee may not have representation from the member's investment banking department. The committee must consider the following factors when reviewing such a research analyst's compensation, if applicable:
	(A) the research analyst's individual performance, including the analyst's productivity and the quality of the analyst's research;
	(B) the correlation between the research analyst's recommendations and the stock price performance; and
	(C) the overall ratings received from clients, sales force, and peers independent of the member's investment banking department, and other independent ratings services.
	The committee may not consider as a factor in reviewing and approving such a research analyst's compensation his or her contributions to the member's investment banking business. The committee must document the basis upon which each such research analyst's compensation was established. The annual attestation required by Rule 2711(i) must certify that the committee reviewed and approved each such research analyst's compensation and documented the basis upon which this compensation was established.
	(e) Prohibition of Promise of Favorable Research
	No member may directly or indirectly offer favorable research, a specific rating or a specific price target, or threaten to change research, a rating or a price target, to a company as consideration or inducement for the receipt of business or compensation.
	(f) Restrictions on Publishing Research Reports and Public Appearances; Termination of Coverage
	(1) No member may publish or otherwise distribute a research report and no research analyst may make a public appearance regarding a subject company for which the member acted as manager or co-manager of:
	(A) an initial public offering, for 40 calendar days following the date of the offering; or
	(B) a secondary offering, for 10 calendar days following the date of the offering; provided that:

European Regulatory Framework for Financial Instruments	U.S. Regulatory Framework for Financial Instruments
	(i) paragraphs (f)(1)(A) and (f)(1)(B) will not prevent a member from publishing or otherwise distributing a research report, or prevent a research analyst from making a public appearance, concerning the effects of significant news or a significant event on the subject company within such 40- and 10-day periods, and provided further that legal or compliance personnel authorize publication of that research report before it is issued or authorize the public appearance before it is made; and

(ii) paragraph (f)(1)(B) will not prevent a member from publishing or otherwise distributing a research report pursuant to SEC Rule 139 regarding a subject company with "actively-traded securities," as defined in Regulation M, 17 CFR 242.101(c)(1), and will not prevent a research analyst from making a public appearance concerning such a company.

(2) No member that has agreed to participate or is participating as an underwriter or dealer (other than as manager or co-manager) of an issuer's initial public offering may publish or otherwise distribute a research report or make a public appearance regarding that issuer for 25 calendar days after the date of the offering.

(3) For purposes of paragraphs (f)(1) and (f)(2), the term "date of the offering" refers to the later of the effective date of the registration statement or the first date on which the security was bona fide offered to the public.

(4) No member that has acted as a manager or co-manager of a securities offering may publish or otherwise distribute a research report or make a public appearance concerning a subject company 15 days prior to and after the expiration, waiver or termination of a lock-up agreement or any other agreement that the member has entered into with a subject company or its shareholders that restricts or prohibits the sale of securities held by the subject company or its shareholders after the completion of a securities offering. This paragraph will not prevent a member from publishing or otherwise distributing a research report concerning the effects of significant news or a significant event on the subject company within such period, provided legal or compliance personnel authorize publication of that research report before it is issued. In addition, this paragraph shall not apply to the publication or distribution of a research report pursuant to SEC Rule 139 regarding a subject company with "actively traded securities," as defined in Regulation M, 17 CFR 242.101(c)(1), or to a public appearance concerning such a subject company.

(5) If a member intends to terminate its research coverage of a subject company, notice |

European Regulatory Framework for Financial Instruments	U.S. Regulatory Framework for Financial Instruments
	of this termination must be made. The member must make available a final research report on the subject company using the means of dissemination equivalent to those it ordinarily uses to provide the customer with its research reports on the subject company. The report must be comparable in scope and detail to prior research reports and must include a final recommendation or rating, unless it is impracticable for the member to produce a comparable report (e.g., if the research analyst covering the subject company or sector has left the member or if the member terminates coverage of the industry or sector). If it is impracticable to produce a final recommendation or rating, the final research report must disclose the member's rationale for the decision to terminate coverage.

(g) Restrictions on Personal Trading by Research Analysts

(1) No research analyst account may purchase or receive any securities before the issuer's initial public offering if the issuer is principally engaged in the same types of business as companies that the research analyst follows.

(2) No research analyst account may purchase or sell any security issued by a company that the research analyst follows, or any option on or derivative of such security, for a period beginning 30 calendar days before and ending five calendar days after the publication of a research report concerning the company or a change in a rating or price target of the company's securities; provided that:

(A) a member may permit a research analyst account to sell securities held by the account that are issued by a company that the research analyst follows, within 30 calendar days after the research analyst began following the company for the member;

(B) a member may permit a research analyst account to purchase or sell any security issued by a subject company within 30 calendar days before the publication of a research report or change in the rating or price target of the subject company's securities due to significant news or a significant event concerning the subject company, provided that legal or compliance personnel pre-approve the research report and any change in the rating or price target.

(3) No research analyst account may purchase or sell any security or any option on or derivative of such security in a manner inconsistent with the research analyst's recommendation as reflected in the most recent research report published by the |

European Regulatory Framework for Financial Instruments	U.S. Regulatory Framework for Financial Instruments
	member.
	(4) Legal or compliance personnel may authorize a transaction otherwise prohibited by paragraphs (g)(2) and (g)(3) based upon an unanticipated significant change in the personal financial circumstances of the beneficial owner of the research analyst account, provided that:
	(A) legal or compliance personnel authorize the transaction before it is entered;
	(B) each exception is granted in compliance with policies and procedures adopted by the member that are reasonably designed to ensure that these transactions do not create a conflict of interest between the professional responsibilities of the research analyst and the personal trading activities of a research analyst account; and
	(C) the member maintains written records concerning each transaction and the justification for permitting the transaction for three years following the date on which the transaction is approved.
	(5) The prohibitions in paragraphs (g)(1) through (g)(3) do not apply to a purchase or sale of the securities of:
	(A) any registered diversified investment company as defined under Section (5)(b)(1) of the Investment Company Act of 1940; or
	(B) any other investment fund over which neither the research analyst nor a member of the research analyst's household has any investment discretion or control, provided that:
	(i) the research analyst accounts collectively own interests representing no more than 1% of the assets of the fund;
	(ii) the fund invests no more than 20% of its assets in securities of issuers principally engaged in the same types of business as companies that the research analyst follows; and
	(iii) if the investment fund distributes securities in kind to the research analyst or household member before the issuer's initial public offering, the research analyst or household member must either divest those securities immediately or the research analyst must refrain from participating in the preparation of research reports concerning that issuer.
	(6) Legal or compliance personnel of the member shall pre-approve all transactions of

European Regulatory Framework for Financial Instruments	U.S. Regulatory Framework for Financial Instruments
	persons who oversee research analysts to the extent such transactions involve equity securities of subject companies covered by the research analysts that they oversee. This pre-approval requirement shall apply to all persons, such as the director of research, supervisory analyst, or member of a committee, who have direct influence or control with respect to the preparation of the substance of research reports or establishing or changing a rating or price target of a subject company's equity securities.
	(h) Disclosure Requirements
	(1) Ownership and Material Conflicts of Interest
	A member must disclose in research reports and a research analyst must disclose in public appearances:
	(A) if the research analyst or a member of the research analyst's household has a financial interest in the securities of the subject company, and the nature of the financial interest (including, without limitation, whether it consists of any option, right, warrant, future, long or short position);
	(B) if, as of the end of the month immediately preceding the date of publication of the research report or the public appearance (or the end of the second most recent month if the publication date is less than 10 calendar days after the end of the most recent month), the member or its affiliates beneficially own 1% or more of any class of common equity securities of the subject company. Computation of beneficial ownership of securities must be based upon the same standards used to compute ownership for purposes of the reporting requirements under Section 13(d) of the Securities Exchange Act of 1934;
	(C) any other actual, material conflict of interest of the research analyst or member of which the research analyst knows or has reason to know at the time of publication of the research report or at the time of the public appearance.
	(2) Receipt of Compensation
	(A) A member must disclose in research reports:
	(i) if the research analyst received compensation:
	a. based upon (among other factors) the member's investment banking revenues; or
	b. from the subject company in the past 12 months.

European Regulatory Framework for Financial Instruments	U.S. Regulatory Framework for Financial Instruments
	(ii) the member or affiliate:
	a. managed or co-managed a public offering of securities for the subject company in the past 12 months;
	b. received compensation for investment banking services from the subject company in the past 12 months; or
	c. expects to receive or intends to seek compensation for investment banking services from the subject company in the next 3 months.
	(iii) if (1) as of the end of the month immediately preceding the date of publication of the research report (or the end of the second most recent month if the publication date is less than 30 calendar days after the end of the most recent month) or (2) to the extent the research analyst or an employee of the member with the ability to influence the substance of the research knows:
	a. the member received any compensation for products or services other than investment banking services from the subject company in the past 12 months; or
	b. the subject company currently is, or during the 12-month period preceding the date of distribution of the research report was, a client of the member. In such cases, the member also must disclose the types of services provided to the subject company. For purposes of this Rule 2711(h)(2), the types of services provided to the subject company shall be described as investment banking services, non-investment banking securities-related services, and non-securities services.
	(iv) if, to the extent the research analyst or an employee of the member with the ability to influence the substance of the research report knows an affiliate of the member received any compensation for products or services other than investment banking services from the subject company in the past 12 months.
	(v) if, to the extent the research analyst or member has reason to know, an affiliate of the member received any compensation for products or services other than investment banking services from the subject company in the past 12 months.
	a. This requirement will be deemed satisfied if such compensation is disclosed in research reports within 30 days after completion of the last calendar quarter, provided that the member has taken steps reasonably designed to identify any such compensation

European Regulatory Framework for Financial Instruments	U.S. Regulatory Framework for Financial Instruments
	during that calendar quarter. This requirement shall not apply to any subject company as to which the member initiated coverage since the beginning of the current calendar quarter.

b. The research analyst and the member will be presumed not to have reason to know whether an affiliate received any compensation for products or services other than investment banking services from the subject company in the past 12 months if the member maintains and enforces policies and procedures reasonably designed to prevent the research analysts and employees of the member with the ability to influence the substance of research reports from, directly or indirectly, receiving information from the affiliate concerning whether the affiliate received such compensation.

(vi) For the purposes of this Rule 2711(h)(2), an employee of the member with the ability to influence the substance of the research report is an employee who, in the ordinary course of that person's duties, has the authority to review the particular research report and to change that research report prior to publication.

(B) A research analyst must disclose in public appearances:

(i) if, to the extent the research analyst knows or has reason to know, the member or any affiliate received any compensation from the subject company in the past 12 months;

(ii) if the research analyst received any compensation from the subject company in the past 12 months; or

(iii) if, to the extent the research analyst knows or has reason to know, the subject company currently is, or during the 12-month period preceding the date of distribution of the research report, was, a client of the member. In such cases, the research analyst also must disclose the types of services provided to the subject company, if known by the research analyst.

(C) A member or research analyst will not be required to make a disclosure required by paragraphs (h)(2)(A)(iii)(b) and (c), (h)(2)(A)(iii)(b), or (h)(2)(B)(i) and (iii) to the extent such disclosure would reveal material non-public information regarding specific potential future investment banking transactions of the subject company.

(3) Position as Officer or Director

A member must disclose in research reports and a research analyst must disclose in |

European Regulatory Framework for Financial Instruments	U.S. Regulatory Framework for Financial Instruments
	public appearances if the research analyst or a member of the research analyst's household serves as an officer, director or advisory board member of the subject company.
	(4) Meaning of Ratings
	If a research report contains a rating, the member must define in the research report the meaning of each rating used by the member in its rating system. The definition of each rating must be consistent with its plain meaning.
	(5) Distribution of Ratings
	(A) Regardless of the rating system that a member employs, a member must disclose in each research report the percentage of all securities rated by the member to which the member would assign a "buy," "hold/neutral," or "sell" rating.
	(B) In each research report, the member must disclose the percentage of subject companies within each of these three categories for whom the member has provided investment banking services within the previous twelve months.
	(C) The information that is disclosed under paragraphs (h)(5)(A) and (h)(5)(B) must be current as of the end of the most recent calendar quarter (or the second most recent calendar quarter if the publication date is less than 15 calendar days after the most recent calendar quarter) and must reflect the distribution of the most recent ratings issued by the member for all subject companies, unless the most recent rating was issued more than 12 months ago.
	(D) The requirements of paragraph (h)(5) shall not apply to any research report that does not contain a rating.
	(6) Price Chart
	If a research report contains either a rating or a price target, and the member has assigned a rating or price target to the subject company's securities rating for at least one year, the research report must include a line graph of the security's daily closing prices for the period that the member has assigned any rating or price target or for a three-year period, whichever is shorter. The line graph must:
	(A) indicate the dates on which the member assigned or changed each rating or price target;

European Regulatory Framework for Financial Instruments	U.S. Regulatory Framework for Financial Instruments
	(B) depict each rating and price target assigned or changed on those dates; and
	(C) be current as of the end of the most recent calendar quarter (or the second most recent calendar quarter if the publication date is less than 15 calendar days after the most recent calendar quarter).
	(7) Price Targets
	If a research report contains a price target, the member must disclose in the research report the valuation methods used to determine the price target. Price targets must have a reasonable basis and must be accompanied by a disclosure concerning the risks that may impede achievement of the price target.
	(8) Market Making
	A member must disclose in research reports if it was making a market in the subject company's securities at the time that the research report was published.
	(9) Disclosure Required by Other Provisions
	In addition to the disclosure required by this rule, members and research analysts must provide disclosure in research reports and public appearances that is required by applicable law or regulation, including FINRA Rule 2210 and the antifraud provisions of the federal securities laws.
	(10) Prominence of Disclosure
	The disclosures required by this paragraph (h) must be presented on the front page of research reports or the front page must refer to the page on which disclosures are found. Disclosures and references to disclosures must be clear, comprehensive and prominent.
	(11) Disclosures in Research Reports Covering Six or More Companies
	When a member distributes a research report covering six or more subject companies (a "compendium report"), for purposes of the disclosures required in paragraph (h), the compendium report may direct the reader in a clear manner as to where they may obtain applicable current disclosures. Electronic compendium reports may include a hyperlink to the required disclosures. Paper-based compendium reports must provide either a toll-free number to call or a postal address to write for the required disclosures and may also include a web address of the member where the disclosures can be found.

European Regulatory Framework for Financial Instruments	U.S. Regulatory Framework for Financial Instruments
	(12) Records of Public Appearances Members must maintain records of public appearances by research analysts sufficient to demonstrate compliance by those research analysts with the applicable disclosure requirements under paragraph (h) of this Rule. Such records must be maintained for three years from the date of the public appearance. **(13) Third-Party Research Reports** (A) Subject to paragraph (h)(13)(B) of this Rule, if a member distributes or makes available any third-party research report, the member must accompany the research report with, or provide a web address that directs the recipient to, the current applicable disclosures, as they pertain to the member, required by paragraphs (h)(1)(B), (h)(1)(C), (h)(2)(A)(ii) and (h)(8) of this Rule. Members must establish written supervisory policies and procedures reasonably designed to ensure the completeness and accuracy of all applicable disclosures. (B) The requirements of paragraph (h)(13)(A) of this Rule shall not apply to independent third-party research reports made available by a member to its customers: (i) upon request; (ii) in connection with a solicited order in which a registered representative has informed the customer, during the solicitation, of the availability of independent research on the solicited equity security, and the customer requests such independent research; or (iii) through a member-maintained web site. (C) Subject to paragraph (h)(13)(D) of this Rule, a registered principal (or supervisory analyst approved pursuant to Rule 344 of the New York Stock Exchange) must approve by signature or initial all third-party research reports distributed by a member. The approval of third-party research shall be based on a review by the designated principal (or supervisory analyst approved pursuant to NYSE Rule 344) to determine that the content of the research report, pursuant to Rule 2210(d)(1)(B), contains no untrue statement of material fact or is otherwise not false or misleading. For the purposes of this Rule only, a member's obligation to review a third-party research report pursuant to Rule 2210(d)(1)(B) extends to any untrue statement of material fact or any false or misleading information that:

European Regulatory Framework for Financial Instruments	U.S. Regulatory Framework for Financial Instruments
	a. should be known from reading the report; or
	b. is known based on information otherwise possessed by the member.
	(D) The requirements of paragraph (h)(13)(C) of this Rule shall not apply to independent third-party research reports distributed or made available by a member.
	(E) For the purposes of this Rule, "third-party research report" shall mean a research report that is produced by a person or entity other than the member and "independent third-party research report" shall mean a third-party research report, in respect of which the person or entity producing the report:
	(i) has no affiliation or business or contractual relationship with the distributing member or that member's affiliates that is reasonably likely to inform the content of its research reports; and
	(ii) makes content determinations without any input from the distributing member or that member's affiliates.
	(i) Supervisory Procedures
	Each member subject to this rule must adopt and implement written supervisory procedures reasonably designed to ensure that the member and its employees comply with the provisions of this rule (including the attestation requirements of Rule 2711(d)(2)), and a senior officer of such a member must attest annually to NASD by April 1 of each year that it has adopted and implemented those procedures.
	(j) Prohibition of Retaliation Against Research Analysts
	No member and no employee of a member who is involved with the member's investment banking activities may, directly or indirectly, retaliate against or threaten to retaliate against any research analyst employed by the member or its affiliates as a result of an adverse, negative, or otherwise unfavorable research report or public appearance written or made by the research analyst that may adversely affect the member's present or prospective investment banking relationship with the subject company of a research report. This prohibition shall not limit a member's authority to discipline or terminate a research analyst, in accordance with the member's policies and procedures, for any cause other than the writing of such an unfavorable research report or the making of such an unfavorable public appearance.

European Regulatory Framework for Financial Instruments	U.S. Regulatory Framework for Financial Instruments
	(k) Exceptions for Small Firms The provisions of paragraph (b) shall not apply to members that over the previous three years, on average per year, have participated in 10 or fewer investment banking services transactions as manager or co-manager and generated $5 million or less in gross investment banking services revenues from those transactions. For purposes of this paragraph (k), the term "investment banking services transactions" includes the underwriting of both corporate debt and equity securities but not municipal securities. Members that qualify for this exemption must maintain records for three years of any communication that, but for this exemption, would be subject to paragraph (b) of this Rule.
• Conduct of business obligations when providing investment services to clients MiFID, level 1, Article 19. 1. Member States shall require that, when providing investment services and/or, where appropriate, ancillary services to clients, an investment firm act honestly, fairly and professionally in accordance with the best interests of its clients and comply, in particular, with the principles set out in paragraphs 2 to 8 bellow. 2. All information, including marketing communications, addressed by the investment firm to clients or potential clients shall be fair, clear and not misleading. Marketing communications shall be clearly identifiable as such. 3. Appropriate information shall be provided in a comprehensible form to clients or potential clients about: • the investment firm and its services, • financial instruments and proposed investment strategies; this should include appropriate guidance on and warnings of the risks	• Conduct of Business Obligations **NASD Rule IM-2310-2. Fair Dealing with Customers** (a) (1) Implicit in all member and registered representative relationships with customers and others is the fundamental **responsibility for fair dealing.** Sales efforts must therefore be undertaken only on a basis that can be judged as being within the ethical standards of the Association's Rules, with particular emphasis on the requirement to deal fairly with the public. (2) This does not mean that legitimate sales efforts in the securities business are to be discouraged by requirements which do not take into account the variety of circumstances which can enter into the member-customer relationship. It does mean, however, **that sales efforts must be judged on the basis of whether they can be reasonably said to represent fair treatment for the persons to whom the sales efforts are directed,** rather than on the argument that they result in profits to customers. (b) District Business Conduct Committees and the Board of Governors have interpreted the Rules, taken disciplinary action and imposed penalties in many

European Regulatory Framework for Financial Instruments	U.S. Regulatory Framework for Financial Instruments
associated with investments in those instruments or in respect of particular investment strategies, • execution venues, and • costs and associated charges so that they are reasonably able to understand the nature and risks of the investment service and of the specific type of financial instrument that is being offered and, consequently, to take investment decisions on an informed basis. This information may be provided in a standardized format. 4. When **providing investment advice or portfolio management the investment firm shall obtain the necessary information regarding the client's or potential client's knowledge and experience in the investment field** relevant to the specific type of product or service, **his financial situation and his investment objectives** so as to enable the firm to recommend to the client or potential client the investment services and financial instruments that are **suitable** for him. 5. Member States shall ensure that investment firms, when providing investment services other than **investment advice or portfolio management (for example simple execution)**, ask the client or potential client **to provide information regarding his knowledge and experience in the investment field relevant to the specific type of product or service offered or demanded so as to enable the investment firm to assess whether the investment service or product envisaged is appropriate for the client.** In case the investment firm considers, on the basis of the information received under the previous subparagraph, that the product or service is not appropriate to the client or potential client, the investment firm shall warn the client or potential client. This warning may be provided in a standardized format. In cases where the client or potential client elects not to provide the information referred to under the first subparagraph, or where he provides insufficient information regarding his knowledge and experience, the investment firm shall warn the client or potential client that such a decision will not allow the firm to determine whether the service or product envisaged is appropriate for him.	situations where members' sales efforts have exceeded the reasonable grounds of fair dealing. Some practices that have resulted in disciplinary action and that clearly violate this responsibility for fair dealing are set forth below, as a guide to members: (1) **Recommending Speculative Low-Priced Securities** Recommending speculative low-priced securities to customers without knowledge of or attempt to obtain information concerning the customers' other securities holdings, their financial situation and other necessary data. The principle here is that this practice, by its very nature, involves a high probability that the recommendation will not be suitable for at least some of the persons solicited. This has particular application to high pressure telephone sales campaigns. (2) **Excessive Trading Activity** Excessive activity in a customer's account, often referred to as "churning" or "overtrading." There are no specific standards to measure excessiveness of activity in customer accounts because this must be related to the objectives and financial situation of the customer involved. (3) **Trading in Mutual Fund Shares** Trading in mutual fund shares, particularly on a short-term basis. It is clear that normally these securities are not proper trading vehicles and such activity on its face may raise the question of Rule violation. (4) **Fraudulent Activity** (A) Numerous instances of fraudulent conduct have been acted upon by the Association and have resulted in penalties against members. Among some of these activities are: (i) **Fictitious Accounts** Establishment of fictitious accounts in order to execute transactions which otherwise would be prohibited, such as the purchase of hot issues, or to disguise transactions which are against firm policy. (ii) **Discretionary Accounts**

European Regulatory Framework for Financial Instruments	U.S. Regulatory Framework for Financial Instruments
6. This warning may be provided in a standardized format. Member States shall allow investment firms when providing investment services that only **consist of execution and/or the reception and transmission of client orders** with or without ancillary services to provide those investment services to their clients **without the need to obtain the information or make the determination provided for in paragraph 5 where all the following conditions are met:** • the above services relate to shares admitted to trading on a Regulated Market or in an equivalent third country market, money market instruments, bonds or other forms of securitized debt (excluding those bonds or securitized debt that embed a derivative), UCITS **and other non-complex financial instruments;** • the service is provided at the initiative of the client or potential client; • the client or potential **client has been clearly informed that in the provision of this service the investment firm is not required to assess the suitability of the instrument** or service provided or offered and that therefore he does not benefit from the corresponding protection of the relevant conduct of business rules; this warning may be provided in a standardized format; • the investment firm complies with its obligations under Article 18 (conflict of interest); 7. The investment firm shall establish a record that includes the document or documents agreed between the firm and the client that set out the rights and obligations of the parties, and the other terms on which the firm will provide services to the client. The rights and duties of the parties to the contract may be incorporated by reference to other documents or legal texts. 8. The client must receive from the investment firm adequate reports on the	Transactions in discretionary accounts in excess of or without actual authority from customers. (iii) **Unauthorized Transactions** Causing the execution of transactions which are unauthorized by customers or the sending of confirmations in order to cause customers to accept transactions not actually agreed upon. (iv) **Misuse of Customers' Funds or Securities** Unauthorized use or borrowing of customers' funds or securities. (B) In addition, other fraudulent activities, such as forgery, non-disclosure or misstatement of material facts, manipulations and various deceptions, have been found in violation of Association Rules. These same activities are also subject to the civil and criminal laws and sanctions of federal and state governments. (5) **Recommending Purchases Beyond Customer Capability** Recommending the purchase of securities or the continuing purchase of securities in amounts which are inconsistent with the reasonable expectation that the customer has the financial ability to meet such a commitment. (c) While most members are fully aware of the fairness required in dealing with customers, it is anticipated that the practices enumerated in paragraph (b), which are not all inclusive, will be of future assistance in the training and education of new personnel. (d) The Commission has also recognized that **brokers and dealers have an obligation of fair dealing** in actions under the general **anti-fraud provisions of the federal securities laws.** The Commission bases this obligation on the principle that when a securities dealer opens his business he is, in effect, representing that the will deal fairly with the public. Certain of the Commission's cases on fair dealing involve practices not covered in the foregoing illustrations. Usually, any breach of the obligation of fair dealing as determined by the Commission under the anti-fraud provisions of the securities laws could be considered a violation of the Association's Rules. (e) **Fair Dealing with Customers with Regard to Derivative Products or New**

European Regulatory Framework for Financial Instruments	U.S. Regulatory Framework for Financial Instruments

service provided to its clients. These reports shall include, where applicable, the costs associated with the transactions and services undertaken on behalf of the client.
 	
9. In cases where an investment service is offered as part of a financial product which is already subject to other provisions of Community legislation or common European standards related to credit institutions and consumer credits with respect to risk assessment of clients and/or information requirements, this service shall not be additionally subject to the obligations set out in this Article.
 	
Relevant provisions from the implementing regulation
    MiFID level 2, directive 2006/73/EC, Article 26
 	
Member States shall ensure that investment firms are not regarded as acting honestly, fairly and professionally in accordance with the best interests of a client if, in relation to the provision of an investment or ancillary service to the client, they pay or are paid any fee or commission, or provide or are provided with any non-monetary benefit, other than the following:
 	
1. a fee, commission or non-monetary benefit paid or provided to or by the client or a person on behalf of the client;
 	
2. a fee, commission or non-monetary benefit paid or provided to or by a third party or a person acting on behalf of a third party, where the following conditions are satisfied:
 	
    i.   the existence, nature and amount of the fee, commission or benefit, or, where the amount cannot be ascertained, the method of calculating that amount, must be clearly disclosed to the client, in a manner that is comprehensive, accurate and understandable, prior to the provision of the relevant investment or ancillary service;
 	
    ii. the payment of the fee or commission, or the provision of the non-monetary benefit must be designed to enhance the quality of the
	Financial Products
	The Board emphasizes members' obligations for fair dealing with customers when making recommendations or accepting orders for new financial products. **As new products are introduced from time to time, it is important that members make every effort to familiarize themselves with each customer's financial situation, trading experience, and ability to meet the risks involved with such products** and to make every effort to make customers aware of the pertinent information regarding the products. Members must follow specific guidelines, set forth below, for qualifying the accounts to trade the products and for supervising the accounts thereafter.
	
	(1) **Security Futures**
	Members must comply with the Rules, regulations and procedures applicable to security futures contained in Rule 2865.
	
	(2) **Index Warrants**
	Members are obliged to comply with the Rules, regulations and procedures applicable to index warrants and foreign currency warrants contained in the Rule 2840 Series.
	
	(3) **Hybrid Securities and Selected Equity-Linked Debt Securities ("SEEDS") Listed on Nasdaq as Global Market Securities**
	With respect to Hybrid Securities and Selected Equity-Linked Debt Securities ("SEEDS") that have been listed as Nasdaq Global Market Securities, members are obliged to comply with any Rules, regulations, or procedures applicable to such securities.
	
	Recommendations to Customers (Suitability)
	
	NASD Rule 2310
	1. **In recommending to a customer the purchase, sale or exchange of any security, a member shall have reasonable grounds for believing that the**

European Regulatory Framework for Financial Instruments	U.S. Regulatory Framework for Financial Instruments
relevant service to the client and not impair compliance with the firm's duty to act in the best interests of the client; 3. proper fees which enable or are necessary for the provision of investment services, such as custody costs, settlement and exchange fees, regulatory levies or legal fees, and which, by their nature, cannot give rise to conflicts with the firm's duties to act honestly, fairly and professionally in accordance with the best interests of its clients. Member States shall permit an investment firm, for the purposes of point (2)(i), to disclose the essential terms of the arrangements relating to the fee, commission or non-monetary benefit in summary form, provided that it undertakes to disclose further details at the request of the client and provided that it honors that undertaking. Article 27, **Conditions with which information must comply in order to be fair, clear and not misleading** 1. Member States shall **require investment firms to ensure that all information they address to, or disseminate in such a way that it is likely to be received by, retail clients or potential retail clients, including marketing communications**, satisfies the following conditions (paragraphs 2 to 8). 2. The information referred to in paragraph 1 shall include the name of the investment firm. It shall be accurate and in particular shall not emphasise any potential benefits of an investment service or financial instrument without also giving a fair and prominent indication of any relevant risks. It shall be sufficient for, and presented in a way that is likely to be understood by, the average member of the group to whom it is directed, or by whom it is likely to be received. It shall not disguise, diminish or obscure important items, statements or warnings. 3. Where the information compares investment or ancillary services, financial instruments, or persons providing investment or ancillary services, the following conditions shall be satisfied:	**recommendation is suitable** for such customer upon the basis of the facts, if any, disclosed by such customer as to his other security holdings and as to his financial situation and needs. 2. Prior to the execution of a transaction **recommended to a non-institutional customer**, other than transactions with customers where investments are limited to money market mutual funds, a member shall make reasonable efforts to obtain information concerning: • the customer's financial status; • the customer's tax status; • the customer's investment objectives; and • such other information used or considered to be reasonable by such member or registered representative in making recommendations to the customer. 3. For purposes of this Rule, the term "non "non-institutional customer" shall mean a customer that does not qualify as an "institutional account" under Rule 3110 **IM-2310-3. Suitability Obligations to Institutional Customers** Rule 2310(a) requires that, In recommending to a customer the purchase, sale or exchange of any security, a member shall have reasonable grounds for believing that the recommendation is suitable for such customer upon the basis of the facts, if any, disclosed by such customer as to his other security holdings and as to his financial situation and needs. This interpretation concerns only the manner in which a member determines that a recommendation is suitable for a particular institutional customer. The manner in which a member fulfills this suitability obligation will vary depending on the nature of the customer and the specific transaction. Accordingly, this interpretation deals only with guidance

European Regulatory Framework for Financial Instruments	U.S. Regulatory Framework for Financial Instruments
a) the comparison must be meaningful and presented in a fair and balanced way; b) the sources of the information used for the comparison must be specified; c) the key facts and assumptions used to make the comparison must be included. 4. Where the information contains an indication of past performance of a financial instrument, a financial index or an investment service, the following conditions shall be satisfied: a) that indication must not be the most prominent feature of the communication; b) the information must include appropriate performance information which covers the immediately preceding 5 years, or the whole period for which the financial instrument has been offered, the financial index has been established, or the investment service has been provided if less than five years, or such longer period as the firm may decide, and in every case that performance information must be based on complete 12-month periods; c) the reference period and the source of information must be clearly stated; d) the information must contain a prominent warning that the figures refer to the past and that past performance is not a reliable indicator of future results; e) where the indication relies on figures denominated in a currency other than that of the Member State in which the retail client or potential retail client is resident, the currency must be clearly stated, together with a warning that the return may increase or decrease as a result of currency fluctuations; f) where the indication is based on gross performance, the effect of commissions, fees or other charges must be disclosed. 5. Where the information includes or refers to simulated past performance, it must relate to a financial instrument or a financial index, and the following conditions shall be satisfied: a) the simulated past performance must be based on the actual past	regarding how a member may fulfill such "customer-specific suitability obligations" under Rule 2310. While it is difficult to define in advance the scope of a member's suitability obligation with respect to a specific institutional customer transaction recommended by a member, the Board (NASD Board) has identified certain factors which may be relevant when considering compliance with Rule 2310. These factors are not intended to be requirements or the only factors to be considered but are offered merely as guidance in determining the scope of a member's suitability obligations. **Considerations Regarding the Scope of Members' Obligations to Institutional Customers** The two most important considerations in determining the scope of a member's suitability obligations in making recommendations to an institutional customer **are the customer's capability to evaluate investment risk independently and the extent to which the customer is exercising independent judgment in evaluating a member's recommendation.** A member must determine, based on the information available to it, the customer's capability to evaluate investment risk. In some cases, the member may conclude that the customer is not capable of making independent investment decisions in general. In other cases, the institutional customer may have general capability, but may not be able to understand a particular type of instrument or its risk. This is more likely to arise with relatively new types of instruments, or those with significantly different risk or volatility characteristics than other investments generally made by the institution. If a customer is either generally not capable of evaluating investment risk or lacks sufficient capability to evaluate the particular product, the scope of a member's customer-specific obligations under the suitability rule would not be diminished by the fact that the member was dealing with an institutional customer. On the other hand, the fact that a customer initially needed help understanding a potential investment need not necessarily imply that the customer did not ultimately develop an understanding and make an independent investment decision. A member may conclude that a customer is exercising independent judgment if the customer's investment decision will be based on its own independent assessment of the

European Regulatory Framework for Financial Instruments	U.S. Regulatory Framework for Financial Instruments
performance of one or more financial instruments or financial indices which are the same as, or underlie, the financial instrument concerned; b) in respect of the actual past performance referred to in point (a), the conditions set out in points (a) to (c), (e) and (f) of paragraph 4 must be complied with; c) the information must contain a prominent warning that the figures refer to simulated past performance and that past performance is not a reliable indicator of future performance. 6. Where the information contains information on future performance, the following conditions shall be satisfied: a) the information must not be based on or refer to simulated past performance; b) it must be based on reasonable assumptions supported by objective data; c) where the information is based on gross performance, the effect of commissions, fees or other charges must be disclosed; d) it must contain a prominent warning that such forecasts are not a reliable indicator of future performance. 7. Where the information refers to a particular tax treatment, it shall prominently state that the tax treatment depends on the individual circumstances of each client and may be subject to change in the future. 8. The information shall not use the name of any competent authority in such a way that would indicate or suggest endorsement or approval by that authority of the products or services of the investment firm. **Article 28, Information concerning client categorization** 1. Member States shall ensure that investment firms notify new clients, and existing clients that the investment firm has newly categorised as required by Directive 2004/39/EC, of their categorization as a retail client, a professional	opportunities and risks presented by a potential investment, market factors and other investment considerations. Where the broker-dealer has reasonable grounds for concluding that the institutional customer is making independent investment decisions and is capable of independently evaluating investment risk, then a member's obligation to determine that a recommendation is suitable for a particular customer is fulfilled.[3] Where a customer has delegated decision-making authority to an agent, such as an investment advisor or a bank trust department, this interpretation shall be applied to the agent. A determination of capability to evaluate investment risk independently will depend on an examination of the customer's capability to make its own investment decisions, including the resources available to the customer to make informed decisions. Relevant considerations could include: • the use of one or more consultants, investment advisers or bank trust departments; • the general level of experience of the institutional customer in financial markets and specific experience with the type of instruments under consideration; • the customer's ability to understand the economic features of the security involved; • the customer's ability to independently evaluate how market developments would affect the security; and • the complexity of the security or securities involved. A determination that a customer is making independent investment decisions will depend on the nature of the relationship that exists between the member and the customer. Relevant considerations could include: • any written or oral understanding that exists between the member and the customer regarding the nature of the relationship between the member and the customer and the services to be rendered by the member; • the presence or absence of a pattern of acceptance of the member's recommendations;

European Regulatory Framework for Financial Instruments	U.S. Regulatory Framework for Financial Instruments
client or an eligible counterparty in accordance with that Directive. 2. Member States shall ensure that investment firms inform clients in a durable medium about any right that client has to request a different categorization and about any limitations to the level of client protection that it would entail. 3. Member States shall permit investment firms, either on their own initiative or at the request of the client concerned: a) to treat as a professional or retail client a client that might otherwise be classified as an eligible counterparty pursuant to Article 24(2) of Directive 2004/39/EC; b) to treat as a retail client a client that is considered as a professional client pursuant to Section I of Annex II to Directive 2004/39/EC. **Article 29, General requirements for information to clients** 1. Member States shall require investment firms, in good time before a retail client or potential retail client is bound by any agreement for the provision of those investment services or ancillary services or before the provision of those services, whichever is the earlier, to provide that client or potential client with the following information: a) the terms of any such agreement; b) the information required by Article 30 relating to that agreement or to those investment or ancillary services. 2. Member States shall require investment firms, in good time before the provision of investment services or ancillary services to retail clients or potential retail clients, to provide the information required under Articles 30 to 33. 3. Member States shall require investment firms to provide professional clients with the information referred to in Article 32 (5) and (6) in good time before the provision of the service concerned.	• the use by the customer of ideas, suggestions, market views and information obtained from other members or market professionals, particularly those relating to the same type of securities; and • the extent to which the member has received from the customer current comprehensive portfolio information in connection with discussing recommended transactions or has not been provided important information regarding its portfolio or investment objectives. Members are reminded that these factors are merely guidelines which will be utilized to determine whether a member has fulfilled its suitability obligations with respect to a specific institutional customer transaction and that the inclusion or absence of any of these factors is not dispositive of the determination of suitability. Such a determination can only be made on a case-by-case basis taking into consideration all the facts and circumstances of a particular member/customer relationship, assessed in the context of a particular transaction. For purposes of this interpretation, an institutional customer shall be any entity other than a natural person. In determining the applicability of this interpretation to an institutional customer, the Association will consider the dollar value of the securities that the institutional customer has in its portfolio and/or under management. While this interpretation is potentially applicable to any institutional customer with at least $10 million invested in securities in the aggregate in its portfolio and/or under management. **FINRA Rule 2114. Recommendations to Customers in OTC Equity Securities** Preliminary Note: The requirements of this Rule are in addition to other existing member obligations under FINRA rules and the federal securities laws, **including obligations to determine suitability of particular securities transactions with customers and to have a reasonable basis for any recommendation made to a customer**. This Rule is not intended to act or operate as a presumption or as a safe harbor for purposes of

European Regulatory Framework for Financial Instruments	U.S. Regulatory Framework for Financial Instruments
4. The information referred to in paragraphs 1 to 3 shall be provided in a durable medium or by means of a website (where that does not constitute a durable medium) provided that the conditions specified in Article 3(2) are satisfied. 5. By way of exception to paragraphs 1 and 2, Member States shall permit investment firms, in the following circumstances, to provide the information required under paragraph 1 to a retail client immediately after that client is bound by any agreement for the provision of investment services or ancillary services, and the information required under paragraph 2 immediately after starting to provide the service: a) the firm was unable to comply with the time limits specified in paragraphs 1 and 2 because, at the request of the client, the agreement was concluded using a means of distance communication which prevents the firm from providing the information in accordance with paragraph 1 or 2; b) in any case where Article 3(3) of Directive 2002/65/EC of the European parliament and of the Council of 23 September 2002 concerning the distance marketing of consumer financial services and amending Council Directive 90/619/EEC and Directives 97/7/EC and 98/27/EC (1) does not otherwise apply, the investment firm complies with the requirements of that Article in relation to the retail client or potential retail client, as if that client or potential client were a 'consumer' and the investment firm were a 'supplier' within the meaning of that Directive. 6. Member State shall ensure that investment firms notify a client in good time about any material change to the information provided under Articles 30 to 33 which is relevant to a service that the firm is providing to that client. That notification shall be given in a durable medium if the information to which it relates is given in a durable medium. 7. Member States shall require investment firms to ensure that information contained in a marketing communication is consistent with any information the firm provides to clients in the course of carrying on investment and ancillary services.	determining suitability or for any other legal obligation or requirement imposed under NASD rules or the federal securities laws. 4. **Review Requirement.** No member or person associated with a member shall recommend that a customer purchase or sell short any equity security that is published or quoted in a quotation medium and that either (1) is not listed on Nasdaq or on a national securities exchange or (2) is listed on a regional securities exchange and does not qualify for dissemination of transaction reports via the Consolidated Tape, unless the member has reviewed the current financial statements of the issuer, current material business information about the issuer, and made a determination that such information, and any other information available, provides a reasonable basis under the circumstances for making the recommendation. 5. **Definitions** (1) For purposes of this Rule, the term "current financial statements" shall include: (A) For issuers that are not foreign private issuers, (i) a balance sheet as of a date less than 15 months before the date of the recommendation; (ii) a statement of profit and loss for the 12 months preceding the date of the balance sheet; (iii) if the balance sheet is not as of a date less than 6 months before the date of the recommendation, additional statements of profit and loss for the period from the date of the balance sheet to a date less than 6 months before the date of the recommendation; (iv) publicly available financial statements and other financial reports filed during the 12 months preceding the date of the recommendation and up to the date of the recommendation with the issuer's principal financial or securities regulatory authority in its home jurisdiction, including the Commission, foreign regulatory authorities, bank and insurance regulators; and (v) all publicly available financial information filed with the Commission

European Regulatory Framework for Financial Instruments	U.S. Regulatory Framework for Financial Instruments
8. Member States shall ensure that, where a marketing communication contains an offer or invitation of the following nature and specifies the manner of response or includes a form by which any response may be made, it includes such of the information referred to in Articles 30 to 33 as is relevant to that offer or invitation: a) an offer to enter into an agreement in relation to a financial instrument or investment service or ancillary service with any person who responds to the communication; b) an invitation to any person who responds to the communication to make an offer to enter into an agreement in relation to a financial instrument or investment service or ancillary service. However, the first subparagraph shall not apply if, in order to respond to an offer or invitation contained in the marketing communication, the potential retail client must refer to another document or documents, which, alone or in combination, contain that information. **Article 30, Information about the investment firm and its services for retail clients and potential retail clients** 1. Member States shall require investment firms to provide retail clients or potential retail clients with the following general information, where relevant: a) the name and address of the investment firm, and the contact details necessary to enable clients to communicate effectively with the firm; b) the languages in which the client may communicate with the investment firm, and receive documents and other information from the firm; c) the methods of communication to be used between the investment firm and the client including, where relevant, those for the sending and reception of orders; d) a statement of the fact that the investment firm is authorized and the name	during the 12 months preceding the date of the recommendation contained in registration statements or Regulation A filings. (B) For foreign private issuers, (i) a balance sheet as of a date less than 18 months before the date of the recommendation; (ii) a statement of profit and loss for the 12 months preceding the date of the balance sheet; (iii) if the balance sheet is not as of a date less than 9 months before the date of the recommendation, additional statements of profit and loss for the period from the date of the balance sheet to a date less than 9 months before the date of the recommendation, if any such statements have been prepared by the issuer; and (iv) publicly available financial statements and other financial reports filed during the 12 months preceding the date of the recommendation and up to the date of the recommendation with the issuer's principal financial or securities regulatory authority in its home jurisdiction, including the Commission, foreign regulatory authorities, bank and insurance regulators. (2) For purposes of this Rule, the term "quotation medium" shall mean any: (A) System of general circulation to brokers or dealers that regularly disseminates quotations or indications of interest of identified brokers or dealers; or (B) Publication, alternative trading system or other device that is used by brokers or dealers to disseminate quotations or indications of interest to others. **(c) Compliance Requirements** (1) A member shall designate a registered person to conduct the review required by this Rule. In making such designation, the member must ensure that: (A) Either the person is registered as a Series 24 principal, or the person's conduct in complying with the provisions of this Rule is

European Regulatory Framework for Financial Instruments	U.S. Regulatory Framework for Financial Instruments
and contact address of the competent authority that has authorized it; e) where the investment firm is acting through a tied agent, a statement of this fact specifying the Member State in which that agent is registered; f) the nature, frequency and timing of the reports on the performance of the service to be provided by the investment firm to the client in accordance with Article 19(8) of Directive 2004/39/EC; g) if the investment firm holds client financial instruments or client funds, a summary description of the steps which it takes to ensure their protection, including summary details of any relevant investor compensation or deposit guarantee scheme which applies to the firm by virtue of its activities in a Member State; h) a description, which may be provided in summary form, of the conflicts of interest policy maintained by the firm in accordance with Article 22; i) at any time that the client requests it, further details of that conflicts of interest policy in a durable medium or by means of a website (where that does not constitute a durable medium) provided that the conditions specified in Article 3(2) are satisfied. 2. Member States shall ensure that, when providing the service of portfolio management, investment firms establish an appropriate method of evaluation and comparison such as a meaningful benchmark, based on the investment objectives of the client and the types of financial instruments included in the client portfolio, so as to enable the client for whom the service is provided to assess the firm's performance. 3. Member States shall require that where investment firms propose to provide portfolio management services to a retail client or potential retail client, they provide the client, in addition to the information required under paragraph 1, with such of the following information as is applicable: a) information on the method and frequency of valuation of the financial instruments in the client portfolio; b) details of any delegation of the discretionary management of all or part of	appropriately supervised by a Series 24 principal; and (B) Such designated person has the requisite skills, background and knowledge to conduct the review required under this Rule. The member shall document the information reviewed, the date of the review, and the name of the person performing the review of the required information. **(d) Additional Review Requirement for Delinquent Filers** If an issuer has not made current filings required by the issuer's principal financial or securities regulatory authority in its home jurisdiction, including the Commission, foreign regulatory authorities, or bank and insurance regulators, such review must include an inquiry into the circumstances concerning the failure to make current filings, and a determination, based on all the facts and circumstances, that the recommendation is appropriate under the circumstances. Such a determination must be made in writing and maintained by the member. **(e) Exemptions** (1) The requirements of this Rule shall not apply to: (A) Transactions that meet the requirements of Rule 504 of Regulation D (related to companies when they offer and sell up to $1,000,000 of their securities in any 12-month period) and transactions with an issuer not involving any public offering pursuant to Section 4(2) of the Securities Act; (B) Transactions with or for an account that qualifies as an "institutional account" under Rule 3110(c)(4) or with a customer that is a "qualified institutional buyer" under Rule 144A promulgated under the Securities Act or "qualified purchaser" under Section 2(a)(51) of the Investment Company Act of 1940; (C) Transactions in an issuer's securities if the issuer has at least $50 million in total assets and $10 million in shareholder's equity as stated in the issuer's most recent audited current financial statements, as defined in this Rule;

European Regulatory Framework for Financial Instruments	U.S. Regulatory Framework for Financial Instruments
the financial instruments or funds in the client portfolio; c) a specification of any benchmark against which the performance of the client portfolio will be compared; d) the types of financial instrument that may be included in the client portfolio and types of transaction that may be carried out in such instruments, including any limits; e) the management objectives, the level of risk to be reflected in the manager's exercise of discretion, and any specific constraints on that discretion. **Article 31, Information about financial instruments** 1. Member States shall require investment firms to provide clients or potential clients with a general description of the nature and risks of financial instruments, taking into account, in particular, the client's categorization as either a retail client or a professional client. That description must explain the nature of the specific type of instrument concerned, as well as the risks particular to that specific type of instrument in sufficient detail to enable the client to take investment decisions on an informed basis. 2. The description of risks shall include, where relevant to the specific type of instrument concerned and the status and level of knowledge of the client, the following elements: a) the risks associated with that type of financial instrument including an explanation of leverage and its effects and the risk of losing the entire investment; b) the volatility of the price of such instruments and any limitations on the available market for such instruments; c) the fact that an investor might assume, as a result of transactions in such instruments, financial commitments and other additional obligations, including contingent liabilities, additional to the cost of acquiring the	(D) Transactions in securities of a bank as defined in Section 3(a)(6) of the Securities Exchange Act of 1934 and/or insurance company subject to regulation by a state or federal bank or insurance regulatory authority; (E) A security with a worldwide average daily trading volume value of at least $100,000 during each month of the six full calendar months immediately before the date of the recommendation; (F) A convertible security, if the underlying security meets the requirement of Section (e)(1)(E) of this Rule; (G) A security that has a bid price, as published in a quotation medium, of at least $50 per share. If the security is a unit composed of one or more securities, the bid price of the unit divided by the number of shares of the unit that are not warrants, options, rights, or similar securities must be at least $50; or (2) Pursuant to the Rule 9600 Series, NASD, for good cause shown after taking into consideration all relevant factors, may exempt any person, security or transaction, or any class or classes of persons, securities or transactions, either unconditionally or on specified terms, from any or all of the requirements of this Rule if it determines that such exemption is consistent with the purpose of this Rule, the protection of investors, and the public interest.

European Regulatory Framework for Financial Instruments	U.S. Regulatory Framework for Financial Instruments
instruments; d) any margin requirements or similar obligations, applicable to instruments of that type. Member States may specify the precise terms, or the contents, of the description of risks required under this paragraph. 3. If an investment firm provides a retail client or potential retail client with information about a financial instrument that is the subject of a current offer to the public and a prospectus has been published in connection with that offer in accordance with Directive 2003/71/EC, that firm shall inform the client or potential client where that prospectus is made available to the public. 4. Where the risks associated with a financial instrument composed of two or more different financial instruments or services are likely to be greater than the risks associated with any of the components, the investment firm shall provide an adequate description of the components of that instrument and the way in which its interaction increases the risks. 5. In the case of financial instruments that incorporate a guarantee by a third party, the information about the guarantee shall include sufficient detail about the guarantor and the guarantee to enable the retail client or potential retail client to make a fair assessment of the guarantee. Article 32, **Information requirements concerning safeguarding of client financial instruments or client funds** 1. Member States shall ensure that, where investment firms hold financial instruments or funds belonging to retail clients, they provide those retail clients or potential retail clients with such of the information specified in paragraphs 2 to 7 as is relevant. 2. The investment firm shall inform the retail client or potential retail client where the financial instruments or funds of that client may be held by a third party on behalf of the investment firm and of the responsibility of the investment firm	

European Regulatory Framework for Financial Instruments	U.S. Regulatory Framework for Financial Instruments
under the applicable national law for any acts or omissions of the third party and the consequences for the client of the insolvency of the third party.	
3. Where financial instruments of the retail client or potential retail client may, if permitted by national law, be held in an omnibus account by a third party, the investment firm shall inform the client of this fact and shall provide a prominent warning of the resulting risks.	
4. The investment firm shall inform the retail client or potential retail client where it is not possible under national law for client financial instruments held with a third party to be separately identifiable from the proprietary financial instruments of that third party or of the investment firm and shall provide a prominent warning of the resulting risks.	
5. The investment firm shall inform the client or potential client where accounts that contain financial instruments or funds belonging to that client or potential client are or will be subject to the law of a jurisdiction other than that of a Member State and shall indicate that the rights of the client or potential client relating to those financial instruments or funds may differ accordingly.	
6. An investment firm shall inform the client about the existence and the terms of any security interest or lien which the firm has or may have over the client's financial instruments or funds, or any right of set-off it holds in relation to those instruments or funds. Where applicable, it shall also inform the client of the fact that a depository may have a security interest or lien over, or right of set-off in relation to those instruments or funds.	
7. An investment firm, before entering into securities financing transactions in relation to financial instruments held by it on behalf of a retail client, or before otherwise using such financial instruments for its own account or the account of another client, shall in good time before the use of those instruments provide	
Article 33, **Information about costs and associated charges**	

European Regulatory Framework for Financial Instruments	U.S. Regulatory Framework for Financial Instruments
Member States shall require investment firms to provide their retail clients and potential retail clients with information on costs and associated charges that includes such of the following elements as are relevant:	
a) the total price to be paid by the client in connection with the financial instrument or the investment service or ancillary service, including all related fees, commissions, charges and expenses, and all taxes payable via the investment firm or, if an exact price cannot be indicated, the basis for the calculation of the total price so that the client can verify it;	
b) where any part of the total price referred to in point (a) is to be paid in or represents an amount of foreign currency, an indication of the currency involved and the applicable currency conversion rates and costs;	
c) notice of the possibility that other costs, including taxes, related to transactions in connection with the financial instrument or the investment service may arise for the client that are not paid via the investment firm or imposed by it;	
d) the arrangements for payment or other performance. For the purposes of point (a), the commissions charged by the firm shall be itemized separately in every case.	
Suitability test.	
MiFID level 2, Directive 2006/73/EC, Article 35, **Assessment of suitability**	
1. Member States shall ensure that investment firms obtain from clients or potential clients such information as is necessary for the firm to understand the essential facts about the client and to have a reasonable basis for believing, giving due consideration to the nature and extent of the service provided, that the specific transaction to be recommended, or entered into in the course of providing a portfolio management service, satisfies the following criteria:	

European Regulatory Framework for Financial Instruments	U.S. Regulatory Framework for Financial Instruments
a) it meets the investment objectives of the client in question; b) it is such that the client is able financially to bear any related investment risks consistent with his investment objectives; c) it is such that the client has the necessary experience and knowledge in order to understand the risks involved in the transaction or in the management of his portfolio. 2. Where an investment firm provides an **investment service** to a **professional client it shall be entitled to assume that, in relation to the products, transactions and services for which it is so classified, the client has the necessary level of experience and knowledge for the purposes of paragraph 1(c).** Where that investment service consists in the **provision of investment advice to a professional client, the investment firm shall be entitled to assume for the purposes of paragraph 1(b) that the client is able financially to bear any related investment risks consistent with the investment objectives of that client.** 3. The information regarding the financial situation of the client or potential client shall include, where relevant, information on the source and extent of his regular income, his assets, including liquid assets, investments and real property, and his regular financial commitments. 4. The information regarding the investment objectives of the client or potential client shall include, where relevant, information on the length of time for which the client wishes to hold the investment, his preferences regarding risk taking, his risk profile, and the purposes of the investment. 5. Where, when **providing the investment service of investment advice or portfolio management,** an investment firm does not obtain the information required under Article 19(4) of Directive 2004/39/EC, the firm shall not recommend investment services or financial instruments to the client or potential client.	

European Regulatory Framework for Financial Instruments	U.S. Regulatory Framework for Financial Instruments
Article 36, Assessment of Appropriateness Member States shall require investment firms, when assessing whether an investment service as referred to in Article 19(5) of Directive 2004/39/EC **(services that do not involve recommendation on the part of an investment firm**, such as only execution for example) is appropriate for a client, to determine whether that client has the necessary experience and knowledge in order to understand the risks involved in relation to the product or investment service offered or demanded. For those purposes an investment firm shall be entitled to assume **that a professional client has the necessary experience and knowledge in order to understand the risks involved in relation to those particular investment services or transactions, or types of transaction or product, for which the client is classified as a professional client.** Article 37, **Provisions common to the assessment of suitability or Appropriateness** 1. Member States shall ensure that the information regarding a client's or potential client's knowledge and experience in the investment field includes the following, to the extent appropriate to the nature of the client, the nature and extent of the service to be provided and the type of product or transaction envisaged, including their complexity and the risks involved: a) the types of service, transaction and financial instrument with which the client is familiar; b) the nature, volume, and frequency of the client's transactions in financial instruments and the period over which they have been carried out; c) the level of education, and profession or relevant former profession of the	

European Regulatory Framework for Financial Instruments	U.S. Regulatory Framework for Financial Instruments
client or potential client. 2. An investment firm shall not encourage a client or potential client not to provide information required for the purposes of assessment of suitability and appropriateness. 3. An investment firm shall be entitled to rely on the information provided by its clients or potential clients unless it is aware or ought to be aware that the information is manifestly out of date, inaccurate or incomplete. **Exemptions from Suitability and Appropriateness:** See eligible counterparties under the Best Execution part Article 39, **Retail client agreement** Member States shall require an investment firm that provides an investment service other than investment advice to a new retail client for the first time after the date of application of this Directive to enter into a written basic agreement, in paper or another durable medium, with the client setting out the essential rights and obligations of the firm and the client. The rights and duties of the parties to the agreement may be incorporated by reference to other documents or legal texts. • Best Execution Rule MiFID, Article 21 1. Member States shall require that investment firms take all reasonable steps to obtain, when executing orders, the best possible result for their clients **taking into account price, costs, speed, likelihood of execution and settlement, size, nature or any other consideration relevant to the execution of the order.** Nevertheless, whenever there is a specific instruction from the client the investment firm shall execute the order following the specific instruction. 2. Member States shall require investment firms to establish and implement	• Best Execution Rule NASD Rule 2320. Best Execution and Interpositioning a. In any transaction for or with a customer or a customer of another broker-dealer, a member and persons associated with a member **shall use reasonable diligence to ascertain the best market for the subject security and buy or sell in such market so that the resultant price to the customer is as favorable as possible under prevailing market conditions.** Among the factors that will be considered in determining whether a member has used "reasonable diligence" are:

European Regulatory Framework for Financial Instruments	U.S. Regulatory Framework for Financial Instruments
effective arrangements for complying with paragraph 1. In particular Member States shall require investment firms to establish and implement an order execution policy to allow them to obtain, for their client orders, the best possible result in accordance with paragraph 1. 3. The order execution policy shall include, in respect of each class of instruments, information on the different venues where the investment firm executes its client orders and the factors affecting the choice of execution venue. It shall at least include those venues that enable the investment firm to obtain on a consistent basis the best possible result for the execution of client orders. Member States shall require that investment firms provide appropriate information to their clients on their order execution policy. Member States shall require that investment firms obtain the prior consent of their clients to the execution policy. Member States shall require that, where the order execution policy provides for the possibility that client orders may be executed outside a Regulated Market or an MTF, the investment firm shall, in particular, **inform its clients about this possibility.** Member States shall require that **investment firms obtain the prior express consent of their clients before** proceeding to execute their orders outside a Regulated Market or an MTF. Investment firms may obtain this consent either in the form of a general agreement or in respect of individual transactions. 4. Member States shall require investment firms to monitor the effectiveness of their order execution arrangements and execution policy in order to identify and, where appropriate, correct any deficiencies. In particular, they shall assess, on a regular basis, whether the execution venues included in the order execution policy provide for the best possible result for the client or whether they need to make changes to their execution arrangements. Member States shall require investment firms to notify clients of any material changes to their order execution arrangements or execution policy. 5. Member States shall require investment firms to be able to demonstrate to	the character of the market for the security, e.g., **price, volatility, relative liquidity, and pressure on available communications;** • the **size and type of transaction;** • the **number of markets checked;** • **accessibility of the quotation;** and • **the terms and conditions of the order** which result in the transaction, as communicated to the member and persons associated with the member. b. In any transaction for or with a customer, no member or person associated with a member shall interject a third party between the member and the best available market except in cases where the member can demonstrate that to his knowledge at the time of the transaction the total cost or proceeds of the transaction, as confirmed to the member acting for or with the customer, was better than the prevailing inter-dealer market for the security. **A member's obligations to his customer are generally not fulfilled when he channels transactions through another broker/dealer or some person in a similar position, unless he can show that by so doing he reduced the costs of the transactions to the customer.** c. When a member **cannot execute directly with a market maker but must employ a broker's broker or some other means in order to insure an execution advantageous to the customer, the burden of showing the acceptable circumstances for doing so is on the retail firm.** Examples of acceptable circumstances are where a customer's order is "crossed" with another retail firm which has a corresponding order on the other side, or where the identity of the retail firm, if known, would likely cause undue price movements adversely affecting the cost or proceeds to the customer. d. Failure to maintain or adequately staff an over-the-counter order room or other department assigned to execute customers' orders cannot be considered justification for executing away from the best available market; nor can channeling orders through a third party as described above as reciprocation

European Regulatory Framework for Financial Instruments	U.S. Regulatory Framework for Financial Instruments
their clients, at their request, that they have executed their orders in accordance with the firm's execution policy. **Best execution criteria** MiFID level 2, Directive 2006/73/EC, Article 44 Implementing measures • Member States shall ensure that, when executing client orders, investment firms take into account the following criteria for determining the relative importance of the factors referred to in Article 21(1) of Directive 2004/39/EC: • the characteristics of the client including the categorization of the client as retail or professional; • the characteristics of the client order; • the characteristics of financial instruments that are the subject of that order; • the characteristics of the execution venues to which that order can be directed. For the purposes of this Article and Article 46, 'execution venue' means a Regulated Market, an MTF, a systematic internaliser, or a market maker or other liquidity provider or an entity that performs a similar function in a third country to the functions performed by any of the foregoing. • An investment firm satisfies its obligation under Article 21(1) of Directive 2004/39/EC to take all reasonable steps to obtain the best possible result for a client to the extent that it executes an order or a specific aspect of an order following specific instructions from the client relating to the order or the specific aspect of the order. 3. Where an investment firm executes an order on behalf of a retail client, the best possible result shall be determined in terms of the total consideration, representing **the price of the financial instrument and the costs related to**	for service or business operate to relieve a member of his obligations. However, the channeling of customers' orders through a broker's broker or third party pursuant to established correspondent relationships under which executions are confirmed directly to the member acting as agent for the customer, such as where the third party gives up the name of the retail firm, are not prohibited if the cost of such service is not borne by the customer. e. A member through whom a retail order is channeled, as described above, and who knowingly is a party to an arrangement whereby the initiating member has not fulfilled his obligations under this Rule, will also be deemed to have violated this Rule. f. The obligations described in paragraphs (1) through (5) above exist not only where the member acts as agent for the account of his customer but also where retail transactions are executed as principal and contemporaneously offset. 1. Except as provided in subparagraph (3) below, in any transaction for or with a customer pertaining to the execution of an order in a non-exchange-listed security (as defined in the Rule 6600 Series), a member or person associated with a member **shall contact and obtain quotations from three dealers** (or all dealers if three or less) **to determine the best inter-dealer market for the subject security.** 2. Members that display priced quotations on a real-time basis for a non-exchange-listed security in two or more quotation mediums that permit quotation updates on a real-time basis must display the same priced quotations for the security in each medium. 3. The requirements described in subparagraph (1) **above shall not apply:** A) when two or more priced quotations for a non-exchange-listed security are displayed in an inter-dealer quotation system that permits quotation updates on a real-time basis; or B) to any transaction for or with a customer pertaining to the execution of an

European Regulatory Framework for Financial Instruments	U.S. Regulatory Framework for Financial Instruments
	order in a non-exchange-listed security of a foreign issuer that is part of the FTSE All-World Index if such transaction is executed during the regular business hours of the foreign market for the foreign security and no trading halt or other similar trading or quoting restriction is in effect in any foreign market on which such foreign security is listed; or C) to any transaction for or with a customer pertaining to the execution of an order in a non-exchange-listed security that is listed on a Canadian exchange, provided that (i) such order is executed by the member or a person associated with the member on a Canadian exchange in an agency or riskless principal capacity; and (ii) the member or a person associated with the member conducts, pursuant to NASD Rule 2320(a) and the duty of best execution, regular and rigorous reviews of the quality of the execution of such orders in such securities. 4. Definitions For purposes of this paragraph (g): A) The term "inter-dealer quotation system" means any system of general circulation to brokers or dealers that regularly disseminates quotations of identified brokers or dealers. B) The term "quotation medium" means any inter-dealer quotation system or any publication or electronic communications network or other device that is used by brokers or dealers to make known to others their interest in transactions in any security, including offers to buy or sell at a stated price or otherwise, or invitations of offers to buy or sell. 5. Pursuant to the Rule 9600 Series, the staff, for good cause shown, after taking into consideration all relevant factors, may exempt any transaction or classes of transactions, either unconditionally or on specified terms, from any or all of the provisions of this paragraph if it determines that such exemption is consistent with the purpose of this Rule, the protection of investors, and the public interest. **Reg NMS: Rule 611 -- Order Protection Rule**
execution, which shall include all expenses incurred by the client which are directly related to the execution of the order, including execution venue fees, clearing and settlement fees and any other fees paid to third parties involved in the execution of the order. For the purposes of delivering best execution where there is more than one competing venue to execute an order for a financial instrument, in order to assess and compare the results for the client that would be achieved by executing the order on each of the execution venues listed in the firm's order execution policy that is capable of executing that order, the firm's own commissions and costs for executing the order on each of the eligible execution venues shall be taken into account in that assessment. 4. Member States shall require that investment firms do not structure or charge their commissions in such a way as to discriminate unfairly between execution venues. 5. Before 1 November 2008 the Commission shall present a report to the European Parliament and to the Council on the availability, comparability and consolidation of information concerning the quality of execution of various execution venues. **Exemption:** An investment firm is not obliged to apply suitability test for **eligible counterparties** (if they choose so) including investment firms, credit institutions, insurance companies, pension funds and their management companies, other financial institutions authorized or regulated under Community legislation or the national law of a Member State (mostly professional clients). Exemptions from Suitability, Appropriateness and Best Execution: Article 24, MiFID level 1, **Transactions executed with eligible counterparties** 1. Member States shall ensure that investment firms authorised to execute	

European Regulatory Framework for Financial Instruments	U.S. Regulatory Framework for Financial Instruments
orders on behalf of clients and/or to deal on own account and/or to receive and transmit orders, **may bring about or enter into transactions with eligible counterparties without being obliged to comply with the obligations under Articles 19, 21 and 22(1) (or suitability, appropriateness and best execution requirements)** in respect of those transactions or in respect of any ancillary service directly related to those transactions.	a. *Reasonable policies and procedures.* 1. A trading center shall establish, maintain, and enforce written policies and procedures that are reasonably designed to prevent trade-throughs on that trading center of protected quotations in NMS stocks that do not fall within an exception set forth in paragraph (b) of this section and, if relying on such an exception, that are reasonably designed to assure compliance with the terms of the exception.
2. Member States shall recognize **as eligible counterparties for the purposes of this Article investment firms, credit institutions, insurance companies, UCITS and their management companies, pension funds and their management companies, other financial institutions authorised or regulated under Community** legislation or the national law of a Member State, undertakings exempted from the application of this Directive under Article 2(1)(k) and (l), national governments and their corresponding offices including public bodies that deal with public debt, central banks and supranational organizations.	2. A trading center shall regularly surveil to ascertain the effectiveness of the policies and procedures required by paragraph (a)(1) of this section and shall take prompt action to remedy deficiencies in such policies and procedures. 3. *Exceptions.* 4. The transaction that constituted the trade-through was effected when the trading center displaying the protected quotation that was traded through was experiencing a failure, material delay, or malfunction of its systems or equipment.
Classification as an eligible counterparty under the first subparagraph shall be without prejudice to the right of such entities to request, either on a general form or on a trade-by-trade basis, treatment as clients whose business with the investment firm is subject to Articles 19, 21 and 22 of MiFID level 1 (suitability, appropriateness and best execution requirements)	5. The transaction that constituted the trade-through was not a regular way contract. 6. The transaction that constituted the trade-through was a single-priced opening, reopening, or closing transaction by the trading center. 7. The transaction that constituted the trade-through was executed at a time when a protected bid was priced higher than a protected offer in the NMS stock.
3. Member States may also recognize as eligible counterparties other undertakings meeting pre-determined proportionate requirements, including quantitative thresholds. In the event of a transaction where the prospective counterparties are located in different jurisdictions, the investment firm shall defer to the status of the other undertaking as determined by the law or measures of the Member State in which that undertaking is established. Member States shall ensure that the investment firm, when it enters into transactions in accordance with paragraph 1 with such undertakings, obtains the express confirmation from the prospective counterparty that it agrees to be treated as an eligible counterparty. Member States shall allow the investment firm to obtain this confirmation either in the form of a general agreement or in	8. The transaction that constituted the trade-through was the execution of an order identified as an intermarket sweep order. 9. The transaction that constituted the trade-through was effected by a trading center that simultaneously routed an intermarket sweep order to execute against the full displayed size of any protected quotation in the NMS stock that was traded through. 10. The transaction that constituted the trade-through was the execution of an order at a price that was not based, directly or indirectly, on the quoted price of

European Regulatory Framework for Financial Instruments	U.S. Regulatory Framework for Financial Instruments
respect of each individual transaction. 4. Member States may recognize as eligible counterparties third country entities equivalent to those categories of entities mentioned in paragraph 2. Member States may also recognize as eligible counterparties third country undertakings such as those mentioned in paragraph 3 on the same conditions and subject to the same requirements as those laid down at paragraph 3. Article 50, MiFID level 2, Directive 2006/73/EC, Eligible counterparties 1. Member States may recognize **an undertaking as an eligible counterparty if that undertaking falls within a category of clients who are to be considered professional clients** in accordance with paragraphs 1, 2 and 3 of Section I of Annex II to Directive 2004/39/EC, excluding any category which is explicitly mentioned in Article 24(2) of that Directive. On request, Member States may also recognize as eligible counterparties undertakings which fall within a category of clients who are to be considered professional clients in accordance with Section II of Annex II to Directive 2004/39/EC. In such cases, however, the undertaking concerned shall be recognized as an eligible counterparty only in respect of the services or transactions for which it could be treated as a professional client. 2. Where, pursuant to the second subparagraph of Article 24(2) of Directive 2004/39/EC, an eligible counterparty requests treatment as a client whose business with an investment firm is subject to Articles 19, 21 and 22 of that Directive, but does not expressly request treatment as a retail client, and the investment firm agrees to that request, the firm shall treat that eligible counterparty as a professional client. However, where that eligible counterparty expressly requests treatment as a retail client, the provisions in respect of requests of non-professional treatment specified in the second, third and fourth sub-paragraphs of Section I of Annex II to Directive 2004/39/EC shall apply.	the NMS stock at the time of execution and for which the material terms were not reasonably determinable at the time the commitment to execute the order was made. 11. The trading center displaying the protected quotation that was traded through had displayed, within one second prior to execution of the transaction that constituted the trade-through, a best bid or best offer, as applicable, for the NMS stock with a price that was equal or inferior to the price of the trade-through transaction. 12. The transaction that constituted the trade-through was the execution by a trading center of an order for which, at the time of receipt of the order, the trading center had guaranteed an execution at no worse than a specified price (a stopped order), where: 13. The stopped order was for the account of a customer; 14. The customer agreed to the specified price on an order-by-order basis; and 15. The price of the trade-through transaction was, for a stopped buy order, lower than the national best bid in the NMS stock at the time of execution or, for a stopped sell order, higher than the national best offer in the NMS stock at the time of execution. 16. *Intermarket sweep orders.* The trading center, broker, or dealer responsible for the routing of an intermarket sweep order shall take reasonable steps to establish that such order meets the requirements set forth in Rule 242.600(b)(30). 17. *Exemptions.* The Commission, by order, may exempt from the provisions of this section, either unconditionally or on specified terms and conditions, any person, security, transaction, quotation, or order, or any class or classes of persons, securities, quotations, or orders, if the Commission determines that such exemption is necessary or appropriate in the public interest, and is consistent with the protection of investors.

European Regulatory Framework for Financial Instruments	U.S. Regulatory Framework for Financial Instruments
• Client order handling rules	• Client order handling rules
	• Order Execution Obligations (*Rules 602-604 of Regulation NMS*)

U.S. Regulatory Framework for Financial Instruments

Rule 604 – Display of Customer Limit Orders

a. *Specialists and OTC market makers. For all NMS stocks:*

1. Each member of a national securities exchange that is registered by that exchange as a specialist, or is authorized by that exchange to perform functions substantially similar to that of a specialist, shall publish immediately a bid or offer that reflects:

   i. **The price and the full size of each customer limit order held by the specialist** that is at a price that would improve the bid or offer of such specialist in such security; and

   ii. The full size of each customer limit order held by the specialist that:

      A. Is priced equal to the bid or offer of such specialist for such security;

      B. Is priced equal to the national best bid or national best offer; and

      C. Represents more than a de minimis change in relation to the size associated with the specialist's bid or offer.

2. Each registered broker or dealer that acts as an OTC market maker shall publish immediately a bid or offer that reflects:

   i. **The price and the full size of each customer limit order held by the OTC market maker** that is at a price that would improve the bid or offer of such OTC market maker in such security; and

   ii. The full size of each customer limit order held by the OTC market maker that:

European Regulatory Framework for Financial Instruments

Client order handling rules

1. Member States shall require that investment firms authorized to execute orders on behalf of clients implement procedures and arrangements which provide for the prompt, fair and expeditious execution of client orders, relative to other client orders or the trading interests of the investment firm. These procedures or arrangements shall allow for the execution of otherwise comparable client orders in accordance with the time of their reception by the investment firm.

2. Member States shall require that, in the case of a client limit order in respect of shares admitted to trading on a Regulated Market which are not immediately executed under prevailing market conditions, investment firms are, unless the client expressly instructs otherwise, to take measures to facilitate the earliest possible execution of that order by making public immediately **that client limit order in a manner which is easily accessible to other market participants**. Member States may decide that investment firms comply with this obligation **by transmitting the client limit order to a Regulated Market and/or MTF**. Member States shall provide that the competent authorities may waive the obligation to make public a limit order that is large in scale compared with normal market size as determined under Article 44(2).

European Regulatory Framework for Financial Instruments	U.S. Regulatory Framework for Financial Instruments
	A. Is priced equal to the bid or offer of such OTC market maker for such security;
	B. Is priced equal to the national best bid or national best offer; and
	C. Represents more than a *de minimis* change in relation to the size associated with the OTC market maker's bid or offer.
	b. *Exceptions.* The requirements in paragraph (a) of this section shall not apply to any customer limit order:
	1. That is executed upon receipt of the order.
	2. That is placed by a customer who expressly requests, either at the time that the order is placed or prior thereto pursuant to an individually negotiated agreement with respect to such customer's orders, that the order not be displayed.
	3. That is an odd-lot order.
	4. That is a block size order, unless a customer placing such order requests that the order be displayed.
	5. That is delivered immediately upon receipt to a national securities exchange or national securities association-sponsored system, or an electronic communications network that complies with the requirements of Rule 242.602(b)(5)(ii) with respect to that order.
	6. That is delivered immediately upon receipt to another exchange member or OTC market maker that complies with the requirements of this section with respect to that order.
	7. That is an all's or none's order.
	c. *Exemptions.* The Commission may exempt from the provisions of this section, either unconditionally or on specified terms and conditions, any responsible broker or dealer, electronic communications network, national securities exchange, or national securities association if the Commission determines that such exemption is consistent with the public interest, the protection of investors and the removal of impediments to and perfection of the mechanism

European Regulatory Framework for Financial Instruments	U.S. Regulatory Framework for Financial Instruments
	of a national market system.
• Obligations related to appointment of tied agents MiFID, level 1, Article 23 **Obligations of investment firms when appointing tied agents** 1. Member States may decide to allow an investment firm to appoint tied agents for the purposes of promoting the services of the investment firm, soliciting business or receiving orders from clients or potential clients and transmitting them, placing financial instruments and providing advice in respect of such financial instruments and services offered by that investment firm. 2. Member States shall require that where an investment firm decides to appoint a tied agent it remains fully and unconditionally responsible for any action or omission on the part of the tied agent when acting on behalf of the firm. Member States shall require the investment firm to ensure that a tied agent discloses the capacity in which he is acting and the firm which he is representing when contacting or before dealing with any client or potential client. Member States may allow, in accordance with Article 13(6), (7) and (8), tied agents registered in their territory to handle clients' money and/or financial instruments on behalf and under the full responsibility of the investment firm for which they are acting within their territory or, in the case of a cross-border operation, in the territory of a Member State which allows a tied agent to handle clients' money. Member States shall require the investment firms to monitor the activities of their tied agents so as to ensure that they continue to comply with this Directive when acting through tied agents. 3. Member States that decide to allow investment firms to appoint tied agents shall establish a public register. Tied agents shall be registered in the public register in the Member State where they are established. Where the Member State in which the tied agent is established has decided, in accordance with paragraph 1, not to allow the investment firms authorised by their competent	• Obligations related to appointment of tied agent. • Guide on registration of Brokers and dealers: There is no differentiation between employees and other associated persons for securities law purposes. Broker-dealers must supervise the securities activities of their personnel regardless of whether they are considered "employees" or "independent contractors" as defined under state law. See, for example, *In the matter of William V. Giordano*, Securities Exchange Act Release No. 36742 (January 19, 1996).

European Regulatory Framework for Financial Instruments	U.S. Regulatory Framework for Financial Instruments
authorities to appoint tied agents, those tied agents shall be registered with the competent authority of the home Member State of the investment firm on whose behalf it acts. Member States shall ensure that tied agents are only admitted to the public register if it has been established that they are of sufficiently good repute and that they possess appropriate general, commercial and professional knowledge so as to be able to communicate accurately all relevant information regarding the proposed service to the client or potential client. Member States may decide that investment firms can verify whether the tied agents which they have appointed are of sufficiently good repute and possess the knowledge as referred to in the third subparagraph. The register shall be updated on a regular basis. It shall be publicly available for consultation. 4. Member States shall require that investment firms appointing tied agents take adequate measures in order to avoid any negative impact that the activities of the tied agent not covered by the scope of this Directive could have on the activities carried out by the tied agent on behalf of the investment firm. Member States may allow competent authorities to collaborate with investment firms and credit institutions, their associations and other entities in registering tied agents and in monitoring compliance of tied agents with the requirements of paragraph 3. In particular, tied agents may be registered by an investment firm, credit institution or their associations and other entities under the supervision of the competent authority. 5. Member States shall require that investment firms appoint only tied agents entered in the public registers referred to in paragraph 3. 6. Member States may reinforce the requirements set out in this Article or add other requirements for tied agents registered within their jurisdiction. • Pre-trade reporting requirements for investment firms MiFID, Article 27	• Pre - trade transparency requirements for brokers and dealers Equities: Rule 602 -- Dissemination of Quotations in NMS Securities

European Regulatory Framework for Financial Instruments	U.S. Regulatory Framework for Financial Instruments

Obligation for investment firms to make public firm quotes
 	
1. Member States shall require systematic internalisers in shares to publish a firm quote in those shares admitted to trading on a Regulated Market for which they are systematic internalisers and for which there is a liquid market. In the case of shares for which there is not a liquid market, systematic internalisers shall disclose quotes to their clients on request.
 	
The provisions of this Article shall be **applicable to systematic internalisers when dealing for sizes up to standard market size.** Systematic internalisers that only deal in sizes above standard market size shall not be subject to the provisions of this Article.
 	
Systematic internalisers may decide the size or sizes at which they will quote. For a particular share each quote shall include a firm bid and/or offer price or prices for a size or sizes which could be up to standard market size for the class of shares to which the share belongs. The price or prices shall also reflect the prevailing market conditions for that share.
 	
2. Systematic internalisers shall make public their quotes on a regular and continuous basis during normal trading hours. They shall be entitled to update their quotes at any time. They shall also be allowed, under exceptional market conditions, to withdraw their quotes. The quote shall be made public in a manner which is easily accessible to other market participants on a reasonable commercial basis.
 	
3. Systematic internalisers shall, while complying with the provisions set down in Article 21, execute the orders they receive from their retail clients in relation to the shares for which they are systematic internalisers at the quoted prices at the time of reception of the order. Systematic internalisers shall execute the orders they receive from their professional clients in relation to the shares for
	b. Obligations of responsible brokers and dealers.
	
	1. Each responsible **broker or dealer shall promptly communicate** to its national securities exchange or national securities association, pursuant to the procedures established by that exchange or association, **its best bids, best offers, and quotation sizes for any subject security.**
	
	2. Subject to the provisions of paragraph b3 of this section, each responsible **broker or dealer shall be obligated to execute** any order to buy or sell a subject security, other than an odd-lot order, presented to it by another broker or dealer, or any other person belonging to a category of persons with whom such responsible broker or dealer customarily deals, **at a price at least as favorable to such buyer or seller as the responsible broker's or dealer's published bid or published offer** (exclusive of any commission, commission equivalent or differential customarily charged by such responsible broker or dealer in connection with execution of any such order) in any amount up to its published quotation size.
	
	3. I. No responsible broker or dealer shall be obligated to execute a transaction for any subject security as provided in paragraph b2 of this section to purchase or sell that subject security in an amount greater than such revised quotation size if:
	
	    (1) Prior to the presentation of an order for the purchase or sale of a subject security, a responsible broker or dealer has communicated to its exchange or association, pursuant to paragraph 1 of this section, a revised quotation size; or
	
	    (2) At the time an order for the purchase or sale of a subject security is presented, a responsible broker or dealer is in the process of effecting a transaction in such subject security, and immediately after the completion of such transaction, it communicates to its exchange or association a revised quotation size, such responsible broker or dealer shall not be obligated by paragraph b2 of this section to purchase or sell that subject security in an amount

European Regulatory Framework for Financial Instruments	U.S. Regulatory Framework for Financial Instruments
which they are systematic internalisers at the quoted price at the time of reception of the order. However, they may execute those orders at a better price in justified cases provided that this price falls within a public range close to market conditions and provided that the orders are of a size bigger than the size customarily undertaken by a retail investor. 4. Furthermore, systematic internalisers may execute orders they receive from their professional clients at prices different than their quoted ones without having to comply with the conditions established in the fourth subparagraph, in respect of transactions where execution in several securities is part of one transaction or in respect of orders that are subject to conditions other than the current market price. 5. The competent authorities shall check: • that investment firms regularly update bid and/or offer prices published in accordance with paragraph 1 and maintain prices which reflect the prevailing market conditions; 6. Systematic internalisers shall be allowed to decide, on the basis of their commercial policy and in an objective nondiscriminatory way, the investors to whom they give access to their quotes. To that end there shall be clear standards for governing access to their quotes. Systematic internalisers may refuse to enter into or discontinue business relationships with investors on the basis of commercial considerations such as the investor credit status, the counterparty risk and the final settlement of the transaction. Relevant provisions from the implementing regulation: Note: This obligation applies only for shares for which investment firms are registered as systematic internalisers. That means that there is no pre-trade transparency requirement	greater than such revised quotation size. II. No responsible broker or dealer shall be obligated to execute a transaction for any subject security as provided in paragraph b2 of this section if: (1) Before the order sought to be executed is presented, such responsible broker or dealer has communicated to its exchange or association pursuant to paragraph b1 of this section, a revised bid or offer; or (2) At the time the order sought to be executed is presented, such responsible broker or dealer is in the process of effecting a transaction in such subject security, and, immediately after the completion of such transaction, such responsible broker or dealer communicates to its exchange or association pursuant to paragraph b1 of this section, a revised bid or offer; provided, however, that such responsible broker or dealer shall nonetheless be obligated to execute any such order in such subject security as provided in paragraph b2 of this section at its revised bid or offer in any amount up to its published quotation size or revised quotation size. 4. Subject to the provisions of paragraph a4 (see under regulated exchanges) of this section: I. No national securities exchange or OTC market maker may make available, disseminate or otherwise communicate to any vendor, directly or indirectly, for display on a terminal or other display device any bid, offer, quotation size, or aggregate quotation size for any NMS security which is not a subject security with respect to such exchange or OTC market maker; and II. No vendor may disseminate or display on a terminal or other display device any bid, offer, quotation size, or aggregate quotation size from any national securities exchange or OTC market maker for any NMS security which is not a subject security with respect to such exchange or

European Regulatory Framework for Financial Instruments	U.S. Regulatory Framework for Financial Instruments

for which firms are not registered as systematic internalisers, but are executed outside the RMs and MTFs. Example for these are brokers & dealers platforms (crossing networks).
 	
Additionally, there is no obligation for pre-trade transparency requirements for bonds, collateralized debt and derivatives.
 	
Provisions from the implementing regulation.
Article 22
Determination of liquid shares
1. A share admitted to trading on a Regulated Market shall be considered to have a liquid market if the share is traded daily, with a free float not less than EUR 500 million, and one of the following conditions is satisfied:
   • the average daily number of transactions in the share is not less than 500;
   • the average daily turnover for the share is not less than EUR 2 million.
   However, a Member State may, in respect of shares for which it is the most relevant market, specify by notice that both of those conditions are to apply. That notice shall be made public.
2. A Member State may specify the minimum number of liquid shares for that Member State. The minimum number shall be no greater than five. The specification shall be made public.
3. Where, pursuant to paragraph 1, a Member State would be the most relevant market for fewer liquid shares than the minimum number specified in accordance with paragraph 2, the competent authority for that Member State may designate one or more additional liquid shares, provided that the total number of shares which are considered in consequence to be liquid shares for which that Member State is the most relevant market does not exceed the minimum number specified by that Member State.
	5. OTC market maker.
	
	I. Entry of any priced order for an NMS security by an exchange market maker or OTC market maker in that security into an electronic communications network that widely disseminates such order shall be deemed to be:
	(1) A bid or offer under this section, to be communicated to the market maker's exchange or association pursuant to this paragraph (b) for at least the minimum quotation size that is required by the rules of the market maker's exchange or association if the priced order is for the account of a market maker, or the actual size of the order up to the minimum quotation size required if the priced order is for the account of a customer; and
	(2) A communication of a bid or offer to a vendor for display on a display device for purposes of paragraph b4 of this section.
	
	II. An exchange market maker or OTC market maker that has entered a priced order for an NMS security into an **electronic communications network** that widely disseminates such order shall be deemed to be in compliance with paragraph 5(1) of this section if the electronic communications network:
	(A)
	(1) Provides to a national securities exchange or national securities association (or an exclusive processor acting on behalf of one or more exchanges or associations) the prices and sizes of the orders at the highest buy price and the lowest sell price for such security entered in, and widely disseminated by, the electronic communications network by exchange market makers and OTC market makers for the NMS security, and such prices and sizes are included in the quotation data made available by such exchange, association, or exclusive processor to vendors pursuant to this

European Regulatory Framework for Financial Instruments	U.S. Regulatory Framework for Financial Instruments
4. The competent authority shall designate the additional liquid shares successively in decreasing order of average daily turnover from among the shares for which it is the relevant competent authority that are admitted to trading on a Regulated Market and are traded daily. For the purposes of the first subparagraph of paragraph 1, the calculation of the free float of a share shall exclude holdings exceeding 5 % of the total voting rights of the issuer, unless such a holding is held by a collective investment undertaking or a pension fund. Voting rights shall be calculated on the basis of all the shares to which voting rights are attached, even if the exercise of such a right is suspended. 5. A share shall not be considered to have a liquid market for the purposes of Article 27 of Directive 2004/39/EC until six weeks after its first admission to trading on a Regulated Market, if the estimate of the total market capitalization for that share at the start of the first day's trading after that admission, provided in accordance with Article 33(3), is less than EUR 500 million. 6. Each competent authority shall ensure the maintenance and publication of a list of all liquid shares for which it is the relevant competent authority. It shall ensure that the list is current by reviewing it at least annually. The list shall be made available to the Committee of European Securities Regulators. It shall be considered as published when it is published by the Committee of European Securities Regulators in accordance with Article 34(5). Article 23 **Standard market size** Article 24 In order to determine the standard market size for liquid shares, those shares shall be grouped into classes in terms of the average value of orders executed in accordance with Table 3 in Annex II.	section; and (2) Provides, to any broker or dealer, the ability to effect a transaction with a priced order widely disseminated by the electronic communications network entered therein by an exchange market maker or OTC market maker that is: I. Equivalent to the ability of any broker or dealer to effect a transaction with an exchange market maker or OTC market maker pursuant to the rules of the national securities exchange or national securities association to which the electronic communications network supplies such bids and offers; and II. At the price of the highest priced buy order or lowest priced sell order, or better, for the lesser of the cumulative size of such priced orders entered therein by exchange market makers or OTC market makers at such price, or the size of the execution sought by the broker or dealer, for such security; or (B) Is an alternative trading system that: (1) Displays orders and provides the ability to effect transactions with such orders under Rule 242.301(b)(3); and (2) Otherwise is in compliance with Regulation ATS (Rule 242.300 through Rule 242.303). c. *Transactions in listed options.* 1. A national securities exchange or national securities association: I. Shall not be required, under paragraph (a) of this section, to collect from responsible brokers or dealers who are members of such exchange or association, or **to make available to vendors, the quotation sizes and aggregate quotation sizes for listed options**, if such exchange or association establishes by rule and periodically publishes the quotation size for which such responsible brokers or dealers are obligated to

European Regulatory Framework for Financial Instruments	U.S. Regulatory Framework for Financial Instruments
Quotes reflecting prevailing market conditions A systematic internaliser shall, for each liquid share for which it is a systematic internaliser, maintain the following: • a quote or quotes which are close in price to comparable quotes for the same share in other trading venues; • a record of its quoted prices, which it shall retain for a period of 12 months or such longer period as it considers appropriate. The obligation laid down in point (b) is without prejudice to the obligation of the investment firm under Article 25(2) of Directive 2004/39/EC to keep at the disposal of the competent authority for at least five years the relevant data relating to all transactions it has carried out. Article 25 **Execution of orders by systematic internalisers** 18. For the purposes of the fifth subparagraph of Article 27(3) of Directive 2004/39/EC, execution in several securities shall be regarded as part of one transaction if that one transaction is a portfolio trade that involves 10 or more securities. For the same purposes, an order subject to conditions other than the current market price means any order which is neither an order for the execution of a transaction in shares at the prevailing market price, nor a limit order. 19. For the purposes of Article 27(6) of Directive 2004/39/EC, the number or volume of orders shall be regarded as considerably exceeding the norm if a systematic internaliser cannot execute those orders without exposing itself to undue risk. In order to identify the number and volume of orders that it can execute without exposing itself to undue risk, a systematic internaliser shall maintain and implement as part of its risk management policy under Article 7 of Commission Directive 2006/73/EC (1) a non-discriminatory policy which takes into account the volume of the transactions, the capital that the firm has available to cover the risk for that type of trade, and the prevailing conditions in the market in which the firm is operating.	execute an order to buy or sell an options series that is a subject security at its published bid or offer under paragraph (b)(2) of this section; II. May establish by rule and periodically publish a quotation size, which shall not be for less than one contract, for which responsible brokers or dealers who are members of such exchange or association are obligated under paragraph (b)(2) of this section to execute an order to buy or sell a listed option for the account of a broker or dealer that is in an amount different from the quotation size for which it is obligated to execute an order for the account of a customer; and III. May establish and maintain procedures and mechanisms for collecting from responsible brokers and dealers who are members of such exchange or association, and making available to vendors, the quotation sizes and aggregate quotation sizes in listed options for which such responsible broker or dealer will be obligated under paragraph (b)(2) of this section to execute an order from a customer to buy or sell a listed option and establish by rule and periodically publish the size, which shall not be less than one contract, for which such responsible brokers or dealers are obligated to execute an order for the account of a broker or dealer. 2. If, pursuant to paragraph (c)(1) of this section, the rules of a national securities exchange or national securities association do not require its members to communicate to it their quotation sizes for listed options, a responsible broker or dealer that is a member of such exchange or association shall: 1. Be relieved of its obligations under paragraph (b)(1) of this section to communicate to such exchange or association its quotation sizes for any listed option; and 2. Comply with its obligations under paragraph (b)(2) of this section by executing any order to buy or sell a listed option, in an amount up to the size established by such exchange's or association's rules under paragraph (c)(1) of this section. 3. *Thirty second response.* Each responsible broker or dealer, within thirty

European Regulatory Framework for Financial Instruments	U.S. Regulatory Framework for Financial Instruments

20. Where, in accordance with Article 27(6) of Directive 2004/39/EC, an investment firm limits the number or volume of orders it undertakes to execute, it shall set out in writing, and make available to clients and potential clients, the arrangements designed to ensure that such a limitation does not result in the discriminatory treatment of clients.
 	
Retail size
 	
Article 26
 	
For the purposes of the fourth subparagraph of Article 27(3) of Directive 2004/39/EC, an order shall be regarded as being of a size bigger than the size customarily undertaken by a retail investor if it exceeds EUR 7 500.
	seconds of receiving an order to buy or sell a listed option in an amount greater than the quotation size established by a national securities exchange's or national securities association's rules pursuant to paragraph (c)(1) of this section, or its published quotation size must:
	
	I. Execute the entire order; or
	II.
	   A. Execute that portion of the order equal to at least:
	     (2) The quotation size established by a national securities exchange's or national securities association's rules, pursuant to paragraph (c)(1) of this section, to the extent that such exchange or association does not collect and make available to vendors quotation size and aggregate quotation size under paragraph (a) of this section; or
	     (3) Its published quotation size; and
	   B. Revise its bid or offer.
	
	4. Notwithstanding paragraph (c)(3) of this section, no responsible broker or dealer shall be obligated to execute a transaction for any listed option as provided in paragraph (b)(2) of this section if:
	I. Any of the circumstances in paragraph (b)(3) of this section exist; or
	II. The order for the purchase or sale of a listed option is presented during a trading rotation in that listed option.
	
	d. *Exemptions*. The Commission may exempt from the provisions of this section, either unconditionally or on specified terms and conditions, any responsible broker or dealer, electronic communications network, national securities exchange, or national securities association if the Commission determines that such exemption is consistent with the public interest, the protection of investors and the removal of impediments to and perfection of the mechanism of a national market system.

European Regulatory Framework for Financial Instruments	U.S. Regulatory Framework for Financial Instruments

• Post-trade reporting requirements for investment firms
 	
MiFID, Article 28
 	
Post-trade disclosure by investment firms
 	
1. Member States shall, at least, require **investment firms** which, either on own account or on behalf of clients, conclude transactions **in shares admitted to trading on a Regulated Market outside a Regulated Market or MTF, to make public the volume and price of those transactions and the time at which they were concluded.** This information shall be made public as close to real-time as possible, on a reasonable commercial basis, and in a manner which is easily accessible to other market participants.
 	
2. Member States shall require that the information which is made public in accordance with paragraph 1 and the time-limits within which it is published comply with the requirements for post-trade transparency requirements for Regulated Markets. Where the measures adopted pursuant to Article 45 (post trade transparency requirements for RMs) provide for deferred reporting for certain categories of transaction in shares (mostly transactions that are large in scale compared with the normal market size for that share or that class of shares), this possibility shall apply mutatis mutandis to those transactions when undertaken outside Regulated Markets or MTFs.
 	
Relevant provisions from the implementing regulation, MiFID level 2, Article 30
 	
Public availability of pre-and post-trade information
 	
Pre-and post-trade information shall be considered to be made public or available to the public if it is made available generally through one of the following to investors located in the Community:
	• Post-trade transparency requirements for brokers and dealers
	
	Rule 601 of Regulation NMS regulates dissemination of transaction reports and last sale data.
	
	According to this rule every exchange and association shall have in place a transaction reporting plan regarding transaction in listed equity and Nasdaq securities executed either through exchange facilities or outside exchanges (association). The trade sale data are collected by exchanges/associations and then consolidated and disseminated. Transaction reporting plans provide more information on responsibilities of brokers and dealers and SROs in this process, as described in this section – Rule 601 is followed by Section 8 from a Consolidated Tape, a joint plan of AMEX, BATS, the BSE, the CBOE, the CHX, the ISE, Nasdaq, the NSX, the NYSE, NYSE Arca and the PHLX
	
	Rule 601 – Dissemination of Transaction Reports and Last Sale Data with Respect to Transactions in NMS Stocks
	
	a. *Filing and effectiveness of transaction reporting plans.*
	
	  1. **Every national securities exchange shall file a transaction reporting plan regarding transactions in listed equity and Nasdaq securities** executed through its facilities, and every national securities association shall file a transaction reporting plan regarding transactions in listed equity and Nasdaq securities executed by its members otherwise than on a national securities exchange.
	
	  2. Any transaction reporting plan, or any amendment thereto, filed pursuant to this section shall be filed with the Commission, and considered for approval, in accordance with the procedures set forth in Rule 242.608(a) and (b). Any such plan, or amendment thereto, shall specify, at a minimum:

European Regulatory Framework for Financial Instruments	U.S. Regulatory Framework for Financial Instruments
1. the facilities of a Regulated Market or an MTF; 2. the facilities of a third party; 3. proprietary arrangements.	i. The listed equity and Nasdaq securities or classes of such securities for which transaction reports shall be required by the plan; ii. Reporting requirements with respect to transactions in listed equity securities and Nasdaq securities, for any broker or dealer subject to the plan; iii. The manner of collecting, processing, sequencing, making available and disseminating transaction reports and last sale data reported pursuant to such plan; iv. The manner in which such transaction reports reported pursuant to such plan are to be consolidated with transaction reports from national securities exchanges and national securities associations reported pursuant to any other effective transaction reporting plan; v. The applicable standards and methods which will be utilized to ensure promptness of reporting, and accuracy and completeness of transaction reports; vi. Any rules or procedures which may be adopted to ensure that transaction reports or last sale data will not be disseminated in a fraudulent or manipulative manner; vii. Specific terms of access to transaction reports made available or disseminated pursuant to the plan; and viii. That transaction reports or last sale data made available to any vendor for display on an interrogation device identify the marketplace where each transaction was executed. 3. No transaction reporting plan filed pursuant to this section, or any amendment to an effective transaction reporting plan, shall become effective unless approved by the Commission or otherwise permitted in accordance with the procedures set forth in Rule

European Regulatory Framework for Financial Instruments	U.S. Regulatory Framework for Financial Instruments
	242.608.
	b. *Prohibitions and reporting requirements.*
	1. No broker or dealer may execute any transaction in, or induce or attempt to induce the purchase or sale of, any NMS stock:
	i. On or through the facilities of a national securities exchange unless there is an effective transaction reporting plan with respect to transactions in such security executed on or through such exchange facilities; or
	ii. Otherwise than on a national securities exchange unless there is an effective transaction reporting plan with respect to transactions in such security executed otherwise than on a national securities exchange by such broker or dealer.
	2. Every broker or dealer who is a member of a national securities exchange or national securities association shall promptly transmit to the exchange or association of which it is a member all information required by any effective transaction reporting plan filed by such exchange or association (either individually or jointly with other exchanges and/or associations).
	c. *Retransmission of transaction reports or last sale data.* Notwithstanding any provision of any effective transaction reporting plan, no national securities exchange or national securities association may, either individually or jointly, by rule, stated policy or practice, transaction reporting plan or otherwise, prohibit, condition or otherwise limit, directly or indirectly, the ability of any vendor to retransmit, for display in moving tickers, transaction reports or last sale data made available pursuant to any effective transaction reporting plan; provided, however, that a national securities exchange or national securities association may, by means of an effective transaction reporting plan, condition such retransmission upon appropriate undertakings to ensure that any charges for the distribution of transaction reports or last sale data in moving tickers

European Regulatory Framework for Financial Instruments	U.S. Regulatory Framework for Financial Instruments
	permitted by paragraph (d) of this section are collected.
	d. *Charges.* Nothing in this section shall preclude any national securities exchange or national securities association, separately or jointly, pursuant to the terms of an effective transaction reporting plan, from imposing reasonable, uniform charges (irrespective of geographic location) for distribution of transaction reports or last sale data.
	e. Appeals. The Commission may, in its discretion, entertain appeals in connection with the implementation or operation of any effective transaction reporting plan in accordance with the provisions of Rule 242.608(d).
	f. *Exemptions.* The Commission may exempt from the provisions of this section, either unconditionally or on specified terms and conditions, any national securities exchange, national securities association, broker, dealer, or specified security if the Commission determines that such exemption is consistent with the public interest, the protection of investors and the removal of impediments to, and perfection of the mechanisms of, a national market system.
	Section 8 (a) of CTA plan. Collection and reporting of last sale data.
	a) Responsibility of Exchange Participants. The AMEX, BATS, the BSE, the CBOE, the CHX, the ISE, Nasdaq, the NSX, the NYSE, NYSE Arca and the PHLX will each collect and report to the Processor all last sale price information to be reported by it relating to transactions in eligible securities taking place on its floor. In addition, FINRA shall collect from its members all last sale price information to be included in the consolidated tape relating to transactions in eligible securities not taking place on the floor of an exchange and shall report all such last sale price information to the Processor. It will be the responsibility of each participant and each other reporting party, to 1) report all last sale price relating to transactions in Eligible Securities as promptly as possible, establish and maintain collection and reporting procedures and facilities such as to assure that under normal conditions not less than 90% of such last sale prices will be

European Regulatory Framework for Financial Instruments	U.S. Regulatory Framework for Financial Instruments
	reported within that period of time in light of experience, and 3) designate as "late" any last sale price not collected and reported in accordance with the above-referenced procedures or as to which reporting party has knowledge that the time interval after the time of execution is significantly greater than the time period referred to above. CTA shall seek to reduce time period for reporting last sale prices to the Processors as conditions warrant.
	b) FINRA responsibility. The FINRA shall develop and adapt rules governing the reporting of last sale price information to be reported by its members to the Processor for inclusion on consolidated tape (see below Rule 6622 for Reporting of OTC transactions).
	c) Description of reporting procedure. Each Participant and each reporting party has prepared and submitted to CTA (and furnished to the SEC) for its information a description of the procedure by which it collects and reports to the processor last sale price information reported by it pursuant to this CTA plan.
	Section 9 of CTA Plan. Receipt and use of CTA information. a) Requirements for receipt and use of information. Pursuant to fair and reasonable terms and conditions, each CTA network's administrator shall provide for: 1) the dissemination of each CTA network's information on terms that are not seasonable discriminatory to vendors, newspapers, Participant, Participant Members and member organizations, and other persons over that network's Ticker and over the high speed line; and 2) the use of that CTA network's information by vendors, subscribers, newspapers, Participants, Participant members and member organization, and other persons.

European Regulatory Framework for Financial Instruments	U.S. Regulatory Framework for Financial Instruments
	FINRA Rule 6622 Transaction Reporting **(a) When and How Transactions are Reported** (1) OTC Market Makers shall, within 90 seconds after execution, transmit to the OTC Reporting Facility last sale reports of transactions in **OTC Equity Securities** executed between the hours of 9:30 a.m. and 4:00 p.m. Eastern Time. Transactions not reported within 90 seconds after execution shall be designated as late. (2) Non-Market Makers shall, within 90 seconds after execution, transmit to the OTC Reporting Facility, or by telephone to the Operations Department if the OTC Reporting Facility is unavailable due to system or transmission failure, last sale reports of transactions in OTC Equity Securities executed between the hours of 9:30 a.m. and 4:00 p.m. Transactions not reported within 90 seconds after execution shall be designated as late. Note: This is a very detailed rule. For the purpose of this table we provided only the first two paragraphs. For the rest please visit FINRA website. (3) **FINRA Rule 6623 Timely Transaction Reporting** FINRA emphasizes the obligations of members to report securities transactions within 90 seconds after execution. All reportable transactions not reported within 90 seconds after execution shall be reported as late, and FINRA routinely monitors members' compliance with the 90-second requirement. If FINRA finds a pattern or practice of unexcused late reporting, that is, repeated reports of executions after 90 seconds without reasonable justification or exceptional circumstances, the member may be found to be in violation of Rule 2010. Exceptional circumstances will be determined on a case-by-case basis and may include instances of system failure by a member or service bureau, or unusual market conditions, such as extreme volatility in a security, or in the market as a whole. Timely reporting of all transactions is necessary and appropriate for the fair and orderly operation of the marketplace, and FINRA will view noncompliance as a rule violation.

European Regulatory Framework for Financial Instruments	U.S. Regulatory Framework for Financial Instruments
	Corporate bonds Reporting FINRA website: NASD introduced TRACE (Trade Reporting and Compliance Engine) in July 2002 in an effort to increase price transparency in the U.S. corporate debt market. The system captures and disseminates consolidated information on secondary market transactions in publicly traded TRACE-eligible securities (investment grade, high yield and convertible corporate debt) - representing all over-the-counter market activity in these bonds.
• Records and Reports MiFID level 1, Article 25 Obligation to uphold integrity of markets, report transactions and maintain records, 1. **Member States shall require investment firms to keep at the disposal of the competent authority, for at least five years, the relevant data relating to all transactions in financial instruments** which they have carried out, whether on own account or on behalf of a client. In the case of transactions carried out on behalf of clients, the records shall contain all the information and details of the identity of the client, and the information required under Council Directive 91/308/EEC of 10 June 1991 on prevention of the use of the financial system for the purpose of money laundering (2). 2. **Member States shall require investment firms which execute transactions in any financial instruments admitted to trading on a Regulated Market to report details of such transactions to the competent authority as quickly as possible, and no later than the close of the following working day.** This obligation shall apply whether or not such transactions were carried out on a Regulated Market. The competent authorities shall, in accordance with Article 58, establish the necessary arrangements in order to ensure that the competent authority of the most relevant market in terms of liquidity (most relevant market in terms of liquidity is defined in implementing regulation, Article 9) for those financial instruments also receives this information.	• Records and Reports Section 17 of the Securities Exchange Act Rules and regulations Records and Reports 1. Every national securities exchange, member thereof, **broker or dealer** who transacts a business in securities through the medium of any such member, registered securities association, registered broker or dealer, registered municipal securities dealer, registered securities information processor, registered transfer agent, nationally recognized statistical rating organization, and registered clearing agency and the Municipal Securities Rulemaking Board **shall make and keep for prescribed periods such records, furnish such copies thereof, and make and disseminate such reports as the Commission, by rule, prescribes as necessary or appropriate in the public interest, for the protection of investors, or otherwise in furtherance of the purposes of this title.** Reg ATS, Rule 302 **Recordkeeping Requirements for Alternative Trading Systems** To comply with the condition set forth in Rule 301, an alternative trading system shall make and keep current the following records: a. A record of subscribers to such alternative trading system (identifying any affiliations between the alternative trading system and subscribers to the alternative trading system, including common directors, officers, or owners);

European Regulatory Framework for Financial Instruments	U.S. Regulatory Framework for Financial Instruments

3. **The reports shall, in particular, include details of the names and numbers of the instruments bought or sold, the quantity, the dates and times of execution and the transaction prices and means of identifying the investment firms concerned.**
 	
4. Member States shall provide for the reports to be made to the competent authority either by the investment firm itself, a third party acting on its behalf or by a trade-matching or reporting system approved by the competent authority or by the Regulated Market or MTF through whose systems the transaction was completed. In cases where transactions are reported directly to the competent authority by a Regulated Market, an MTF, or a trade-matching or reporting system approved by the competent authority, the obligation on the investment firm laid down in paragraph 3 may be waived.
 	
5. When, in accordance with Article 32(7), reports provided for under this Article are transmitted to the competent authority of the host Member State, it shall transmit this information to the competent authorities of the home Member State of the investment firm, unless they decide that they do not want to receive this information.
 	
6. In order to ensure that measures for the protection of market integrity are modified to take account of technical developments in financial markets, and to ensure the uniform application of paragraphs 1 to 5, the Commission may adopt, in accordance with the procedure referred to in Article 64(2), implementing measures which define the methods and arrangements for reporting financial transactions, the form and content of these reports and the criteria for defining a relevant market in accordance with paragraph 3.
 	
Relevant provisions in implementing regulation: EC No 1287/2006 Articles 9 – 14.
	b. Daily summaries of trading in the alternative trading system including:
	  1. Securities for which transactions have been executed;
	  2. Transaction volume, expressed with respect to equity securities in:
	    i. Number of trades;
	    ii. Number of shares traded; and
	    iii. Total settlement value in terms of U.S. dollars; and
	  3. Transaction volume, expressed with respect to debt securities in:
	    i. Number of trades; and
	    ii. Total U.S. dollar value; and
	c. Time-sequenced records of order information in the alternative trading system, including:
	  1. Date and time (expressed in terms of hours, minutes, and seconds) that the order was received;
	  2. Identity of the security;
	  3. The number of shares, or principal amount of bonds, to which the order applies;
	  4. An identification of the order as related to a program trade or an index arbitrage trade as defined in New York Stock Exchange Rule 80A;
	  5. The designation of the order as a buy or sell order;
	  6. The designation of the order as a short sale order;
	  7. The designation of the order as a market order, limit order, stop order, stop limit order, or other type or order;
	  8. Any limit or stop price prescribed by the order;
	  9. The date on which the order expires and, if the time in force is less than one day, the time when the order expires;
	  10. The time limit during which the order is in force;
	  11. Any instructions to modify or cancel the order;
	  12. The type of account, i.e., retail, wholesale, employee, proprietary, or any

European Regulatory Framework for Financial Instruments	U.S. Regulatory Framework for Financial Instruments
	other type of account designated by the alternative trading system, for which the order is submitted; 13. Date and time (expressed in terms of hours, minutes, and seconds) that the order was executed; 14. Price at which the order was executed; 15. Size of the order executed (expressed in number of shares or units or principal amount); and 16. Identity of the parties to the transaction. • Transparency requirement for ATS (same as for exchanges and broker-dealers) Alternative trading venues register with the SEC as broker & dealers (unless because of large trading volume they register as exchanges in which case they are subject to the rules for the exchanges) and therefore are subject to the same rules as brokers and dealers. Reg ATS Summary of Final Rules (Section II-B) The framework the Commission adopts today uses the Commission's new exemptive authority to allow most alternative trading systems to choose to be regulated either as exchanges or as broker-dealers. Rule 3a1-1 exempts most alternative trading systems from the definition of "exchange," and therefore the requirement to register as an exchange, if they comply with Regulation ATS. However, any system exercising self-regulatory powers, such as regulating its members' or subscribers' conduct when engaged in activities outside of that trading system, must register as an exchange or be operated by a national securities association. This is because self-regulatory activities in the securities markets must be subject to Commission oversight under Section 19 of the Exchange Act.[24] Thus any system exercising self-regulatory powers will not be permitted the option of registering as a broker-dealer. In addition, the Commission can determine that a dominant alternative trading system should be registered as an
• Additional Trading Transparency Requirements for MTFs **MiFID level 1, Article 14** **Trading process and finalization of transactions in an MTF** 1. Member States shall require that investment firms or market operators operating an MTF, in addition to meeting the requirements laid down in Article 13, establish transparent and non-discretionary rules and procedures for fair and orderly trading and establish objective criteria for the efficient execution of orders. 2. Member States shall require that investment firms or market operators operating an MTF establish transparent rules regarding the criteria for determining the financial instruments that can be traded under its systems. Member States shall require that, where applicable, investment firms or market operators operating an MTF provide, or are satisfied that there is access to, sufficient publicly available information to enable its users to form an investment judgement, taking into account both the nature of the users and the types of instruments traded. 3. Member States shall ensure that Articles 19, 21 and 22 are not applicable to the transactions concluded under the rules governing an MTF between its members or participants or between the MTF and its members or participants in relation to the use of the MTF. However, the members or participants in	

European Regulatory Framework for Financial Instruments	U.S. Regulatory Framework for Financial Instruments
the MTF shall comply with the obligations provided for in Articles 19, 21 and 22 with respect to their clients when, acting on behalf of their clients, they execute their orders through the systems of an MTF. 4. Member States shall require that investment firms or market operators operating an MTF establish and maintain transparent rules, based on objective criteria, governing access to its facility. 5. Member States shall require that investment firms or market operators operating an MTF clearly inform its users of their respective responsibilities for the settlement of the transactions executed in that facility. Member States shall require that investment firms or market operators operating an MTF have put in place the necessary arrangements to facilitate the efficient settlement of the transactions concluded under the systems of the MTF. 6. Where a transferable security, which has been admitted to trading on a Regulated Market, is also traded on an MTF without the consent of the issuer, the issuer shall not be subject to any obligation relating to initial, ongoing or ad hoc financial disclosure with regard to that MTF. 7. Member States shall require that any investment firm or market operator operating an MTF comply immediately with any instruction from its competent authority pursuant to Article 50(1) to suspend or remove a financial instrument from trading. • Pre-trade transparency requirements for MTFs Article 29, MiFID level 1 1. Member States shall, at least, require that **investment firms and market operators operating an MTF make public current bid and offer prices and the depth of trading interests** at these prices which are advertised through their systems in respect of shares admitted to trading on a Regulated Market. Member States shall provide for this information to be made available to the	exchange. An alternative trading system would first have to exceed certain volume levels and the Commission, after notice and an opportunity for the alternative trading system to respond, would have to determine that an exemption from exchange regulation is not necessary or appropriate in the public interest or consistent with the protection of investors, taking into account the requirements of exchange registration and the objectives of the national market system. At this time, however, the Commission does not believe that it is necessary or appropriate under this provision that any alternative trading system register as an exchange. • Pre-trade Transparency for ATS Alternative trading systems register with the SEC as broker&dealers (unless because of large trading volume they register as exchanges) and therefore are subject to the same rules as brokers and dealers.

European Regulatory Framework for Financial Instruments	U.S. Regulatory Framework for Financial Instruments
public on reasonable commercial terms and on a continuous basis during normal trading hours.	Additional Rules set in Reg ATS: Rule 301:
2. Member States shall provide for the competent authorities to be able to waive the obligation for investment firms or market operators operating an MTF to make public the information referred to in paragraph 1 based on the market model or the type and size of orders in the cases defined in accordance with paragraph 3. In particular, the competent authorities shall be able to waive the obligation in respect of transactions that are large in scale compared with normal market size for the share or type of share in question.	1. Order display and execution access.
	i. An alternative trading system shall comply with the requirements set forth in paragraph (ii) of this section, with respect to any NMS stock in which the alternative trading system:
	A. Displays subscriber orders to any person (other than alternative trading system employees); and
3. In order to ensure the uniform application of paragraphs 1 and 2, the Commission shall, in accordance with the procedure referred to in Article 64(2) adopt implementing measures as regards:	B. During at least 4 of the preceding 6 calendar months, had an average daily trading volume of 5 percent or more of the aggregate average daily share volume for such NMS stock as reported by an effective transaction reporting plan.
(a) the range of bid and offers or designated market‑maker quotes, and the depth of trading interest at those prices, to be made public;	ii. Such alternative trading system shall provide to a national securities exchange or national securities association the prices and sizes of the orders at the highest buy price and the lowest sell price for such NMS stock, displayed to more than one person in the alternative trading system, for inclusion in the quotation data made available by the national securities exchange or national securities association to vendors pursuant to Rule 242.602.
(b) the size or type of orders for which pre‑trade disclosure may be waived under paragraph 2;	iii. (With respect to any order displayed pursuant to paragraph (ii) of this section, an alternative trading system shall provide to any broker-dealer that has access to the national securities exchange or national securities association to which the alternative trading system provides the prices and sizes of displayed orders pursuant to paragraph (ii) of this section, the ability to effect a transaction with such orders that is:
(c) the market model for which pre‑trade disclosure may be waived under paragraph 2 and in particular, the applicability of the obligation to trading methods operated by an MTF which conclude transactions under their rules by reference to prices established outside the systems of the MTF or by periodic auction.	A. Equivalent to the ability of such broker-dealer to effect a transaction with other orders displayed on the exchange or by the association; and
Except where justified by the specific nature of the MTF, the content of these implementing measures shall be equal to that of the implementing measures provided for in Article 44 for Regulated Markets.	B. At the price of the highest priced buy order or lowest priced sell order displayed for the lesser of the cumulative size of such priced orders entered therein at such price, or the size of the execution

European Regulatory Framework for Financial Instruments	U.S. Regulatory Framework for Financial Instruments
• Post-trade transparency requirements for MTFs MiFID, Article 30 **Post-trade transparency requirements for MTFs** 1. Member States shall, at least, require that investment firms and market operators operating an MTF make public the price, volume and time of the transactions executed under its systems in respect of shares which are admitted to trading on a Regulated Market. Member States shall require that details of all such transactions be made public, on a reasonable commercial basis, as close to real-time as possible. This requirement shall not apply to details of trades executed on an MTF that are made public under the systems of a Regulated Market. 2. Member States shall provide that the competent authority may authorise investment firms or market operators operating an MTF to provide for deferred publication of the details of transactions based on their type or size. In particular, the competent authorities may authorize the deferred publication in respect of transactions that are large in scale compared with the normal market size for that share or that class of shares. Member States shall require MTFs to obtain the competent authority's prior approval to proposed arrangements for deferred trade publication, and shall require that these arrangements be clearly disclosed to market participants and the investing public. 3. In order to provide for the efficient and orderly functioning of financial markets, and to ensure the uniform application of paragraphs 1 and 2, the Commission shall, in accordance with the procedure referred o in Article 64(2) adopt implementing measures in respect of: (a) the scope and content of the information to be made available to the public; (b) the conditions under which investment firms or market operators	sought by such broker-dealer. • Post-trade transparency requirements for alternative trading systems Same as for brokers and dealers unless registered as exchanges when the rules for exchanges shall apply.

European Regulatory Framework for Financial Instruments	U.S. Regulatory Framework for Financial Instruments

operating an MTF may provide for deferred publication of trades and the criteria to be applied when deciding the transactions for which, due to their size or the type of share involved, deferred publication is allowed.
 	
Except where justified by the specific nature of the MTF, the content of these implementing measures shall be equal to that of the implementing measures provided for in Article 45 for Regulated Markets.
 	
Relevant provisions from the implementing regulation, MiFID level 2, Article 18
 	
Waivers based on market model and type of order or transaction
 	
1.   Waivers in accordance with Article 29(2) (MTFs) and 44(2) (RMs) of Directive 2004/39/EC may be granted by the competent authorities for systems operated by an MTF or a Regulated Market, if those systems satisfy one of the following criteria:
 	
   (a) they must be based on a trading methodology by which the price is determined in accordance with a reference price generated by another system, where that reference price is widely published and is regarded generally by market participants as a reliable reference price;
 	
   (b) they formalize negotiated transactions, each of which meets one of the following criteria:
 	
      (i) it is made at or within the current volume weighted spread reflected on the order book or the quotes of the market makers of the Regulated Market or MTF operating that system or, where the share is not traded continuously, within a percentage of a suitable reference price, being a percentage and a reference price set in advance by the system operator;
 	
      (ii) it is subject to conditions other than the current market	

European Regulatory Framework for Financial Instruments	U.S. Regulatory Framework for Financial Instruments
price of the share. For the purposes of point (b), the other conditions specified in the rules of the Regulated Market or MTF for a transaction of this kind must also have been fulfilled. In the case of systems having functionality other than as described in points (a) or (b), the waiver shall not apply to that other functionality. 3. Waivers in accordance with Articles 29(2) and 44(2) of Directive 2004/39/EC based on the type of orders may be granted only in relation to orders held in an order management facility maintained by the Regulated Market or the MTF pending their being disclosed to the market. Article 20 **Waivers in relation to transactions which are large in scale** An order shall be considered to be large in scale compared with normal market size if it is equal to or larger than the minimum size of order specified in Table 2 in Annex II of the Directive. For the purposes of determining whether an order is large in scale compared to normal market size, all shares admitted to trading on a Regulated Market shall be classified in accordance with their average daily turnover, which shall be calculated in accordance with the procedure set out in Article 33.	
Regulated Markets • Authorization MiFID, Article 36 1. Member States shall reserve authorization as a Regulated Market to those systems which comply with the provisions of this Title. Authorization as a Regulated Market shall be granted only where the	**National Exchanges** • Registration of Exchanges Section 6 (a) of Securities Exchange Act Registration An exchange may be registered as a national securities exchange by filing with the Commission **an application for registration** containing the rules of the exchange and other information and documents as the Commission, by rule, may prescribe as

European Regulatory Framework for Financial Instruments	U.S. Regulatory Framework for Financial Instruments
competent authority is satisfied that both the market operator and the systems of the Regulated Market comply at least with the requirements laid down in this Title. In the case of a Regulated Market that is a legal person and that is managed or operated by a market operator other than the Regulated Market itself, Member States shall establish how the different obligations imposed on the market operator under this Directive are to be allocated between the Regulated Market and the market operator. 2. The operator of the Regulated Market shall provide all information, including a programme of operations setting out inter alia the types of business envisaged and the organisational structure, necessary to enable the competent authority to satisfy itself that the Regulated Market has established, at the time of initial authorization, all the necessary arrangements to meet its obligations under the provisions of this Title. 3. Member States shall require the operator of the Regulated Market to perform tasks relating to the organisation and operation of the Regulated Market under the supervision of the competent authority. Member States shall ensure that competent authorities keep under regular review the compliance of Regulated Markets with the provisions of this Title. They shall also ensure that competent authorities monitor that Regulated Markets comply at all times with the conditions for initial authorization established under this Title. 4. Member States shall ensure that the market operator is responsible for ensuring that the Regulated Market that he manages complies with all requirements under this Title. Member States shall also ensure that the market operator is entitled to exercise the rights that correspond to the Regulated Market that he manages by virtue of this Directive. 5. Without prejudice to any relevant provisions of Directive 2003/6/ EC, the public law governing the trading conducted under the systems of the Regulated Market shall be that of the home Member State of the Regulated Market.	necessary or appropriate in the public interest or for the protection of investors. Registration of securities exchange is conditional upon fulfillment of the organizational requirements as discussed in the section 27 of this table (Section 6 (b) of the Securities Exchange Act).

European Regulatory Framework for Financial Instruments	U.S. Regulatory Framework for Financial Instruments
6. The competent authority may withdraw the authorization issued to a Regulated Market where it: (a) does not make use of the authorization within 12 months, expressly renounces the authorization or has not operated for the preceding six months, unless the Member State concerned has provided for authorization to lapse in such cases; (b) has obtained the authorization by making false statements or by any other irregular means; (c) no longer meets the conditions under which authorization was granted; (d) has seriously and systematically infringed the provisions adopted pursuant to this Directive; (e) falls within any of the cases where national law provides for withdrawal.	
• Requirements for the Management of Regulated Markets (reputational and professional tests) MiFID, Article 37 2. Member States shall require the persons who effectively direct the business and the operations of the Regulated Market to be of sufficiently good repute and sufficiently experienced as to ensure the sound and prudent management and operation of the Regulated Market. Member States shall also require the operator of the Regulated Market to inform the competent authority of the identity and any other subsequent changes of the persons who effectively direct the business and the operations of the Regulated Market. The competent authority shall refuse to approve proposed changes where there are objective and demonstrable grounds for believing that they pose a material threat to the sound and prudent management and operation of the Regulated Market.	• Requirements for the Management of Exchanges • NA

European Regulatory Framework for Financial Instruments	U.S. Regulatory Framework for Financial Instruments
2. Member States shall ensure that, in the process of authorization of a Regulated Market, the person or persons who effectively direct the business and the operations of an already authorized Regulated Market in accordance with the conditions of this Directive are deemed to comply with the requirements laid down in paragraph 1.	
• Requirements related to people exercising significant influence (reputational and when required professional tests) MiFID level 1, Article 38 1. Member States shall require the persons who are in a position to exercise, directly or indirectly, significant influence over the management of the Regulated Market to be suitable. 2. Member States shall require the operator of the Regulated Market: (a) to provide the competent authority with, and to make public, information regarding the ownership of the Regulated Market and/or the market operator, and in particular, the identity and scale of interests of any parties in a position to exercise significant influence over the management; (b) to inform the competent authority of and to make public any transfer of ownership which gives rise to a change in the identity of the persons exercising significant influence over the operation of the Regulated Market. 3. The competent authority shall refuse to approve proposed changes to the controlling interests of the Regulated Market and/or the market operator where there are objective and demonstrable grounds for believing that they would pose a threat to the sound and prudent management of the Regulated Market.	• NA
• Organizational Requirements for Regulated Markets MiFID, Article 39	• Organizational Requirements for Exchanges Section 6 of the Securities Exchange Act

European Regulatory Framework for Financial Instruments	U.S. Regulatory Framework for Financial Instruments
Member States shall require the Regulated Market: (a) to have arrangements to identify and manage the potential adverse consequences, for the operation of the Regulated Market or for its participants, of any conflict of interest between the interest of the Regulated Market, its owners or its operator and the sound functioning of the Regulated Market, and in particular where such conflicts of interest might prove prejudicial to the accomplishment of any functions delegated to the Regulated Market by the competent authority; (b) to be adequately equipped to manage the risks to which it is exposed, to implement appropriate arrangements and systems to identify all significant risks to its operation, and to put in place effective measures to mitigate those risks; (c) to have arrangements for the sound management of the technical operations of the system, including the establishment of effective contingency arrangements to cope with risks of systems disruptions; (d) to have transparent and non-discretionary rules and procedures that provide for fair and orderly trading and establish objective criteria for the efficient execution of orders; (e) to have effective arrangements to facilitate the efficient and timely finalization of the transactions executed under its systems; (f) to have available, at the time of authorization and on an ongoing basis, sufficient financial resources to facilitate its orderly functioning, having regard to the nature and extent of the transactions concluded on the market and the range and degree of the risks to which it is exposed.	1) **An Exchange shall be so organized** and have the capacity to be able to carry out the purposes of Securities Exchange Act and to comply and to enforce compliance by its members and persons associated with its members, with the provisions of this chapter, the rules and regulations thereunder, and the rules of the exchange. 2) Subject to the provisions of subsection (c) of section 78f, the rules of the exchange provide that any registered broker or dealer or natural person associated with a registered broker or dealer may become a member of such exchange and any person may become associated with a member thereof. 3) The rules of the exchange assure a fair representation of its members in the selection of its directors and administration of its affairs and provide that one or more directors shall be representative of issuers and investors and not be associated with a member of the exchange, broker, or dealer. 4) The rules of the exchange provide for the equitable allocation of reasonable dues, fees, and other charges among its members and issuers and other persons using its facilities. 5) The rules of the exchange are designed to prevent fraudulent and manipulative acts and practices, to promote just and equitable principles of trade, to foster cooperation and coordination with persons engaged in regulating, clearing, settling, processing information with respect to, and facilitating transactions in securities, to remove impediments to and perfect the mechanism of a free and open market and a national market system, and, in general, to protect investors and the public interest; and are not designed to permit unfair discrimination between customers, issuers, brokers, or dealers, or to regulate by virtue of any authority conferred by this chapter matters not related to the purposes of this chapter or the administration of the exchange. 6) The rules of the exchange provide that (subject to any rule or order of the Commission pursuant to section 78q(d) or 78s(g)l(2) of this title) its members and persons associated with its members **shall be appropriately disciplined** for violation of the provisions of this chapter, the rules or regulations

European Regulatory Framework for Financial Instruments	U.S. Regulatory Framework for Financial Instruments	
	7)	thereunder, or the rules of the exchange, by expulsion, suspension, limitation of activities, functions, and operations, fine, censure, being suspended or barred from being associated with a member, or any other fitting sanction.
		The rules of the exchange are in accordance with the provisions of subsection (d) of this section, and in general, provide a fair procedure for the disciplining of members and persons associated with members, the denial of membership to any person seeking membership therein, the barring of any person from becoming associated with a member thereof, and the prohibition or limitation by the exchange of any person with respect to access to services offered by the exchange or a member thereof.
	8)	The rules of the exchange do not impose any burden on competition not necessary or appropriate in furtherance of the purposes of this chapter.
	9)	The rules of the exchange prohibit the listing of any security issued in a limited partnership rollup transaction (as such term is defined in paragraphs (4) and (5) of section 78n(h)of the Securities Exchange Act), unless such transaction was conducted in accordance with procedures designed to protect the rights of limited partners, including –
		(a) the right of dissenting limited partners to one of the following:
		(1) an appraisal and compensation;
		(2) retention of a security under substantially the same terms and conditions as the original issue;
		(3) approval of the limited partnership rollup transaction by not less than 75 percent of the outstanding securities of each of the participating limited partnerships;
		(4) the use of a committee of limited partners that is independent, as determined in accordance with rules prescribed by the exchange, of the general partner or sponsor, that has been approved by a majority of the outstanding units of each of the participating limited partnerships, and that has such authority as is necessary

European Regulatory Framework for Financial Instruments	U.S. Regulatory Framework for Financial Instruments
	to protect the interest of limited partners, including the authority to hire independent advisors, to negotiate with the general partner or sponsor on behalf of the limited partners, and to make a recommendation to the limited partners with respect to the proposed transaction; or
	(5) other comparable rights that are prescribed by rule by the exchange and that are designed to protect dissenting limited partners;
	b) the right not to have their voting power unfairly reduced or abridged
	c) the right not to bear an unfair portion of the costs of a proposed limited partnership rollup transaction that is rejected; and
	d) restrictions on the conversion of contingent interests or fees into non-contingent interests or fees and restrictions on the receipt of a non-contingent equity interest in exchange for fees for services which have not yet been provided.
	As used in this paragraph, the term "dissenting limited partner" means a person who, on the date on which soliciting material is mailed to investors, is a holder of a beneficial interest in a limited partnership that is the subject of a limited partnership rollup transaction, and who casts a vote against the transaction and complies with procedures established by the exchange, except that for purposes of an exchange or tender offer, such person shall file an objection in writing under the rules of the exchange during the period during which the offer is outstanding.
• Admission of financial instruments to trading MiFID, Article 40	• Registration Requirements for Securities Sec. 12 of the Securities Exchange Act.

European Regulatory Framework for Financial Instruments	U.S. Regulatory Framework for Financial Instruments
1. Member States shall require that Regulated Markets have clear and transparent rules regarding the admission of financial instruments to trading. Those rules shall ensure that any financial instruments admitted to trading in a Regulated Market are capable of being traded in a fair, orderly and efficient manner and, in the case of transferable securities, are freely negotiable.	(a) General requirement of registration It shall be unlawful for any member, broker, or dealer to effect any transaction in any security (other than an exempted security) on a national securities exchange unless a registration is effective as to such security for such exchange in accordance with the provisions of this chapter and the rules and regulations thereunder. The provisions of this subsection shall not apply in respect of a security futures product traded on a national securities exchange.
2. In the case of derivatives, the rules shall ensure in particular that the design of the derivative contract allows for its orderly pricing as well as for the existence of effective settlement conditions.	b) Procedure for registration; information A security may be registered on a national securities exchange by the issuer filing an application with the exchange (and filing with the Commission such duplicate originals thereof as the Commission may require), which application shall contain -
3. In addition to the obligations set out in paragraphs 1 and 2, Member States shall require the Regulated Market to establish and maintain effective arrangements to verify that issuers of transferable securities that are admitted to trading on the Regulated Market comply with their obligations under Community law in respect of initial, ongoing or ad hoc disclosure obligations. Member States shall ensure that the Regulated Market establishes arrangements which facilitate its members or participants in obtaining access to information which has been made public under Community law.	1) Such information, in such detail, as to the issuer and any person directly or indirectly controlling or controlled by, or under direct or indirect common control with, the issuer, and any guarantor of the security as to principal or interest or both, as the Commission may by rules and regulations require, as necessary r appropriate in the public interest or for the protection of investors, in respect of the following: a) the organization, financial structure, and nature of the business;
4. Member States shall ensure that Regulated Markets have established the necessary arrangements to review regularly the compliance with the admission requirements of the financial instruments which they admit to trading.	b) the terms, position, rights, and privileges of the different classes of securities outstanding;
5. A transferable security that has been admitted to trading on a Regulated Market can subsequently be admitted to trading on other Regulated Markets, even without the consent of the issuer and in compliance with the relevant provisions of Directive 2003/71/EC of on the prospectus to be published when securities are offered to the public or admitted to trading and amending Directive 2001/34/EC (1). The issuer shall be informed by the Regulated Market of the fact that its securities are traded on that Regulated Market. The issuer shall not be subject to any obligation to provide information required under paragraph 3 directly to any Regulated Market which has admitted the issuer's securities to trading without its consent.	c) the terms on which their securities are to be, and during he preceding three years have been, offered to the public or otherwise;
6. In order to ensure the uniform application of paragraphs 1 to 5, the Commission	d) the directors, officers, and underwriters, and each security holder of record holding more than 10 per centum of any class of any equity security of the issuer (other than an

European Regulatory Framework for Financial Instruments	U.S. Regulatory Framework for Financial Instruments
shall, in accordance with the procedure referred to in Article 64(2) adopt implementing measures which:	exempted security), their remuneration and their interests in the securities of, and their material contracts with, the issuer and any person directly or indirectly controlling or controlled by, or under direct or indirect common control with, he issuer;
(a) specify the characteristics of different classes of instruments to be taken into account by the Regulated Market when assessing whether an instrument is issued in a manner consistent with the conditions laid down in the second subparagraph of paragraph 1 for admission to trading on the different market segments which it operates;	e) remuneration to others than directors and officers exceeding $20,000 per annum;
	f) bonus and profit-sharing arrangements;
	g) management and service contracts;
	h) options existing or to be created in respect of their securities;
(b) clarify the arrangements that the Regulated Market is to implement so as to be considered to have fulfilled its obligation to verify that the issuer of a transferable security complies with its obligations under Community law in respect of initial, ongoing or ad hoc disclosure obligations;	i) material contracts, not made in the ordinary course of business, which are to be executed in whole or in part at or after the filing of the application or which were made not more than two years before such filing, and every material patent or contract for a material patent right shall be deemed a material contract;
(c) clarify the arrangements that the Regulated Market has to establish pursuant to paragraph 3 in order to facilitate its members or participants in obtaining access to information which has been made public under the conditions established by Community law.	j) balance sheets for not more than the three preceding fiscal years, certified if required by the rules and regulations of the Commission by a registered public accounting firm;
	k) profit and loss statements for not more than the three preceding fiscal years, certified if required by the rules and regulations of the Commission by a registered public accounting firm; and
	l) any further financial statements which the Commission may deem necessary or appropriate for the protection of investors.
	2) Copies of articles of incorporation, bylaws, trust indentures, or corresponding documents, underwriting arrangements, and other similar documents of, and voting trust agreements with respect to, the issuer and any person directly or indirectly controlling or controlled by, or under direct or indirect common control

European Regulatory Framework for Financial Instruments	U.S. Regulatory Framework for Financial Instruments
	with, the issuer as the Commission may require as necessary or appropriate for the proper protection of investors and to insure fair dealing in the security.
	3) Such copies of material contracts, referred to in paragraph
	1) (I) above, as the Commission may require as necessary or appropriate for the proper protection of investors and to insure fair dealing in the security.
	c) Additional or alternative information If in the judgment of the Commission any information required under subsection (b) of this section is inapplicable to any specified class or classes of issuers, the Commission shall require in lieu thereof the submission of such other information of comparable character as it may deem applicable to such class of issuers.
	d) Effective date of registration; withdrawal of registration If the exchange authorities certify to the Commission that the security has been approved by the exchange for listing and registration, the registration shall become effective thirty days after the receipt of such certification by the Commission or within shorter period of time as the Commission may determine. A security registered with a national securities exchange may be withdrawn or stricken from listing and registration in accordance with the rules of the exchange and, upon such terms as the Commission may deem necessary to impose for the protection of investors, upon application by the issuer or the exchange to the Commission; whereupon the issuer shall be relieved from further compliance with the provisions of this section and section 78m of this title and any rules or regulations under such sections as to the securities so withdrawn or stricken. An unissued security may be registered only in accordance with such rules and regulations as the Commission may prescribe as necessary or appropriate in the public interest or for the protection of investors.
	(f) Unlisted trading privileges for security originally listed on another national exchange

European Regulatory Framework for Financial Instruments	U.S. Regulatory Framework for Financial Instruments
	1)(a) Notwithstanding the preceding subsections of this section, any national securities exchange, in accordance with the requirements of this subsection and the rules hereunder, may extend unlisted trading privileges to - (1) any security that is listed and registered on a national securities exchange, subject to subparagraph (b); and (2) any security that is otherwise registered pursuant to this section, or that would be required to be so registered except for the exemption from registration provided in subparagraph (b) or (g) of subsection (g)(2) of this section, subject to subparagraph (e) of this paragraph.
• Suspension or Removal of Instruments from Trading MiFID, level 1, Article 41 1. Without prejudice to the right of the competent authority under Article 50(2)(j) and (k) to demand suspension or removal of an instrument from trading, the operator of the Regulated Market may suspend or remove from trading a financial instrument which no longer complies with the rules of the Regulated Market unless such a step would be likely to cause significant damage to the investors' interests or the orderly functioning of the market. Notwithstanding the possibility for the operators of Regulated Markets to inform directly the operators of other Regulated Markets, Member States shall require that an operator of a Regulated Market that suspends or removes from trading a financial instrument make public this decision and communicates relevant information to the competent authority. The competent authority shall inform the competent authorities of the other Member States. 2. A competent authority which demands the suspension or removal of a financial instrument from trading on one or more Regulated Markets shall immediately	• Trading Suspensions **Section, Securities and Exchange Act** **Authority of the Commission:** Trading suspensions; emergency authority (1) Trading suspensions If in its opinion the public interest and the protection of investors so require, the Commission is authorized by order - (A) summarily to suspend trading in any security (other than an exempted security) for a period not exceeding 10 business days, and (B) summarily to suspend all trading on any national securities exchange or otherwise, in securities other than exempted securities, for a period not exceeding 90 calendar days. For exchanges: see the organizational requirements for national exchanges which

European Regulatory Framework for Financial Instruments	U.S. Regulatory Framework for Financial Instruments
make public its decision and inform the competent authorities of the other Member States. Except where it could cause significant damage to the investors' interests or the orderly functioning of the market the competent authorities of the other Member States shall demand the suspension or removal of that financial instrument from trading on the Regulated Markets and MTFs that operate under their authority.	provide for the enforcement power for the exchanges.

• Access to Regulated Markets
MiFID Article 42
 	
1. Member States shall require the Regulated Market to establish and maintain transparent and non-discriminatory rules, based on objective criteria, governing access to or membership of the Regulated Market.
2. Those rules shall specify any obligations for the members or participants arising from:
 	
   (a) the constitution and administration of the Regulated Market;
   (b) rules relating to transactions on the market;
   (c) professional standards imposed on the staff of the investment firms or credit institutions that are operating on the market;
   (d) the conditions established, for members or participants other than investment firms and credit institutions, under paragraph 3;
   (e) the rules and procedures for the clearing and settlement of transactions concluded on the Regulated Market.
 	
3. Regulated Markets may admit as members or participants investment firms, credit institutions authorized under Directive 2000/12/EC and other persons who:
	• Access to Exchanges
	
	See organizational requirements for National Exchanges.

European Regulatory Framework for Financial Instruments	U.S. Regulatory Framework for Financial Instruments
(a) are fit and proper; (b) have a sufficient level of trading ability and competence; (c) have, where applicable, adequate organizational arrangements; (d) have sufficient resources for the role they are to perform, taking into account the different financial arrangements that the Regulated Market may have established in order to guarantee the adequate settlement of transactions. 4. Member States shall ensure that, for the transactions concluded on a Regulated Market, members and participants are not obliged to apply to each other the obligations laid down in Articles 19, 21 and 22. However, the members or participants of the Regulated Market shall apply the obligations provided for in Articles 19, 21 and 22 (conduct of business rules) with respect to their clients when they, acting on behalf of their clients, execute their orders on a Regulated Market. 5. Member States shall ensure that the rules on access to or membership of the Regulated Market provide for the direct or remote participation of investment firms and credit institutions. 6. Member States shall, without further legal or administrative requirements, allow Regulated Markets from other Member States to provide appropriate arrangements on their territory so as to facilitate access to and trading on those markets by remote members or participants established in their territory. The Regulated Market shall communicate to the competent authority of its home Member State the Member State in which it intends to provide such arrangements. The competent authority of the home Member State shall communicate, within one month, this information to the Member State in which the Regulated Market intends to provide such arrangements. The competent authority of the home Member State of the Regulated Market shall, on the request of the competent authority of the host Member State and within a reasonable time, communicate the identity of the members or participants of	

European Regulatory Framework for Financial Instruments	U.S. Regulatory Framework for Financial Instruments
7. the Regulated Market established in that Member State. Member States shall require the operator of the Regulated Market to communicate, on a regular basis, the list of the members and participants of the Regulated Market to the competent authority of the Regulated Market.	
• Reporting irregularities and non-compliance in trading **MiFID, Article 43** **Monitoring of compliance with the rules of the Regulated Market and with other legal obligations** 1. Member States shall require that Regulated Markets establish and maintain effective arrangements and procedures for the regular monitoring of the compliance by their members or participants with their rules. Regulated Markets shall monitor the transactions undertaken by their members or participants under their systems in order to identify breaches of those rules, disorderly trading conditions or conduct that may involve market abuse. 2. Member States shall require the operators of the Regulated Markets to report significant breaches of their rules or disorderly trading conditions or conduct that may involve market abuse to the competent authority of the Regulated Market. Member States shall also require the operator of the Regulated Market to supply the relevant information without delay to the authority competent for the investigation and prosecution of market abuse on the Regulated Market and to provide full assistance to the latter in investigating and prosecuting market abuse occurring on or through the systems of the Regulated Market.	• Reporting irregularities and non-compliance in trading See organizational requirements for Regulated Markets.
• Pre-trade Transparency requirements for Regulated Markets MiFID (level 1) Article 44 1. Member States shall, at least, require Regulated Markets to make public current bid and offer prices and the depth of trading interests at those prices which are advertised through their systems for shares admitted to trading.	• Pre-trade Transparency requirements for exchanges Rule 602 -- Dissemination of Quotations in NMS Securities a. *Dissemination requirements for national securities exchanges and national securities associations*

European Regulatory Framework for Financial Instruments	U.S. Regulatory Framework for Financial Instruments
1. Member States shall require this information to be made available to the public on reasonable commercial terms and on a continuous basis during normal trading hours. Regulated Markets may give access, on reasonable commercial terms and on a non-discriminatory basis, to the arrangements they employ for making public the information under the first subparagraph to investment firms which are obliged to publish their quotes in shares pursuant to Article 27. 2. Member States shall provide that the competent authorities are to be **able to waive the obligation for Regulated Markets** to make public the information referred to in paragraph 1 based on the market model or the type and size of orders in the cases defined in accordance with paragraph 3. In particular, the competent authorities shall be able to waive the obligation in respect of transactions that are large in scale compared with normal market size for the share or type of share in question. 3. In order to ensure the uniform application of paragraphs 1 and 2, the Commission shall, in accordance with the procedure referred to in Article 64(2) adopt implementing measures as regards: • the range of bid and offers or designated market maker quotes, and the depth of trading interest at those prices, to be made public; • the size or type of orders for which pre-trade disclosure may be waived under paragraph 2; • the market model for which pre-trade disclosure may be waived under paragraph 2, and in particular, the applicability of the obligation to trading methods operated by Regulated Markets which conclude transactions under their rules by reference to prices established outside the Regulated Market or by periodic auction.	1. Every national securities exchange and national securities association shall establish and maintain procedures and mechanisms for collecting bids, offers, quotation sizes, and aggregate quotation sizes from responsible brokers or dealers who are members of such exchange or association, processing such bids, offers, and sizes, and making such bids, offers, and sizes available to vendors, as follows: • Each national securities exchange shall at all times such exchange is open for trading, collect, process, and make available to vendors **the best bid, the best offer, and aggregate quotation sizes for each subject security listed or admitted to unlisted trading** privileges which is communicated on any national securities exchange by any responsible broker or dealer, but shall not include: (1) Any bid or offer executed immediately after communication and any bid or offer communicated by a responsible broker or dealer other than an exchange market maker which is cancelled or withdrawn if not executed immediately after communication; and (2) Any bid or offer communicated during a period when trading in that security has been suspended or halted, or prior to the commencement of trading in that security on any trading day, on that exchange. • Each national securities association shall, at all times that last sale information with respect to NMS securities is reported pursuant to an effective transaction reporting plan, collect, process, and make available to vendors the best bid, best offer, and quotation sizes communicated otherwise than on an exchange by each member of such association acting in the capacity of an OTC market maker for each subject security and the identity of that member (excluding any bid or offer executed immediately after communication), except during any period when over-the-counter trading in that security has been suspended. 1. Each national securities exchange shall, with respect to each published bid and published offer representing a bid or offer of a member for a subject

European Regulatory Framework for Financial Instruments	U.S. Regulatory Framework for Financial Instruments
	security, establish and maintain procedures for ascertaining and disclosing to other members of that exchange, upon presentation of orders sought to be executed by them in reliance upon paragraph (b)(2) of this section, the identity of the responsible broker or dealer who made such bid or offer and the quotation size associated with it.
	2.
	• If, at any time a national securities exchange is open for trading, such exchange determines, pursuant to rules approved by the Commission pursuant to section 19(b)(2) of the Act, that the level of trading activities or the existence of unusual market conditions is such that the exchange is incapable of collecting, processing, and making available to vendors the data for a subject security required to be made available pursuant to paragraph (a)(1) of this section in a manner that accurately reflects the current state of the market on such exchange, such exchange shall immediately notify all specified persons of that determination. Upon such notification, responsible brokers or dealers that are members of that exchange shall be relieved of their obligation under paragraphs (b)(2) and (c)(3) of this section and such exchange shall be relieved of its obligations under paragraphs 1 and 2 of this section for that security; provided, however, that such exchange will continue, to the maximum extent practicable under the circumstances, to collect, process, and make available to vendors data for that security in accordance with paragraph 1 of this section.
	• During any period a national securities exchange, or any responsible broker or dealer that is a member of that exchange, is relieved of any obligation imposed by this section for any subject security by virtue of a notification made pursuant to paragraph 3(1) of this section, such exchange shall monitor the activity or conditions which formed the basis for such notification and shall immediately renotify all specified persons when that exchange is

European Regulatory Framework for Financial Instruments	U.S. Regulatory Framework for Financial Instruments
	once again capable of collecting, processing, and making available to vendors the data for that security required to be made available pursuant to paragraph 1 of this section in a manner that accurately reflects the current state of the market on such exchange. Upon such renotification, any exchange or responsible broker or dealer which had been relieved of any obligation imposed by this section as a consequence of the prior notification shall again be subject to such obligation. 4. Nothing in this section shall preclude any national securities exchange or national securities association from making available to vendors indications of interest or bids and offers for a subject security at any time such exchange or association is not required to do so pursuant to paragraph 1 of this section. 5. • Any national securities exchange may make an election for purposes of the definition of *subject security* in Rule 242.600(b)(73) for any NMS security, by collecting, processing, and making available bids, offers, quotation sizes, and aggregate quotation sizes in that security; except that for any NMS security previously listed or admitted to unlisted trading privileges on only one exchange and not traded by any OTC market maker, such election shall be made by notifying all specified persons, and shall be effective at the opening of trading on the business day following notification. • Any member of a national securities association acting in the capacity of an OTC market maker may make an election for purposes of the definition of *subject security* in Rule 242.600(b)(73) for any NMS security, by communicating to its association bids, offers, and quotation sizes in that security; except that for any other NMS security listed or admitted to unlisted trading privileges on only one exchange and not traded by any other OTC market maker, such election shall be made by notifying its association and all

European Regulatory Framework for Financial Instruments	U.S. Regulatory Framework for Financial Instruments
	specified persons, and shall be effective at the opening of trading on the business day following notification. • The election of a national securities exchange or member of a national securities association for any NMS security pursuant to this paragraph 5 shall cease to be in effect if such exchange or member ceases to make available or communicate bids, offers, and quotation sizes in such security.
• Post-trade transparency requirements for Regulated Markets **MiFID Article 45** 1. Member States shall, at least, require Regulated Markets to make public the price, volume and time of the transactions executed in respect of shares admitted to trading. Member States shall require details of all such transactions to be made public, on a reasonable commercial basis and as close to real-time as possible. Regulated Markets may give access, on reasonable commercial terms and on a non-discriminatory basis, to the arrangements they employ for making public the information under the first subparagraph to investment firms which are obliged to publish the details of their transactions in shares pursuant to Article 28. 2. Member States shall provide that the competent authority may authorise Regulated Markets to provide for deferred publication of the details of transactions based on their type or size. In particular, the competent authorities may authorise the deferred publication in respect of transactions that are large in scale compared with the normal market size for that share or that class of shares. Member States shall require Regulated Markets to obtain the competent authority's prior approval of proposed arrangements for deferred trade-publication, and shall require that these arrangements be clearly disclosed to market participants and the investing public.	• Post-trade transparency requirements for exchanges NMS Regulation rule 601, FINRA reporting rules and consolidated tape associations plans. See the post-trade transparency requirements for brokers&dealers.

European Regulatory Framework for Financial Instruments	U.S. Regulatory Framework for Financial Instruments
3. In order to provide for the efficient and orderly functioning of financial markets, and to ensure the uniform application of paragraphs 1 and 2, the Commission shall, in accordance with the procedure referred to in Article 64(2) adopt implementing measures in respect of: (a) the scope and content of the information to be made available to the public; (b) the conditions under which a Regulated Market may provide for deferred publication of trades and the criteria to be applied when deciding the transactions for which, due to their size or the type of share involved, deferred publication is allowed. Relevant provision from implementing regulation, MiFID level 2, Article 18 **Waivers based on market model and type of order or transaction** 3. Waivers in accordance with Article 29(2) (MTFs) and 44(2) (RMs) of Directive 2004/39/EC may be granted by the competent authorities for systems operated by an MTF or a Regulated Market, if those systems satisfy one of the following criteria: (a) they must be based on a trading methodology by which the price is determined in accordance with a reference price generated by another system, where that reference price is widely published and is regarded generally by market participants as a reliable reference price; (b) they formalise negotiated transactions, each of which meets one of the following criteria: (i) it is made at or within the current volume weighted spread reflected on the order book or the quotes of the market makers of the Regulated Market or MTF operating that system or, where the share is not traded continuously, within a percentage of a suitable reference	

European Regulatory Framework for Financial Instruments	U.S. Regulatory Framework for Financial Instruments
price, being a percentage and a reference price set in advance by the system operator;	
(ii) it is subject to conditions other than the current market price of the share. For the purposes of point (b), the other conditions specified in the rules of the Regulated Market or MTF for a transaction of this kind must also have been fulfilled. In the case of systems having functionality other than as described in points (a) or (b), the waiver shall not apply to that other functionality.	
4. Waivers in accordance with Articles 29(2) and 44(2) of Directive 2004/39/EC based on the type of orders may be granted only in relation to orders held in an order management facility maintained by the Regulated Market or the MTF pending their being disclosed to the market.	
Article 20	
Waivers in relation to transactions which are large in scale	
An order shall be considered to be large in scale compared with normal market size if it is equal to or larger than the minimum size of order specified in Table 2 in Annex II of Directive. For the purposes of determining whether an order is large in scale compared to normal market size, all shares admitted to trading on a Regulated Market shall be classified in accordance with their average daily turnover, which shall be calculated in accordance with the procedure set out in Article 33.	
• Designation of Competent Authorities	• Designation of SEC and SROs
MiFID Article 48	Section 4 of Securities exchange Act
1. Each Member State shall designate the competent authorities which are to carry out each of the duties provided for under the different provisions of this Directive. Member States shall inform the Commission and the competent authorities of other	Securities and Exchange Commission, Self-Regulatory Organizations (put here rules on SROs)

European Regulatory Framework for Financial Instruments	U.S. Regulatory Framework for Financial Instruments
2. Member States of the identity of the competent authorities responsible for enforcement of each of those duties, and of any division of those duties. The competent authorities referred to in paragraph 1 shall be public authorities, without prejudice to the possibility of delegating tasks to other entities where that is expressly provided for in Articles 5(5), 16(3), 17(2) and 23(4). Any delegation of tasks to entities other than the authorities referred to in paragraph 1 may not involve either the exercise of public authority or the use of discretionary powers of judgment. Member States shall require that, prior to delegation, competent authorities take all reasonable steps to ensure that the entity to which tasks are to be delegated has the capacity and resources to effectively execute all tasks and that the delegation takes place only if a clearly defined and documented framework for the exercise of any delegated tasks has been established stating the tasks to be undertaken and the conditions under which they are to be carried out. These conditions shall include a clause obliging the entity in question to act and be organised in such a manner as to avoid conflict of interest and so that information obtained from carrying out the delegated tasks is not used unfairly or to prevent competition. In any case, the final responsibility for supervising compliance with this Directive and with its implementing measures shall lie with the competent authority or authorities designated in accordance with paragraph 1. Member States shall inform the Commission and the competent authorities of other Member States of any arrangements entered into with regard to delegation of tasks, including the precise conditions regulating such delegation. 3. The Commission shall publish a list of the competent authorities referred to in paragraphs 1 and 2 in the *Official Journal of the European Union* at least once a year and update it continuously on its website.	Securities and Exchange Commission (a) Establishment; composition; limitations on commissioners; terms of office There is hereby established a Securities and Exchange Commission (hereinafter referred to as the "Commission") to be composed of five commissioners to be appointed by the President by and with the advice and consent of the Senate. Not more than three of such commissioners shall be members of the same political party, and in making appointments members of different political parties shall be appointed alternately as nearly as may be practicable. No commissioner shall engage in any other business, vocation, or employment than that of serving as commissioner, nor shall any commissioner participate, directly or indirectly, in any stock-market operations or transactions of a character subject to regulation by the Commission pursuant to this chapter. Each commissioner shall hold office for a term of five years and until his successor is appointed and has qualified, except that he shall not so continue to serve beyond the expiration of the next session of Congress subsequent to the expiration of said fixed term of office, and except (1) any commissioner appointed to fill a vacancy occurring prior to the expiration of the term for which his predecessor was appointed shall be appointed for the remainder of such term, and (2) the terms of office of the commissioners first taking office after June 6, 1934, shall expire as designated by the President at the time of nomination, one at the end of one year, one at the end of two years, one at the end of three years, one at the end of four years, and one at the end of five years, after June 6, 1934. (b) Appointment and compensation of staff and leasing authority

European Regulatory Framework for Financial Instruments	U.S. Regulatory Framework for Financial Instruments
	(1) Appointment and compensation The Commission shall appoint and compensate officers, attorneys, economists, examiners, and other employees in accordance with section 4802 of title 5. (3) Reporting of information In establishing and adjusting schedules of compensation and benefits for officers, attorneys, economists, examiners, and other employees of the Commission under applicable provisions of law, the Commission shall inform the heads of the agencies referred to under section 1833b of title 12 and Congress of such compensation and benefits and shall seek to maintain comparability with such agencies regarding compensation and benefits. (4) Leasing authority Notwithstanding any other provision of law, the Commission is authorized to enter directly into leases for real property for office, meeting, storage, and such other space as is necessary to carry out its functions, and shall be exempt from any General Services Administration space management regulations or directives. (c) Acceptance of travel support for Commission activities from non-Federal sources; regulations Notwithstanding any other provision of law, in accordance with regulations which the Commission shall prescribe to prevent conflicts of interest, the Commission may accept payment and reimbursement, in cash or in kind, from non-Federal agencies, organizations, and individuals for travel, subsistence, and other necessary expenses incurred by Commission members and employees in attending meetings and conferences concerning the functions or activities of the Commission. Any payment or reimbursement accepted shall be credited to the appropriated funds of the Commission. The amount of travel, subsistence, and other necessary expenses for members and employees paid or reimbursed under this subsection may exceed per diem amounts

European Regulatory Framework for Financial Instruments	U.S. Regulatory Framework for Financial Instruments
	established in official travel regulations, but the Commission may include in its regulations under this subsection a limitation on such amounts.
	(d) Acceptance of relocation expenses from former employers by professional fellows program participants Notwithstanding any other provision of law, former employers of participants in the Commission's professional fellows programs may pay such participants their actual expenses for relocation to Washington, District of Columbia, to facilitate their participation in such programs, and program participants may accept such payments.
	(e) Fee payments. Notwithstanding any other provision of law, whenever any fee is required to be paid to the Commission pursuant to any provision of the securities laws or any other law, the Commission may provide by rule that such fee shall be paid in a manner other than in cash and the Commission may also specify the time that such fee shall be determined and paid relative to the filing of any statement or document with the Commission.
	(f) Reimbursement of expenses for assisting foreign securities authorities. Notwithstanding any other provision of law, the Commission may accept payment and reimbursement, in cash or in kind, from a foreign securities authority, or made on behalf of such authority, for necessary expenses incurred by the Commission, its members, and employees in carrying out any investigation pursuant to section 78u(a)(2) of this title or in providing any other assistance to a foreign securities authority. Any payment or reimbursement accepted shall be considered a reimbursement to the appropriated funds of the Commission.
	SROs. The Financial Industry Regulatory Authority (FINRA), is the largest non-governmental regulator for all securities firms doing business in the United States. FINRA

European Regulatory Framework for Financial Instruments	U.S. Regulatory Framework for Financial Instruments
	oversees nearly 5,000 brokerage firms, about 173,000 branch offices and approximately 656,000 registered securities representatives. **FINRA touches virtually every aspect of the securities business—from registering and educating industry participants to examining securities firms; writing rules; enforcing those rules and the federal securities laws; informing and educating the investing public;** providing trade reporting and other industry utilities; and administering the largest dispute resolution forum for investors and registered firms. It also performs market regulation under contract for The NASDAQ Stock Market, the American Stock Exchange, the International Securities Exchange and the Chicago Climate Exchange.
• Scope of power for CAs MiFID, Article 50 1. Competent authorities shall be given all supervisory and investigatory powers that are necessary for the exercise of their functions. Within the limits provided for in their national legal frameworks they shall exercise such powers: • directly; or • in collaboration with other authorities; or • under their responsibility by delegation to entities to which tasks have been delegated according to Article 48(2); or • by application to the competent judicial authorities. 2. The powers referred to in paragraph 1 shall be exercised in conformity with national law and shall include, at least, the rights to: • have access to any document in any form whatsoever and to receive a copy of it; • demand information from any person and if necessary to summon and question a person with a view to obtaining information; • carry out on-site inspections; • require existing telephone and existing data traffic records;	• Scope of power for regulators Securities Exchange Act assigns important responsibilities to SEC. http://www.sec.gov/about/laws.shtml - With the Securities Exchange Act from 1934, Congress created the Securities and Exchange Commission. The Act empowers the SEC with broad authority over all aspects of the securities industry. This includes the power to register, regulate, and oversee brokerage firms, transfer agents, and clearing agencies as well as the nation's securities self regulatory organizations (SROs). For the scope of power of SROs please see the Paper (Part 1: Regulatory Framework and oversight)

European Regulatory Framework for Financial Instruments	U.S. Regulatory Framework for Financial Instruments
• require the cessation of any practice that is contrary to the provisions adopted in the implementation of this Directive; • request the freezing and/or the sequestration of assets; • request temporary prohibition of professional activity; • require authorized investment firms and Regulated Markets' auditors to provide information; • adopt any type of measure to ensure that investment firms and Regulated Markets continue to comply with legal requirements; • require the suspension of trading in a financial instrument; • require the removal of a financial instrument from trading, whether on a Regulated Market or under other trading arrangements; • refer matters for criminal prosecution; • allow auditors or experts to carry out verifications or investigations.	
• Anti-Money Laundering MiFID level 1, Article 25 Par. 2. Member States shall require investment firms to keep at the disposal of the competent authority, for at least five years, the relevant data relating to all transactions in financial instruments which they have carried out, whether on own account or on behalf of a client. In the case of transactions carried out on behalf of clients, the records shall contain all the information and details of the identity of the client, and the information required under Council Directive 91/308/EEC of 10 June 1991 on prevention of the use of the financial system for the purpose of money laundering (2).	• Anti-Money Laundering **NASD Rule 3011. Anti-Money Laundering Compliance Program** On or before April 24, 2002, each member shall develop and implement a written anti-money laundering program reasonably designed to achieve and monitor the member's compliance with the requirements of the Bank Secrecy Act (31 U.S.C. 5311, *et seq.*), and the implementing regulations promulgated thereunder by the Department of the Treasury. Each member's anti-money laundering program must be approved, in writing, by a member of senior management. The anti-money laundering programs required by this Rule shall, at a minimum, (a) Establish and implement policies and procedures that can be reasonably expected to detect and cause the reporting of transactions required under 31 U.S.C. 5318(g) and the implementing regulations thereunder; (b) Establish and implement policies, procedures, and internal controls reasonably designed to achieve compliance with the Bank Secrecy Act and the implementing regulations thereunder;

European Regulatory Framework for Financial Instruments	U.S. Regulatory Framework for Financial Instruments
	(c) Provide for annual (on a calendar-year basis) independent testing for compliance to be conducted by member personnel or by a qualified outside party, unless the member does not execute transactions for customers or otherwise hold customer accounts or act as an introducing broker with respect to customer accounts (e.g., engages solely in proprietary trading or conducts business only with other broker-dealers), in which case such "independent testing" is required every two years (on a calendar-year basis); (d) Designate and identify to NASD (by name, title, mailing address, e-mail address, telephone number, and facsimile number) an individual or individuals responsible for implementing and monitoring the day-to-day operations and internal controls of the program (such individual or individuals must be an associated person of the member) and provide prompt notification to NASD regarding any change in such designation(s); and (e) Provide ongoing training for appropriate personnel. **CFR 103.178: Due diligence programs for private banking accounts.** (a) *In general.* A covered financial institution shall maintain a due diligence program that includes policies, procedures, and controls that are reasonably designed to detect and report any known or suspected money laundering or suspicious activity conducted through or involving any private banking account that is established, maintained, administered, or managed in the United States by such financial institution. The due diligence program required by this section shall be a part of the anti-money laundering program otherwise required by this subpart. (b) *Minimum requirements.* The due diligence program required by paragraph (a) of this section shall be designed to ensure, at a minimum, that the financial institution takes reasonable steps to: (1) Ascertain the identity of all nominal and beneficial owners of a private banking account; (2) Ascertain whether any person identified under paragraph (b)(1) of this section is a

European Regulatory Framework for Financial Instruments	U.S. Regulatory Framework for Financial Instruments
• Directive 2005/60/EC of 26 October 2005 on the prevention of the use of the financial system for the purpose of money laundering and terrorist financing • Section 3, Article 13.4 4. In respect of transactions or business relationships with politically exposed persons residing in another Member State or in a third country, Member States shall require those institutions and persons covered by this Directive to: (a) have appropriate risk-based procedures to determine whether the customer is a politically exposed person; (b) have senior management approval for establishing business relationships with such customers; (c) take adequate measures to establish the source of wealth and source of funds that are involved in the business relationship or transaction; (d) conduct enhanced ongoing monitoring of the business relationship.	senior foreign political figure; (3) Ascertain the source(s) of funds deposited into a private banking account and the purpose and expected use of the account; and (…) (c) *Special requirements for senior foreign political figures.* (1) In the case of a private banking account for which a senior foreign political figure is a nominal or beneficial owner, the due diligence program required by paragraph (a) of this section shall include enhanced scrutiny of such account that is reasonably designed to detect and report transactions that may involve the proceeds of foreign corruption
• Directive 2006/70/EC of 1 August 2006 as regards the definition of "politically exposed person" • Article 2 Politically exposed persons 1. For the purposes of Article 3(8) of Directive 2005/60/EC, 'natural persons who are or have been entrusted with prominent public functions' shall include the following: (a) heads of State, heads of government, ministers and deputy or assistant ministers; (b) members of parliaments; (c) members of supreme courts, of constitutional courts or of other high-level judicial bodies whose decisions are not subject to further appeal, except in exceptional circumstances; (d) members of courts of auditors or of the boards of central banks;	CFR 103.175: **Definitions** (r) *Senior foreign political figure.* (1) The term *senior foreign political figure* means: (i) A current or former: (A) Senior official in the executive, legislative, administrative, military, or judicial branches of a foreign government (whether elected or not); (B) Senior official of a major foreign political party; or (C) Senior executive of a foreign government-owned commercial enterprise; (ii) A corporation, business, or other entity that has been formed by, or for the benefit of, any such individual; (iii) An immediate family member of any such individual; and (iv) A person who is widely and publicly known (or is actually known by the relevant covered financial institution) to be a close associate of such individual. (2) For purposes of this definition: (i) *Senior official or executive* means an individual with substantial authority over policy,

European Regulatory Framework for Financial Instruments	U.S. Regulatory Framework for Financial Instruments
(e) ambassadors, chargés d'affaires and high-ranking officers in the armed forces; (f) members of the administrative, management or supervisory bodies of State-owned enterprises. None of the categories set out in points (a) to (f) of the first subparagraph shall be understood as covering middle ranking or more junior officials. The categories set out in points (a) to (e) of the first subparagraph shall, where applicable, include positions at Community and international level. 2. For the purposes of Article 3(8) of Directive 2005/60/EC, 'immediate family members' shall include the following: (a) the spouse; (b) any partner considered by national law as equivalent to the spouse; (c) the children and their spouses or partners; (d) the parents. 3. For the purposes of Article 3(8) of Directive 2005/60/EC, 'persons known to be close associates' shall include the following: (a) any natural person who is known to have joint beneficial ownership of legal entities or legal arrangements, or any other close business relations, with a person referred to in paragraph 1 (b) any natural person who has sole beneficial ownership of a legal entity or legal arrangement which is known to have been set up for the benefit de facto of the person referred to in paragraph 1	operations, or the use of government-owned resources; and (ii) *Immediate family member* means spouses, parents, siblings, children and a spouse's parents and siblings.

References

Biais, B., F. Declerck, J. Dow, R. Portes, and E-L von Thadden. 2006. "European Corporate Bonds Market: Transparency, Liquidity Efficiency." Centre for Economic Policy Research, London.

Black, Barbara. 2008. "Are Retail Investors Better Off Today?" University of Cincinnati Public Law Research Paper 07-34, January.

Committee of European Securities Regulators, The (CESR). 2009. "Impact of MiFID on Equity Secondary Markets Functioning." 10 June. CESR, Paris.

———. 2009b. "Questions and Answers on MiFID." May. CESR, Paris.

Clifford Chance, 2009. "US Regulatory Reform Would Impose Strict Limits on Investments and Activities of Systemically Significant Financial Firms." Client Memorandum, June. Clifford Chance US LLP. www.cliffordchance.com

European Commission. 2009a. Communication on European Financial Supervision, COM (2009) 232, 27 May.

———. 2009b Communication on Ensuring Efficient, Safe and Sound Derivatives Markets, COM (2009) 332, 3 July.

EC Directive 2003/6/EC of 28 January 2003 on insider dealing and market manipulation (market abuse).

EC Directive 2003/71/EC of 4 November 2003 on the prospectus to be published when securities are offered to the public or admitted to trading.

EC Directive 2004/109/EC of 15 December 2004 on the harmonization of transparency requirements in relation to information about issuers whose securities are admitted to trading on a Regulated Market.

EC Directive 2006/48/EC of 14 June 2006 relating to the taking up and pursuit of the business of credit institutions.

EC Directive 2006/49/EC of 14 June 2006 on the capital adequacy of investment firms and credit institutions.

EC Directive 2004/39/EC of 21 April 2004 on markets in financial instruments.

EC Directive 2006/73/EC of 10 August 2006 implementing directive 2004/39/EC of the European Parliament and the Council as regards organizational requirements and operating conditions for investment firms and defined terms for the purpose of that directive.

Commission Regulation 1287/2006 of 10 August 2006 implementing directive 2004/39/EC as regards record-keeping obligations for investment firms, transaction reporting, market transparency, admission of financial instruments to trading, and defined terms for the purpose of that directive.

EC Directive 2007/44/EC of 5 September 2007 as regards procedural rules and evaluation criteria for the prudential assessment of acquisitions and increase of holdings in the financial sector.

G20. 2009. Declaration on Strengthening the Financial System, London, 2 April.

Krause Reinhardt. 2008. "Dark Pools Let Big Institutions Trade Quietly." *Investors' Business Daily*, November.

O'Hare, Jennifer. 2007. "Retail Investor Remedies Under Rule 10b-5." Villanova Law/Public Policy Research Paper No. 2007-19, October. *University of Cincinnati Law Review* (forthcoming).

Petrella, Giovanni. 2009. "MiFID, Reg NMS and Competition Across Trading Venues in Europe and United States." Milan Catholic University, January.

Rosenblatt Securities. 2009. "Market Structure Analysis and Trading Strategy, Let There Be Light." *Trading Talk: 2008 in Review* (Special Issue), January 19.

Securities and Exchange Act, 1934.

Securities and Exchange Commission, Reg ATS, 1998. Washington, DC.

———. 1999. "On-line Brokerage: Keeping Apace of Cyberspace." Washington, DC.

———. Reg NMS, 2004. Washington, DC.

———. 2005. "Order Granting Exemption to Liquidnet, Inc. from Certain Provisions of Regulation ATS under the Securities Exchange Act of 1934." September 27. Washington, DC.

———. 2007. Final Rules to Implement the Bank "Broker" Provisions of the Gramm-Leach-Bliley Act. Washington, DC.

———. 2008a. "Guide to Broker-Dealer Registration." April. Washington, DC.

———. 2008b. Keynote Speech by Erik Sirri, Director, Division of Trading and Markets, at the SIFMA 2008 Dark Pools Symposium, February 1.

———. 2009. Remarks by the SEC Chairman at the IOSCO Technical Committee Conference, October 8.

Statement by Senator Carl Levin before Homeland Security and Governmental Affairs Committee. January 21, 2009. "Where Were the Watchdogs? The Financial Crisis and the Breakdown of Financial Governance." Washington, DC.

Tabb Group. 2009. Liquidity Matrix. April. Westborough, MA.

U.S. Treasury Department. 2009. "Financial Regulatory Reform: A New Foundation." 17 June. Washington, DC.

Eco-Audit

Environmental Benefits Statement

The World Bank is committed to preserving Endangered Forests and natural resources. We print World Bank Working Papers and Country Studies on postconsumer recycled paper, processed chlorine free. The World Bank has formally agreed to follow the recommended standards for paper usage set by Green Press Initiative—a nonprofit program supporting publishers in using fiber that is not sourced from Endangered Forests. For more information, visit www.greenpressinitiative.org.

In 2008, the printing of these books on recycled paper saved the following:

Trees*	Solid Waste	Water	Net Greenhouse Gases	Total Energy
355	16,663	129,550	31,256	247 mil.
*40 feet in height and 6–8 inches in diameter	Pounds	Gallons	Pounds CO$_2$ Equivalent	BTUs

green
press
INITIATIVE